Lords of the Golden Horn
From Suleiman the Magnificent to Kamal Ataturk

Noel Barber has written over twenty books, many of them historical reconstructions. *The War of the Running Dogs*, a bestseller in this country, was also the History Book Club of America choice in 1972. *Sinister Twilight* has been translated into eight languages. He is married to an Italian and has two children. He lives in Chelsea and in the south of France.

Noel Barber
Lords of the Golden Horn

From Suleiman the Magnificent to Kamal Ataturk

Pan Books London and Sydney

First published 1973 by Macmillan London Ltd
This edition published 1976 by Pan Books Ltd,
Cavaye Place, London SW10 9PG
© Filmtransac AG 1973
ISBN 0 330 24735 2
Printed and bound in Great Britain by
Richard Clay (The Chaucer Press) Ltd, Bungay, Suffolk

For
Titina and Simonetta
with love

Contents

List of maps

List of illustrations

Illustration acknowledgements

Bibliothèque Nationale: 1
Popperfoto: 5, 6, 7, 8, 12
Topkapi Museum; photographed by Necati Orbay: 3, 4
Rodney Searight Collection: 2, 10, 11, 13, 14, 15, 16, 17, 18, 20
Istanbul University Library: 9
Radio Times Hulton Picture Library: 19, 21, 22, 23

Acknowledgements

This is a book about people; it does not pretend to be a history of the Ottoman Empire. What I have tried to do is to show the decline of a mighty and colourful empire through the eyes and actions of the Sultans and their concubines in the harem (who at times wielded immense power) from the time of Suleiman the Magnificent to the death of a leader of a different stamp – Kamal Ataturk.

It is not so much the story of great battles as of the events leading up to them, though I have made an exception with the siege of Plevna, partly because it provides a superb example of the Turkish talent for bulldog defence, but also (to be truthful) because it is such a rattling good yarn that I could not resist it.

I have not cluttered up the text with more footnotes than necessary, but those who are interested will find details of my major sources in the Notes on further reading at the end of the book.

Since there are often half a dozen different ways of spelling a Turkish name, I have used the simplest European versions.

It is impossible for me to thank individually the many friends who helped me during my eighteen months of research but I must mention Haldun Simavi who opened every door for me in Turkey; Ilban Oz, the Director of Topkapi (as the Grand Seraglio is now called) who allowed me unlimited freedom to explore the harem so that I could place my characters correctly, and who also provided me with most useful documents; Halusi Ozso, my constant companion for many weeks and at one time Ataturk's bodyguard; and those two indefatigable brothers Vahit and Baki Celikbas.

I owe a great debt to the librarians who searched out documents for me in libraries and universities in many European capitals as well as in Turkey itself. My special thanks to Donald Dinsley for his painstaking research in many parts of the world while I was writing in Turkey. I would like to express my thanks also to those authors and publishers who have kindly given me permission to publish extracts from their books.

Last but by no means least, my most grateful thanks to Julian Bach, my friend and agent, who first suggested writing this book.

Noel Barber, Istanbul, 1970–72

The Othman dynasty

This volume opens during the reign of the tenth sultan of the Ottoman dynasty, Suleiman the Magnificent.

Part 1
The years of decline

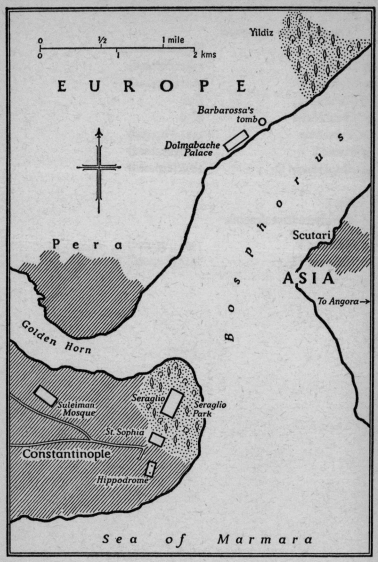

Constantinople

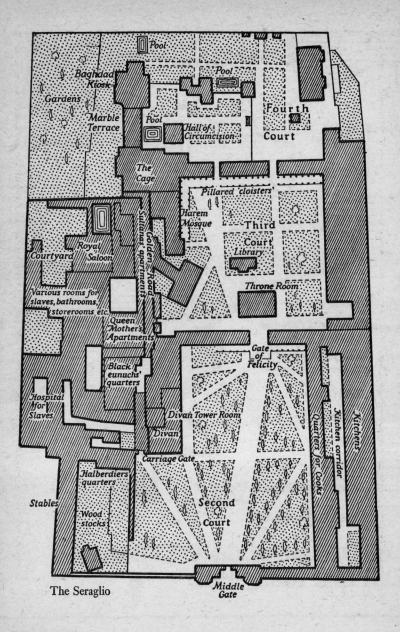

Pool

Baghdad
Kiosk

Gardens

Marble
Terrace

Pool

The Cage

Courtyard

Royal
Saloon

Various rooms for
slaves, bathrooms,
storerooms etc.

Queen
Mother's
Apartments

Black
eunuchs'
quarters

Hospital
for
Slaves

Pool

Pool

Hall of
Circumcision

Harem
Mosque

Sultanas' apartments

Golden Road

Fourth
Court

Pillared 'cloisters'

Third
Court
Library

Throne Room

Gate
of
Felicity

Divan Tower Room

Divan

Kitchen corridor

Kitchens

Quarters for Cooks

Carriage Gate

Halberdiers'
quarters

Stables

Wood
stocks

Second
Court

The Seraglio

Middle
Gate

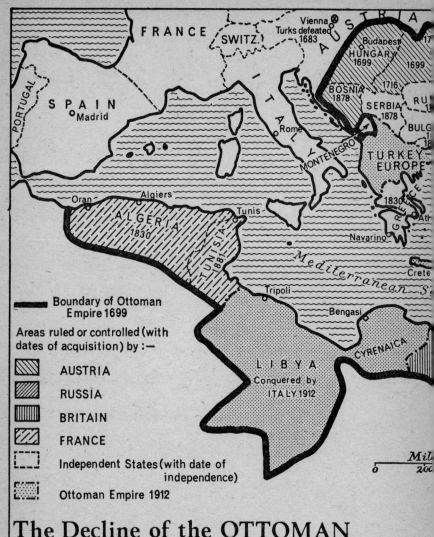

The Decline of the OTTOMAN
EMPIRE 1683–1912

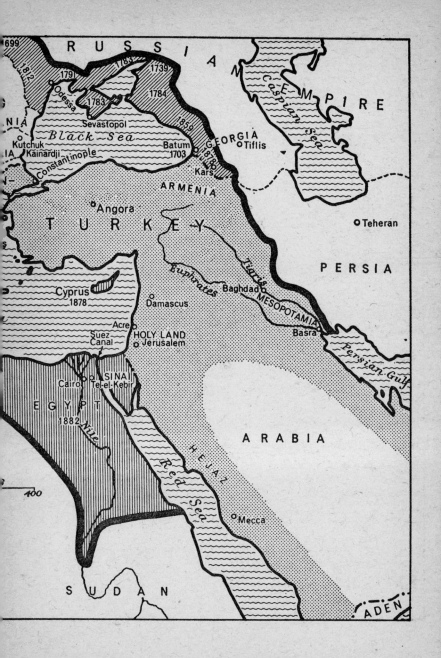

RUSSIAN 1699

1812

1791

1783

1783

1739

1784

1859

1878

1703

Odessa

Sevastopol

Black Sea

Kutchuk
Kainardji

NIA

IA

Constantinople

Batum

GEORGIA
Kars

Tiflis

Caspian Sea

EMPIRE

ARMENIA

TURKEY

Angora

Teheran

PERSIA

Euphrates

Tigris

Baghdad

MESOPOTAMIA

Basra

Cyprus
1878

Damascus

Acre

Suez
Canal

HOLY LAND
Jerusalem

SINAI

Persian Gulf

Cairo
Tel-el-Kebir

EGYPT

1882

Nile

Red Sea

HEJAZ

ARABIA

400

Mecca

SUDAN

ADEN

Part 1
The years of decline

Chapter one
The Grand Seraglio

In those last days of untarnished glory in the mid sixteenth century, when the Ottoman Empire extended from the gates of Vienna to the Yemen and Aden, from Persia to Oran, when the Sultan Suleiman ruled over six of the seven wonders in the world, there was no place more magnificent in its oriental splendour than the private world that lay behind the arch of the Imperial Gate in Constantinople – the Grand Seraglio of the Sultan. The sea walls of this impregnable fortress were lapped by the Sea of Marmora and the Golden Horn. It was a town of five thousand people within a city; its heart – beyond the inner Gate of Felicity – beat in the harem with its hundreds of odalisques and slave girls zealously guarded by pot-bellied or wrinkled black eunuchs.

Constantinople itself was the world's most beautiful city. Standing on seven hills, wrapped in the Bosporus, the Sea of Marmora and the Golden Horn, water was as much a part of the city as the gently sloping forests of cypress or the bustling 'suburb' of Pera with its tiled-roofed houses across the Horn. It was cosmopolitan too. The Patriarch of the Orthodox Church prayed almost within earshot of the stables where Sultan Suleiman kept his four thousand horses; in the great covered market Jews and Moors, most of them refugees from the Spain of Ferdinand and Isabella, worked side by side. Behind the market the Serbs lived in the quarter they had nostalgically named Belgrade. Berbers and Arabs from Africa and the Red Sea toiled in the warehouses lining the shore, protecting the spices, ivory, silk and pearls imported by their masters. It was a city of many peoples and – by the violent standards of the Empire – it was a city at peace. Perhaps the beauty of the ever-present waters, alive with skimming caïques, helped. Perhaps the monuments to bygone Byzantium that still remained – the Hippodrome, the Churches of St Irene and St Sophia – helped too. The narrow streets of Constantinople might have been made of clay, the new houses of flimsy wood ready to crackle at the first touch of fire, but the streets hummed with the life of citizens whose skins varied in colour as much as their gaudy clothes, but who might have been ten thousand miles away from the vast parks and villas of the Grand Seraglio which lay in their midst on a tongue of land, a hillside gently sloping to the sea which three-parts girded it, with the green shores of Asia ahead and the trees behind.

This was a hidden world of golden domes and pointed minarets reaching for the sky like manicured fingers; of dark cypress groves hiding kiosks, or villas, their walls of marble, glittering mosaics or exquisite tiles; of artificial lakes and pleasure gardens, of the mingled scents of herbs and fruit trees and roses, of an imperative silence broken only by the tinkling of scores of fountains. In the latter half of the sixteenth century, when the Ottoman Empire was at its zenith, poised at the very moment in history before its triumph was flawed, no court in Europe was its equal, even though Europe was enjoying a golden age dominated by the spirit of the Renaissance: Visili Ivanovitch, the Grand Prince of Moscow, was laying the foundations of Russia's greatness; Pope Leo X was turning Rome into 'an intellectual garden'; Henry VIII ruled England, Charles V Spain, François I France, and, further south, Gritti, 'the Doge of Venice', the one city above all others that was the gateway to the Levant. Barely thirty years had passed since Columbus stepped on to the shores of a new world.

Europe was coming of age, having built up its first naval squadrons, its first permanent armies, and having discovered the principles and use of artillery. Yet Suleiman was superior to all the European powers in battle, while at home he was, with his architect Sinan, building mosques, schools and hospitals which rivalled the works of the master builders of Europe; Michelangelo was at this time struggling to raise the dome of St Peter's and François I had started to rebuild the Louvre. Despite the thirteen wars in which he personally led his soldiers into battle, Suleiman had time to produce an improved code of justice – and incidentally to execute corrupt officials (including one son-in-law) for acts of injustice. He husbanded his vast treasures; his standing army of fifty thousand was well paid. He had a literary bent, was a disciple of Aristotle (and his hero was Alexander the Great); he kept a daily diary when at war, he wrote poetry when at peace.

The Venetian envoy to Constantinople at the time described him as a man of commanding personality, tall, thin, with a prominent brow, startling black eyes and an aquiline nose above long moustaches and a forked beard, which partly softened the thin mouth with its trace of hereditary cruelty. His complexion, he said, was 'as if smoked'. He was relentless and proud, and a stickler for protocol, particularly for the Friday prayers when the streets were lined with people.

Friday was, of course, the Moslem 'Sabbath', when Suleiman usually prepared to go to prayer in St Sophia. The Master of the Wardrobe had laid out all his clothes, scenting them with aloes. Suleiman wore a gown of heavy silk and over it a sleeveless robe trimmed with ermine. On his head he wore a wide oval turban with an aigrette of peacock feathers held in place by a clasp of diamonds. His white horse was ready, its heavy leather saddle studded with precious gems.

Outside, in the first court of the Grand Seraglio, ringed by a wall three miles long, a cast of characters drawn from the Arabian Nights awaited the moment when their lord and master would emerge and ride along its paved paths past the higgledy-piggledy workaday buildings needed to sustain a town of five thousand people – a bakery on the right, a giant wood-store on the left, big enough to hold five hundred shiploads, and guarded by the Tressed Halberdiers whose headgear incorporated wigs on either side of their faces in case they tried to steal a glance at the Sultan's odalisques when carrying wood for the harem fires.

'There seemed to be no rhyme or reason for the throng of people,' wrote the Venetian envoy after watching Suleiman set off for prayers. He was mistaken (or misleading), for if the harem were the heart of the Seraglio, the Seraglio was the heart of the Empire; it was not merely Suleiman's residence, but the seat of government, a curious mixture of private and public, as though Buckingham Palace and Whitehall lay within the same walled garden.

Envoys from vassal states waited to bow before him and present gifts to God's Vice-Regent on earth – on this particular day some desert horses, two elephants, a cargo of priceless furs, an egg-sized emerald, and a group of fair-skinned Circassian virgins. Filing through their ranks were the Janissaries, the privileged troops drawn from captured Christian boys, welded into the Empire from an early age, swaggering in their white turbans, loose jackets and yellow boots. Ambassadors in scarlet and gold, with their retinue and escort, waited to pay their respects near the gate to the Divan and the second court, leading to a medieval-looking gate with its towers and conical tops 'like candle-snuffers' which concealed a dungeon from where the severed heads of men of rank were carried out and placed on iron spikes by the gate to blacken in the sun. (Those of rank below pasha were exposed in niches by the main gate.)

The Grand Vizier, or chief minister, arrived, preceded by two officials in fur-trimmed robes who struck the ground with silver staffs as they slowly stalked five paces ahead of him – and though the Grand Vizier was changed with disconcerting frequency, often violently, everyone recognized him by his conical turban ringed with gold.

A thousand minor characters, often parasites such as astronomers and dervishes, crowded the first court: the Chief Cook, wearing a pointed cap not unlike a champagne bottle and with a gigantic spoon on his shoulder; the Chief Armourer, carrying the Sultan's sabre in its velvet case; the Chief Huntsman in his horn-shaped cap of gold; the overseers of the Sultan's perfumes; the Chief Keeper of the Nightingales; the Custodian of the Heron's Plume. This was the age of flashing jewels on turban and scimitar, of ostrich plumes, of flowing robes, of immense pantaloons or drawers, of sable-lined pelisses, but each man knew his neighbour instantly by the clothes which strict law demanded he must wear; these laws governed the colour or shape of a turban or sleeve, so that viziers (or ministers) wore green, muftis (or priests) white, court chamberlains scarlet, sheiks blue.

Above all towered the one man who, apart from the Sultan, was feared by all, the Chief Black Eunuch, the Kislar Aga, literally 'Master of the Girls'. He was a man of immense power and wealth – entitled to his own retinue of slaves – for he was in control of the harem and was its only link with the outside world. He waited, a grotesque, ugly, castrated man, by the Gate of Felicity, dressed in his ceremonial robes of flowered silk and broad sash, his sable-trimmed pelisse reaching almost to the ground, and on his head a cylindrical headdress twenty-five inches high, shaped like a sugar loaf. Yet for all this display of ostentation the Kislar Aga was a man who had been castrated in Africa, sold as a slave for a few piastres and, despite the power he wielded, was crude, ignorant, corrupt and, because of his physical state, often dangerously capricious.

Suleiman emerged, hedged in by the main officers of his Privy Chamber – the master of the keys, the master of the stirrup, the master of the turbans, the sword-bearer, even one official who carried his raincoat. Around them all, a group of soldiers shielded the Sultan from the inquisitive by the simple expedient of wearing hats that consisted mainly of huge sprays of feathers rising into the air, forming, in the words of the Venetian envoy, 'the effect of a muslin canopy through which you could catch only the occasional glimpse of the Sultan's grave, stern face'.

As the procession, led by the heralds, moved under the Imperial Gate and into the streets of the capital, two palace pages rode ahead, carrying two of the Sultan's turbans which at times they inclined to the left or right, as though saluting the waiting crowds – which in fact they were, for the custom had started in order to provide the Sultan with a change of turbans when he reached the mosque, but now was regarded merely as a preliminary greeting from the Sultan.

When Suleiman reached the mosque the head of the Janissary troops removed his boots and replaced them with a pair of velvet slippers, for no man could defile the rugs of the mosque which every true believer touched with his forehead during prayer. Only then could Suleiman climb the flight of stairs leading to his private pew, perfumed with incense and decorated with flowers and fruit.

The service over, the Sultan was escorted back to his palace for a banquet of great splendour; on most Fridays guests were bidden to eat with the Sultan; even the groaning tables of Henry VIII, who was three years older than Suleiman the Magnificent,* could not match the gargantuan meals of fifty courses served by two hundred attendants in red silk and gold-embroidered hats who formed a file from the kitchens 'standing close to each other, just as if they had been painted figures'. As the guests arrived in a room with carpets and cloth-of-gold hanging from the walls the attendants – all youths – saluted them, placing their hands on their thighs and bowing as low as they could. When the ceremony of welcome was over and the guests were seated at a silver table,

---

* A title bestowed on him by Europeans. Within the Empire he was known as Suleiman the Legislator.

each dish, protected by a cover of black felt lined with white, was passed from man to man until it reached the Sultan and his guests. Only meat killed 'in the name of God' was allowed to be eaten: this meant that the animals' throats were cut so as to sever the windpipe and carotid arteries. Once each course was finished, the empty dish was, by protocol, borne away with the black-and-white cover reversed.

Food reached Constantinople from every quarter of the Empire: dates, plums and prunes from Egypt; honey (a substitute for sugar) from Candia; oil from Greece; butter from Moldavia, packed in ox hides and shipped across the Black Sea. Pastromani (beef preserved in barrels and the forerunner of today's pastrami) was from cows in calf because Suleiman found it more savoury. A hundred and fifty cooks sweated in ten enormous domed kitchens, cooking up to two hundred sheep for the main course of a dinner which would end with fruit and Turkish Delight, the favourite sweet of the Empire, called Rahat Lokum, or 'Giving rest to the throat'.

There was little alcohol, but there was an abundance of sherbets, iced with snow carried in felt sacks on mules from Mount Olympus to Mudania on the Sea of Marmora, whence it was shipped the seventy miles to Constantinople and stored in special pits. (Nero refrigerated his ice in much the same way.)

Thousands of underlings pandered to every whim of the Sultan. The Head Gardener, who combined his duties with those of Chief Executioner, headed a staff of a thousand under-gardeners easily recognizable in their tall cylindrical hats of red felt. A hundred court calligraphers worked in the Tower of the Commissioner of Stationery, writing all day long on special coloured paper, watermarked even in those days. Every craft, every trade, had its niche, from the sixty carpet-layers, two hundred falconers, fifty confectioners, to nearly two hundred bakers, whose task was to bake pure white loaves for the Sultan, made of goat's milk and grain specially imported from the city of Bursa in Anatolia. Each man according to rank received a ration – a pasha, for instance, was given ten loaves a day. Bread for the 'middle classes' was not so white, the Bursa flour being mixed with Greek grain, while the court pages ate black Greek bread. Good bread was so treasured that the bakers had their own mosque and received an annual gift of a robe in addition to their fixed salary.

*

No doubt Suleiman breathed a sigh of relief when the festivities were ended, and though we cannot, of course, follow his footsteps for the rest of the day the likelihood is that, as the Divan was not in session,* he left the Selamlik, the men's 'greeting-quarters' where no woman could venture, for the harem, its doors closed to all but the Sultan and his eunuchs.

There were five gates leading into the harem, but the main entrances lay in the second court behind the Divan, or from the third court, in itself a startling contrast to the semi-public atmosphere of the first and second courts; in the third court, beyond the Gate of Felicity, the scene changed abruptly. The dusty outside courtyards, the milling crowds of officials, gave way to an extensive garden, in the centre of which Suleiman's pavilion blazed with cloth-of-gold hangings and shining marble walls. In one corner of the third court a door opened on to the Golden Road, the link between the male and female worlds, a long, cobbled corridor, leading past the suites of the Queen Mother, the rooms of those slaves elevated to the status of 'wives', to the harem mosque.

The harem was not a single building, but a warren of pavilions, kiosks, villas, some with terraced gardens or courtyards with pergolas, built almost at random on ground sloping from the crest of the hill to the water's edge, and it centred round the most important woman in the Ottoman Empire – the Queen Mother, mother of the ruler, the Sultan Valideh. She ruled the harem and often the fortunes of the Empire too, for though a sultan could have a thousand concubines he could only have one mother; the Prophet himself having decreed that, 'Paradise is under the feet of thy mother.' When her son became Sultan the new Queen Mother exacted an oath of obedience from every member of the harem. Even the Sultan's semi-official wives could not see her unless an audience had been requested and granted. Not even the greatest favourite of the Sultan dared to visit her except in 'full dress', and with her arms crossed over her breasts as she addressed the Queen Mother by her title of 'Crown of Veiled Heads'.

A strict hierarchy had arisen in the harem since it had first started as a convenience for a nation's warriors too busy fighting to be saddled with the canker of jealousy. Away from home for long periods, they found it

* The Divan, or Turkish Parliament, sat four days a week, from Saturday to Tuesday inclusive.

much simpler to lock their women up when they were not there, and guard them with eunuchs. Out of this practical arrangement, a court with orders of precedence had evolved. Its members ranged from the lowliest slaves sleeping ten to a room until the moment when they might 'catch Suleiman's eye'; those who had been pleasured by him but who had not borne him children; until, directly below the Queen Mother, were the sultanas* – semi-official wives called *kadins*, elevated to that position after bearing a son and from that moment onwards living in their own suites with their own retinues. They were usually limited to the first four who produced boys: after that the court abortionist was called in. Even the sultanas had their ruthless order of precedence, and no second sultana (though she might be the Sultan's current favourite) could lord it over the woman who had borne an heir before her; yet every woman in the harem had entered it as a slave (which meant, incidentally, that each sultan in the Ottoman Empire was the son of a slave).

Over the years the growth of protocol in the harem had spilled over, even to the royal bed. The preliminaries in choosing a partner for the night must have been extremely irksome to a warm-blooded man. First he had to make a long and profound obeisance to his mother; only then were the young odalisques paraded before him. If one took his fancy he signalled her out, and then there were hours of frenzied preparation before the girl went to his bed. She was scrubbed and bathed, often by a procession of virgins who, after pummelling her and shaving her body of every vestige of hair, cleansed her with a mudpack of oil and riceflour, dyed her nails, perfumed and pomaded her, using henna to prevent perspiration, and painted her eyelashes with kohl, made of lemons and plumbago over a brazier.

Since (in theory anyway) Suleiman had the pick of the Empire's most beautiful slaves, one might have hoped that protocol would be dispensed with in the bedchamber but, in fact, when a virgin was led to the Sultan's rooms women guarded the doors zealously and two enormous candles burned throughout the night. The Sultan invariably went to bed first, and with the dawn he rose first, and made for his bath (cleanliness being

* The word 'sultana' is westernized and not strictly correct. The Ottomans used 'Sultan' for both men and women, placing it before a man's name and after a woman's.

extremely close to godliness in the Moslem world) where he lingered some time. His bathing quarters consisted of a three-roomed suite in white marble. The anteroom was furnished with golden hangings encrusted with pearls. The bathroom itself was, even in the time of Suleiman, astonishingly modern – the bath very much the same shape as ours today, only with a seat at each end, complete with back and arm rest, all in marble. Water heated in an invisible copper boiler gushed in through fountains.

While the Sultan bathed, the girl was busy examining his clothes, for all money in his pockets was automatically hers by right. The date was then carefully entered into a special register (in case anything should happen nine months later), after which the girl returned to her quarters. If she did not produce an heir, and become a sultana, she might never see the Sultan again.

It must have seemed very romantic, at any rate to the indefatigable lady traveller, Frances Elliott. She wrote in her *Diary of an Idle Woman in Constantinople*, 'Here was to be seen the Kislar Aga of the black eunuchs, gorgeous with ringing plaques of gold, sounding like bells, conducting a bevy of princesses ... another, escorting the stately Valideh, closely veiled, to visit her son, followed by her court of slaves; a third, guarding the Sultana of the day, setting forth for the bath; or awaiting fresh convoys of beauties, to be drilled and educated to take their places when the imperial appetite is satiated; Albanian, Greek, Georgian and Circassian, offered as tribute, or stolen by pirates, or purchased in Asiatic markets – all perfumed, painted and apparelled to catch the eye. A world as of magic, in which the eunuchs rule, and the Sultan, however often he changes, is exalted to a god.'

In truth the romantic picture of beautiful perfumed odalisques reclining on silken cushions was tinged with much sadness. Except for the lucky ones, it must have been dull. Only a few inmates were caught in its intrigues, only a handful of aspiring – and often calculating – harem girls ever slept with the Sultan. The monotonous life, the absence of male companionship led to many sexual indulgences, including 'love affairs' with eunuchs, all of whom were examined regularly by the palace doctors to make sure that the operation of castration had been perfectly performed. Not only eunuchs but castrated page-boys frequently became the favourites of harem women. These boys had been carefully trained, were always dressed in brilliant silks, and were invariably called by flower names – Hyacinth, Narcissus, Rose, Carnation.

The eunuchs may have provided a certain distraction, but the most prevalent vice in the harem was, of course, the easiest – lesbianism. The girls, it was said, indulged in lesbian love affairs 'as often as the pages [training for war or diplomacy] indulged in homosexuality'. Despite the ever-watchful eyes of the eunuchs we find Ottaviano Bon, a Venetian envoy to the capital, writing of the 'young, lustie and lascivious wenches' in the harem, 'Now, it is not lawfull for any one to bring ought in unto them, with which they may commit deeds of beastly uncleannesse; so that if they have a will to eate Cucumbers, they are sent in unto them sliced, to deprive them of the meanes of playing the wantons.'

The lack of a normal life was bad enough, but it was even worse when the lord and master was deposed or died. The new Sultan instantly banished all his predecessor's odalisques to an older palace, in effect nothing more than a boarding-house for compulsorily retired females and called by the Turks 'The Palace of Tears'. Occasionally a favourite would be married off to some luckless pasha. For the most part the women passed their declining years in a hopeless living death.

*

The harem of Suleiman the Magnificent contained three hundred odalisques living in its bewildering assortment of rooms, each one carefully trained in the art of pleasing her lord, each one proud to be bedded. Yet the harem posed a particular problem to Suleiman – one that would have astonished, even outraged, his ancestors. Soon after one slave had borne him an heir and had thus become First Sultana, the Sultan was presented with a newly captured Russian slave.

Nine months later she bore him a son, and became Second Sultana. From that moment, the Sultan never looked at another woman. He was faithful to her until she died. With an irony hard to match even in a work of fiction, it was this act of faithfulness, this deep love for one woman, that caused the first cracks in Suleiman's dynasty – cracks that would eventually widen, until the foundations were so weakened that the greatest empire on earth lay in a heap of ruins.

Chapter two
The fatal flaws

Suleiman came to the throne in 1520 at the age of twenty-six, and three factors contributed to the auspicious start to his reign. An only son, he was spared the agony of enforcing the Moslem law of fratricide, which had caused one of his ancestors to slaughter his two brothers and eight nephews; an enlightened father had sent him to spend sixteen years learning the art of government in provincial capitals; and he had something else, rare in those days of intrigue: as firm and close a friend as any man could wish.

This was Ibrahim, born a Christian Greek at Parga on the Ionian Sea, captured by corsairs, sold as a slave to a Turkish widow who was so impressed by his talents that she educated him in music, philosophy and languages so that he spoke Turkish, Persian, Greek and Italian.

Suleiman first met Ibrahim when a youth, and attached him to his princely retinue. He was one year older than Suleiman, below average height, swarthy, but with a long face full of animation. Inevitably, when Suleiman became Sultan, Ibrahim joined the royal court, and the pair remained inseparable. They ate their meals together, went boating, and in times of war shared a tent – or even the same bed, thus convincing some future historians that the two men had a sexual attachment; not that it would have raised an eyebrow in those days.

Ibrahim was a loyal friend and a valuable adviser, in some ways more discerning than his master. Within three years, having started his career at court in the comparatively humble post of Grand Falconer and Master of the Pages, he had become in succession First Officer of the Royal Bedchamber, governor of a province, Vizier and finally Grand Vizier. Even by Ottoman standards, in which preferment was often the result of a despotic whim, this was an astonishingly rapid rise to power.

Over the years the two men had forged a deep bond of friendship which had started in the comparatively careless rapture of youth, and now Ibrahim fitted perfectly into the off-duty pursuits of a man's man like Suleiman. When each August the Sultan moved his court (and harem) to the more bracing climate of Adrianople, he and Ibrahim spent days together engaged in falconry, hunting in a vast area of semi-swamp and floodwater abounding in wild geese, heron, hawks, eagles. Here Suleiman laid out many square miles of gardens on the banks of the Maritza river, filling them with roses and wild quince, and in their splendid tents each evening Ibrahim was always ready with his music, or at hand if the Sultan felt the urge to write a poem. Sometimes they spent months in Adrianople, only returning to Constantinople when 'the frogs begin to be a nuisance with their croaking'.

It can never have crossed their minds that one day their relationship would end in tragedy fomented by harem jealousies. Suleiman's first 'wife', a Montenegrin called Gulbehar ('Rose of Spring'), had automatically become Sultana when she bore Suleiman a son, Mustafa. 'Rose of Spring' was apparently a woman who, in the best tradition of wifeliness, was perfectly content to bask in the love of a wise husband who was not a voluptuary, until suddenly, without warning, the tranquil life of the harem was shattered.

Within a few days of Ibrahim's appointment as Grand Vizier in June 1523, Turkish raiders in Galicia captured a bevy of slaves, including a Russian girl of such infectious wit that they promptly christened her 'Khurrem' (the 'Laughing One'), and singled her out for the royal harem, where, because of her Russian origin, she was to become better known as Roxelana, a corruption of Russolana.

Roxelana was not particularly beautiful but she had a slight, graceful figure, great charm and a sense of humour that soon enabled her to gain the complete affections of the Sultan. A Bellini portrait of her shows a striking profile with red hair hanging down her back in two braids. Round her neck are several rows of huge pearls. She looks every inch a Slav, and Suleiman fell passionately in love with her. Within the year she presented him with a son (the first of her five children), which the delighted Suleiman christened Selim after his father.

Roxelana was now Second Sultana, and third woman in the harem hierarchy, after the Queen Mother and 'Rose of Spring', and before long it was rumoured that the Sultan was not only interested in sharing his bed with Roxelana but enjoyed spending hours talking to her, discussing problems of state, walking with her past the ornamental ponds, through the gardens with their tame gazelles and ostriches. Roxelana had all the clear-sighted shrewdness of a peasant girl, and there seems to be no doubt that Suleiman sought her advice. It was an entirely new phenomenon.

No doubt Roxelana genuinely loved her lord, but her lust for power was something new to the harem. She was clever and played her cards patiently, but before long there was trouble, possibly because Suleiman was happiest with a few intimates, and regularly visited 'Rose of Spring', whose son, the heir-apparent, was growing into a fine boy. Whether or not he and Rose remained lovers no one knows. Since it *is* known that his passion for Roxelana was insatiable the visits may well have had no more significance than those of a man visiting an estranged wife to see the son he loves; on the other hand, each sultana had the conjugal rights of a wife, and the Sultan, in theory anyway, was obliged to sleep with her when it was her *nobet gecesi*, or 'night turn'.

Certainly, after one royal visit to Rose of Spring's private apartments Roxelana flew into a rage, and the two women had a stand-up fist-fight. A jealous Roxelana forced her way past the black eunuchs into Rose's sitting-room with its gold-leafed walls, flew at her, fists flailing in fury. In fact, before the two girls fighting on the floor could be separated, Roxelana had got the worst of it. Rose of Spring tore out a handful of her tawny hair and scratched her severely in the face.

If this were a desperate attempt by Rose of Spring to hold on to her marital rights, it failed dismally. For several days Roxelana refused to appear before the Sultan, using the perfectly valid excuse that her face was disfigured. At the same time she was careful enough to make no complaint. In the end, Suleiman gave in. The battle in the harem had, of course, become court gossip, and so was the result: though Rose of Spring still remained the First Sultana, she was, according to a report by Pietro Bragadino, Venetian envoy in Constantinople, completely displaced in the Sultan's affections, 'her lord not concerning himself with her any more'.

Patiently Roxelana waited until she could get rid of Rose of Spring, and this she did when Mustafa reached his majority. Rose's son was appointed governor of the Province of Magnesia and his mother went with him, spending much of the year away from the capital. Shortly afterwards the Queen Mother died, and Roxelana found herself in fact, if not in name, first woman of the harem, a position she made more secure by having Mustafa (and his mother) transferred to provinces even more distant.

Now her power over Suleiman was such that another Venetian wrote, 'He bears her such love and keeps such faith to her that all of his subjects marvel and say that she has bewitched him, and they call her the ziadi [jadi], or the witch. On this account the army and the court hate her and her children, but because he loves her, no one dares to protest: for myself I have always heard everyone speak ill of her and of her children, and well of the first-born and his mother.'

Suleiman was certainly so besotted – the only instance in Ottoman history of a Sultan's exclusive devotion – that Roxelana now made the ultimate demand: marriage. Even Suleiman must have been astounded. The rights she enjoyed as Sultana placed her virtually on a par with the absent Rose of Spring. Suleiman's love put her above all others. Not for six centuries had a sultan married, since the wife of one of Suleiman's forebears was taken prisoner and was forced by her conqueror to strip naked and serve him at table. To prevent any further humiliations, marriage had never been entertained since.

Roxelana, however, was no ordinary woman, and put forward arguments which the Sultan found hard to refute. To ensure Suleiman's faithfulness, Roxelana had persuaded him to marry off many younger, prettier harem-slaves. Some had done very well for themselves, and Roxelana argued that while they were now wives, with privileges and property of their own, she, the lover of the most exalted man on earth, was still a slave.

It did not, she argued, seem fair, particularly as she had by now become a true believer and for some time had been doling out large sums of (Suleiman's) money to mosques and other institutions (thus gaining the support of *ulema*, or the religious body). In fact, she knew she held the love of a man who was sufficiently independent to ignore tradition if he chose.

While Constantinople gasped in disbelief the wedding took place quietly before a judge of the law to whom Suleiman promised, 'This woman, I set free from slavery and make her a wife. All that belongs to her shall be her property.'

As one of the clerks at the Genoese Bank of St George wrote, 'This week, there has occurred in this city a most extraordinary event, one absolutely unprecedented in the history of the Sultans. The Grand Signor Suleiman has taken unto himself a slave woman from Russia called Roxelana, as his Empress, and there has been great feasting, and much rejoicing, in consequence. The ceremony took place within the Palace,' adding with obvious perplexity: 'There is great talk all over this country about this marriage and no one can understand exactly what it means.'*

The ceremony that made Roxelana the Sultan's acknowledged consort may have been a simple affair, but the party that followed was a very different matter. Over the years Suleiman's court had reached a state of 'unprecedented luxury and display [which] were the wonder of Europe'. But nothing, not even the royal circumcision feasts which started during Suleiman's reign, surpassed the 'wedding breakfast'.

Within an hour of breakfast – bread and olives for the poor; cheese, fruit, bread and rose-leaf jam for the wealthier – the streets of Constantinople were jammed for the celebration. The main streets were festooned with flowers, the scarlet flags of the Ottoman Empire, the green flags of Islam. Mounds of fruit – mardin plums, Azerbaizan pears, Smyrna grapes, Temesvir prunes – were on sale at one street corner; at the next there would be haggis cooked on portable stoves for the crowds who lined the streets. The sherbet sellers did a roaring trade, pouring the sherbet through a lump of snow stuck on the end of the vessel's spout: sherbets of lemon juice and snow flavoured with honey, amber and musk; others of water lilies, together with the favourite (but more expensive) sherbet made of violets and honey. There were squares of rice-jelly sprinkled with rose-water, served with a brass shovel, or fruit soup with ice floating in it. The coffee sellers were also doing well, for Suleiman had just permitted the first Arab to open a coffee house in the city, to sell what one contemporary, contemptuous Turk described as 'the black enemy of sleep and copulation'.

From all over the country offerings had been sent to the Sultana, and these were first shown in a staggering procession of two hundred mules loaded with carpets, furniture, gold and silver vases. Each mule was led

* Quoted in R. Davey, *The Sultan and His Subjects.*

by two slaves in splendid livery. They were followed by two hundred camels heavily laden with 'sumptuous gifts sent to the Empress by the great ones of the nation, even from very distant parts of the Empire'. A hundred and sixty magnificently dressed eunuchs – half of them black, half white – brought up the rear. They, too, were presents – to enter the service of Roxelana.

This procession was followed by one of another sort – the city's master bakers baking bread on dozens of wagons, throwing the hot little loaves covered with sesame and fennel seeds to the crowds, while, as a centre of attraction, an enormous loaf, certainly the size of an average room, was dragged on a raft of poles by ten oxen. It had been baked slowly in a pit lined and covered with cinders.

The festivities continued for a week. As each dusk fell, and the city sparkled with thousands of lanterns, a tribune was set up in the Hippodrome – where the Byzantines had raced their chariots – for the Sultan and his court. One part was screened so that Roxelana and the harem could see through gilded lattices everything that happened in the arena. There were tournaments, wrestling, archery, tumblers, jugglers and a procession of strange-looking animals from Asia and Africa including, as the Genoese bank clerk noted, 'two giraffes with necks so long that they seemed to reach the sky'.

Thousands lined the edge of the arena, even climbing trees to catch a glimpse of the Sultan or to receive the gifts of money or silk which the Sultana's slaves were showering among the crowds, together with 'a liberal distribution of bread and fruit'. There was no doubt a certain amount of drinking, for though alcohol was officially prohibited by the Koran, Suleiman was not averse to the occasional glass of wine, and only if a man became a nuisance did the usually blind eye of the law see anything amiss – fortunately for transgressors, as the punishments for drunkenness ranged from the bastinado to an enforced gulp of molten lead.

*

The marriage of Roxelana was the first link in the chain of events that brought about the downfall of the Ottoman Empire, for now – and for the next century and a half – the influence of the harem in state affairs was all-powerful.

As she watched and waited before dealing with rivals who stood in her way, Roxelana faced one minor but irritating problem: that of the distance between the Seraglio and the harem, which until the middle of the sixteenth century had always been housed in another building, the Old Seraglio, built by Mahomet the Conqueror after taking the city in 1453, but long since discarded by the sultans as a centre of government. Roxelana felt that life would be easier if she and her husband lived literally under the same roof, and chance played into her hands. Constantinople, with its flimsy wooden buildings, was like a tinder-box, with constant threats of fire, and one of the worst in its history swept the city in 1541. Starting on the waterfront the flames were fanned up to the gimcrack buildings of the Old Palace, where odalisques screaming with terror fled as it burned the heart of the harem to a pile of grey ash.

Suleiman's wife obviously had to live somewhere. So Roxelana moved into the Grand Seraglio which, since the time of Mahomet the Conqueror, had been in effect a government office, with sleeping-quarters for the Sultan when he did not visit the harem. When Roxelana arrived even Suleiman must have been startled, for she was accompanied by an entourage of a hundred ladies-in-waiting, a guard of eunuchs, together with servants, her dressmaker and purveyor, who was 'very richly dressed, coming and going out of the palace whenever he liked, and always being accompanied by thirty slaves'.

No husband could have made more than a feeble protest in these circumstances. The gutted Old Palace – in which a sultan's ransom of treasures had perished – seemed to take a long time to rebuild. A private door was cut between Roxelana's new quarters and the Sultan's modest two-roomed apartment. Now she was installed by his side, and it was a simple matter for the Sultana to walk down the Golden Road until she reached a stairway leading to the tower where Suleiman had constructed a latticed window overlooking the Divan, so that he could listen to its proceedings without his ministers knowing whether he was there or not. Here Roxelana learned the art of government.

It seemed that Roxelana had achieved the ultimate ambition, but even now two clouds darkened her horizon. Mustafa, the heir-apparent, was the idol of the people and stood in the way of her son Selim; and she was jealous of the power which the Sultan had bestowed on Ibrahim.

*

During these years the Sultan had not, of course, spent all his time lolling on harem divans in the arms of his lover. There is much misconception about the sexual life (and prowess) of the Ottoman sultans, and though it was the debauchery and depravity of many sultans after Suleiman which helped to bring about the fall of the Empire there were many whose thirst for fighting was the equal of their thirst for women (with both conveniently easy to slake). The Turks really loved fighting. As *Tractatus** puts it, they 'come together for war as though they had been invited to a wedding.' Suleiman was above all a warrior-ruler, who watched every aspect of his country's fortunes, but preferred the battlefield to the council chamber. True, his countrymen gave him the title of the Legislator, but in fact his legislation included few startling innovations; rather did he try to provide laws to fill in loopholes in the everyday life as it then was. He gained his reputation as a great legislator partly because his achievements were set in contrast to the absence of any law-makers among his immediate predecessors. But it was because he enjoyed going to war that he built up a remarkable school for slaves. With each campaign thousands of new slaves arrived, and as Sultan, one in five became his personal property. In addition there were the 'tribute boys', victims of a process under which agents scoured the Empire every four years to wrest the most promising youths from non-Moslem families and train them for the royal service. They were picked out by 'a body of officials more skilled in judging boys than trained horse-dealers are in judging colts'. It was cruel; though well-behaved, intelligent Christian boys stood far better chances of preferment in the Seraglio than in spartan mountain-farms. When they were inducted into the palace school they became members of the Sultan's slave family, from which all the highest posts in the land were chosen. Their training in scholarship exceeded that of the then new university at Bologna; they were hardened by physical games of prowess, so that, as in Plato's Republic, Suleiman was cultivating intelligence inside toughened bodies.

Their training was harsh. Each boy had a daily bath and a weekly manicure and pedicure. He had to shave twice a week, have a clean

* *Tractatus* was the title of a volume published in the fifteenth century containing miscellaneous information and sayings by a number of authors. It gave the word 'tract' to the English language.

handkerchief daily, a haircut once a month. He was searched daily for hidden sweets or spices (the latter being regarded as encouraging sexual desires) and for love letters – presumably from other boys, since they were cut off from all female company. No doubt the incidence of homosexuality was high and, 'for Sultans who were inclined to such pleasures, it must have been a happy hunting ground.'

Of course, tribute boys had to be staunch teetotallers, except when ill, for in the infirmary they were allowed wine which the palace gardeners lowered by rope over the palace wall. But there was no malingering. No tribute boy could enter the infirmary without Suleiman's express permission; nor could he have a tooth extracted without his sanction, and if the dentist made a mistake he lost one of his own teeth.

Despite the hardships, every boy had equal opportunities to rise to the highest positions in the land, for the Ottoman Empire was never ruled by Turks, but by a huge slave family elevated in status after an enforced and gruelling education had fitted them to rule better than the average Turk. The Venetian envoy Gianfrancesco Morosini summed it up, when he said that they, 'take great pride in being able to say, "I am a slave of the Grand Signor"; since they know that this is a government or commonwealth of slaves, where it is theirs to command.' In fact, Suleiman even faced the problem of trying to exclude unwanted boys who pretended they had been chosen. When the Sultan went to war, he could leave behind a government of which every single member belonged to him personally as a slave. He held the power of life and death over them – which was why he could at a stroke make or break a grand vizier.

He held the same power over his troops, for while the brainiest boys became diplomats the brawniest became soldiers in the élite corps of the Janissaries, a praetorian guard formed in 1330 exclusively from tribute boys or slaves. There was no force in the world quite like them. Absolute obedience was the first article of their charter. The men wore dark blue uniforms and magnificent white felt hats, those of the senior officers being adorned with prodigious bird-of-paradise plumes. They took an oath of celibacy, were well paid, and so well fed that all their military terms reflected the pleasures of the kitchen. One grade of officer was called *chorbaji* (literally 'soup kitchen'). Sergeants and corporals were called 'Head Cook' and 'Head Water-carrier'. The cauldrons in which their pilaff was cooked became the equivalent of our regimental colours, and if the Janissaries had a grievance to air they overturned them, as a gesture that they would no longer eat the Sultan's food.

With diplomats and soldiers of such unquestioning obedience and loyalty, Suleiman no doubt felt easy in his mind when, within a year of his accession, he set off on his first campaign against Christian Europe. The goal was the fortified citadel of Belgrade, 'The White City', on the southern shore of the Danube.

War in those days demanded a strict sense of protocol. It had to be legitimized by the highest Moslem spiritual leaders in the Divan, after which the first measure was to throw the enemy's ambassador into jail. The Grand Vizier then received a charger, brilliantly caparisoned, and a jewelled sabre at a magnificent reception. The Court Astrologer fixed the time of the attack, the enemy always being offered the opportunity to surrender.

On 16 February 1521, the Sultan left Constantinople for Belgrade in a scene of unparalleled splendour. Three thousand camels carrying ammunition and supplies had gone ahead by the time the Sultan reviewed picked troops in the first courtyard of the Grand Seraglio. The horsemen's mounts were caparisoned in cloth-of-silver with gold and precious stones, each rider plumed in black feathers and wearing cloth-of-gold or silk or satin according to rank and regiment; each rider had two sheaths, one for his bow, the other filled with arrows, a spear in his right hand and a gem-studded scimitar and a steel club hanging from his saddle. The infantry units wore enormous plumes that gave one watcher the impression of 'a moving forest', and they were followed by the redoubtable Janissaries with their muskets. The Sultan in cloth-of-gold rode last, on a magnificent charger, followed by three pages carrying his water-flask, his cloak and his bow.

The discipline of the troops was stricter than anywhere in the world. Paolo Giovio in Rome wrote that, 'Their discipline under arms is due to their justice and severity, which surpasses that of the ancient Romans. They surpass our soldiers for three reasons: they obey their commanders without question: they seem to care nothing at all for their lives in battle: they go for a long time without bread or wine, being content with barley and water.' The troops could also live for long periods on iron rations, very necessary when marching through areas laid waste by the enemy. Their meagre diet consisted mainly of flour, spices and salt, which they mixed with water and boiled until the swollen 'porridge' filled a bowl. Some carried a small sack of powdered, dried beef, which they warmed in the same way; sometimes they ate horseflesh, and of course they lived off the country when they could.

Twice before, Suleiman's ancestors had failed to take Belgrade, but now, aided by another thirty thousand camels from Asia carrying more supplies, Suleiman laid siege to the city and succeeded, helped to no small degree by the infantry, whose task it was 'to aid in filling the moats by their own bodies'. If they lived they were rewarded; if (as usual) they died, they went as martyrs straight to heaven.

Little more than six months after leaving Constantinople Suleiman was back, a hero. Belgrade, the last major barrier on the northern route to Europe, had fallen – a victory which the Doge of Venice described in a letter to England as 'lamentable, and of importance to all Christians'.

Suleiman wasted no time. Within a year he attacked the island of Rhodes, with its fortress housing the famous Knights of St John of Jerusalem and succeeded in capturing it after a siege of 145 days. But the victory had been earned only at fearful cost to the Turks, who lost ten times as many men as the heroic defenders, and not for three years did Suleiman go to war again.

This was the period of Ibrahim's meteoric rise to fame, and of a friendship that seemed to become firmer and closer each day. At times the two men even wore each other's clothes; they exchanged notes when apart; they often slept in the same quarters. No wonder the Ottoman court was scandalized. To them it was totally unsuitable for the world's greatest emperor to show such favour to a slave.

Gradually Ibrahim's mode of life changed, as he lapped up the luxuriance of the Byzantine age which almost suffocated Constantinople with its ostentation. It seemed as though Ibrahim were trying to out-do his master in splendour. He lived in a palace modelled on the Sultan's. He received vast gifts from those who sought to work under him. He had his private barge with twelve pairs of oars, eight guards of honour, twelve led horses. The Sultan even offered him a salary nearly twice as large as that earned by the preceding grand vizier, though this was of little consequence because the property of a grand vizier was always returned to the State on his death or deposition.

And finally, in May 1524, the Sultan offered Ibrahim his own sister in marriage, the ceremony being followed by nine days of rejoicing in the Hippodrome, with the streets 'full of pleasure from end to end'.

The Sultan's faith in Ibrahim as a warrior and prime minister was fully justified. He may have been boastful and conceited, and he certainly was not averse to taking presents (including a magnificent ruby ring once worn by François I), but he performed his duties brilliantly, both in war and as a diplomat.

When the war against Hungary was renewed, after years of sporadic fighting in the border areas, Ibrahim distinguished himself in the final battle on the plain of Mohacs. It was a savage battle in which the Turks took no prisoners, enabling Suleiman to note on 31 August 1526 in his diary (using the third person as he always did), 'The Emperor, seated on a golden throne receives the homage of the viziers and beys: massacre of 2,000 prisoners,' adding the laconic homely touch, 'The rain falls in torrents.' In all 200,000 were massacred and 100,000 slaves taken back to Constantinople.

*

Suleiman was now thirty-two, and Bragadino, the Venetian envoy, found him 'deadly pale, slender, with an aquiline nose and a long neck; of no great apparent strength, but his hand is very strong, as I observed when I kissed it, and he is said to be able to bend a stiffer bow than anyone else. He is by nature melancholy, much addicted to women, liberal, proud, hasty and yet sometimes very gentle.'

This was the ruler of the greatest empire on earth, won in three centuries since the little clan of the Othmans first moved west, and won by an army which, with irresistible impetus, and an individual ferocity unknown in Europe, plus unrivalled artillery, seemed to have no limits to its horizons other than its own ambitions.

The towns, countries, rivers under the jurisdiction of Suleiman read like a gazetteer of famous landmarks. 'The Turkish dominions in his time comprised all the most celebrated cities of biblical and classical history, except Rome, Syracuse, and Persepolis,' wrote Stanley Lane-Poole. 'The sites of Carthage, Memphis, Tyre, Nineveh, Babylon, and Palmyra were

Ottoman ground; and the cities of Alexandria, Jerusalem, Smyrna, Damascus, Nice, Prusa, Athens, Philippi, and Adrianople, besides many of later but scarce inferior celebrity, such as Algiers, Cairo, Mekka, Medina, Basra, Baghdad, and Belgrade, obeyed the Sultan of Constantinople. The Nile, the Jordan, the Orontes, the Euphrates, the Tigris, the Danube, the Hebrus, and the Ilyssus, rolled their waters "within the shadow of the Horsetails". The eastern recess of the Mediterranean, the Propontis, the Palus Maeotis, the Euxine, and the Red Sea, were Turkish lakes. The Ottoman crescent touched the Atlas and the Caucasus; it was supreme over Athos, Sinai, Ararat, Mount Carmel, Mount Taurus, Ida, Olympus, Pelion, Hacmus, the Carpathian and the Acroceraunian Heights.'

Suleiman was always looking to Europe; and he knew a great deal about it. He had inherited from his father a copy of the chart which Columbus had drawn (and later lost) as he sailed to the New World. It is astonishing to think that 'the barbarians', as the Christians contemptuously called the Ottomans, were plotting their campaigns aided by a map showing the western shores of Spain, France, Africa, the Atlantic and the east coast of Central and North America.

Now, with Hungary finally subjected, he turned his sights on the final gateway into Europe: Vienna, at that time a small city of churches and monasteries ringed round the cathedral of St Steven.

Not for eight centuries, since the battle of Tours, had Christianity been so threatened, yet the European powers were facing so many military threats that, incredibly, little help was offered to the garrison at Vienna, which Suleiman and Ibrahim invested in the last days of September 1529, after taking Buda on the way. There seemed no reason why the city should not fall quickly. Suleiman had nearly a quarter of a million troops and three hundred guns. Vienna was defended by only sixteen thousand troops and seventy-two guns behind an encircling wall five feet thick and without bastions. For miles around the city the tents of Suleiman filled the plain while his cavalry ravaged the country with unmentionable ferocity and cruelty. Four hundred small Turkish boats were ferried up the Danube. But Suleiman's siege guns had been left half-way along the route, bogged down in the worst storms for years, and though Suleiman attacked remorselessly for three weeks, it was in vain. The countryside had been so denuded that he had not even enough food to feed his men.

Suleiman had no alternative but to raise the siege. On the last night the enormous amount of booty taken was burned below the walls of Vienna. The best-looking women were selected for the slave markets, and the rest of the prisoners – mostly local peasantry who had nothing to do with the war – were hurled into the raging fire in full view of the Viennese.

Suleiman and Ibrahim retreated without pursuit to Constantinople, where his failure to break the resistance of Vienna was concealed by fanciful accounts of his 'success'. Nothing, however, could disguise the fact that for the first time in seventeen years the Ottoman Empire had been checked, and by inferior forces.

One other sobering point, doubtless not appreciated at the time, cannot be denied: that, in fact, Suleiman *should* have taken Vienna and that the history of the world would have been changed had not torrential rains prevented him from bringing up his heavy guns.

*

Suleiman's golden age had now reached its zenith. Not only was he victorious on land but, equally remarkable, his navy ruled the Mediterranean under the most fearsome admiral of his time – Barbarossa, a murderous red-bearded, hooked-nosed pirate whom Suleiman had cleverly persuaded to serve under the Ottoman flag. Suleiman gave him a jewelled sword, the title of Lord High Admiral, and constructed an entirely new fleet for him of fast, wicked-looking war-galleys driven by fifty long oars, with cannon on their foredecks. Built like today's racing shells – their length was eight times their beam – they were manned by wretched galley-slaves chained to the long oars, mostly men captured in war but at times slaves from Turkish homes who were hired out in the summer season.

Barbarossa ravaged the coasts of Africa and Europe in daring raids – Italy, Spain, Sardinia and even the Adriatic coast. In Africa he took the city of Tunis, using as a pretext for aggression the fact that the Sultan Boni Hafss was a degenerate reprobate. He certainly was – for 'he spent his energies in recruiting a harem of four hundred good-looking lads'.

Barbarossa, like Ibrahim, always took care, when enriching himself, to propitiate the Sultan with suitable gifts; when he returned to Constantinople from a season of plunder he 'dressed two hundred boys in scarlet, bearing in their hands flasks and goblets of gold and silver. Behind them followed thirty others, each carrying on his shoulders a purse of gold; after these came two hundred men, each carrying a purse of money; and lastly, two hundred infidels wearing collars, each bearing a roll of cloth on his back. These he took as a present to the Emperor, and having kissed the royal hand, was presented with robes of the most splendid kind.'*

When Barbarossa died, Suleiman built for him a tomb the cunning old pirate might have chosen himself – grey granite, almost lapped by the Bosporus, engraved with three Arabic words that meant 'Dead is the Captain of the Sea'.

*

With the Empire's armies and navies pouring in untold wealth, the splendour of court life grew. Suleiman's favourite kiosk behind the Gate of Felicity had marble walls inlaid with precious stones, the coloured windows laced in gold. Here, during the day he took the occasional nap on two mattresses, one embroidered in gold, one in silver. At night he slept on three, covered in red velvet.

The Sultan never wore the same clothes twice – they were always perfumed with aloe wood – not even the sable pelisses studded with rubies. He dined on a silver table off jewel-encrusted silver plates – lobster, swordfish and sturgeon from the Bosporus, stuffed pheasants, venison from the hunting-grounds. He drank wine from a goblet cut out of one piece of turquoise.

Even his four barges were sumptuously appointed, with curtained pavilions at the stern inlaid with mother of pearl, the roof edged with marquetry of rubies and turquoises. There can be no doubt that Suleiman was becoming enticed by the sybaritic life of the Byzantine Age that was all around him: the imperial wealth, the indolence, colonnades, churches, even new mosques influenced by Byzantine architecture, all pointed to the fact that the hard-living Turks who had captured Constantinople were being steadily corrupted.

At forty, in 1534, the Venetian Daniello de Ludovisi found Suleiman 'tall, thin, with an aquiline nose'; there were indications that the Sultan was leaving the reins of government more and more in the hands of Ibrahim. Ludovisi felt that the Sultan was 'given rather to ease than

* Recorded by G. E. Hubbard in *The Day of the Crescent*.

business, orthodox in his faith and of decent life; his intellect, however, it is commonly said, is not very alert, nor has he the force and prudence which ought to belong to so great a prince, seeing that he has given the government of his empire into the hands of another, his Grand Vizier Ibrahim, without whom neither he nor any of his court undertake any important deliberations, while Ibrahim does everything without consulting the Grand Signor or any other person.'

As with other men who have risen to power quickly, Ibrahim's vanity had been growing over the years, and was becoming dangerous. At a reception in 1533 foreign envoys were required to kiss the hem of the Grand Vizier's cloth-of-gold caftan before offering gifts. When they had all assembled, Ibrahim made an astonishing speech. 'It is I who govern this vast empire,' he announced. 'What I do is done; I have all the power, all offices, all the rule. What I wish to give is given and cannot be taken away; what I do not give is not confirmed by anyone. If ever the great Sultan wishes to give, or has given anything, if I do not please it is not carried out. All is in my hands: peace, war, treasure; I do not say these things for no reason, but to give you courage to speak freely.'

This was not the first time he had been so outspoken and it gave great consolation to his enemies of whom he had many – including, of course, Roxelana; and there can be little doubt that she was largely responsible for starting the whispering campaign against him.

Throughout these years she had been relentlessly pursuing one goal – the throne for her son, Selim. Mustafa, the Rose of Spring's son, blocked the way. And so, to a lesser degree, did Ibrahim, because of his influence on her husband. Ibrahim, she maintained, was usurping the Sultan's power, and there were many who agreed with her. We shall never know Suleiman's secret thoughts at having to choose between his old friend and his lover in head-on collision, but he must have known that it could only end in tragedy. He must have realized that Ibrahim had never betrayed him; on the other hand, Roxelana's attacks were convincing, particularly when she quoted from the Grand Vizier's speeches. And, indeed, Ibrahim seemed to have gone mad. Dozens of scandalized court functionaries heard him announce scornfully that 'If he [the Sultan] orders a thing and I disapprove, it is not executed; but if I order a thing he disapproves, it is done nevertheless.'

It must have taken many months of anguish, but Suleiman was finally convinced that Ibrahim was a menace to his power. Yet he faced a crisis of conscience, for he had given his word never to disgrace Ibrahim while he lived, and now required a dispensation. It came from a legal counsellor of the Divan, who told him, 'You have sworn not to put him to death while you are living. Cause him to be strangled while you are asleep. He that sleeps doth not truly live so you may punish his disloyalty and not violate your oath.' *

Whether this incident is apocryphal or not – it certainly seems plausible and in keeping with Turkish custom – Suleiman now acted secretly, silently, swiftly. On 15 March 1536, Ibrahim went, as he so often did, to dine with his master in the Seraglio. He can have had no suspicions, for the Sultan did not confront him or challenge his honesty. Instead, historians tell us that they dined quietly, as if they would meet the next morning as usual. When Suleiman was about to retire he suggested that Ibrahim remain for the night in the adjoining room, where his usual mattress was waiting for him.

He was never seen alive again. The next morning his strangled body was found at the Seraglio gate, but all the evidence pointed to a violent struggle between the Grand Vizier and the deaf mutes sent to murder him. The walls of the room were splashed with blood that remained there for a century. It was said at the time that Suleiman could not sleep, but that he was smothered with kisses by Roxelana so that he could not hear the fight in the next room. The story is colourful, but probably apocryphal.

*

Three unimportant grand viziers followed Ibrahim. The first was so occupied with the harem that he had forty cradles in his palace at the same time, and left 120 children when he died of plague. The second lasted a year and was pensioned off. The third was a eunuch, deposed in 1544. It was the fourth who mattered, for this was Rustem Pasha, and he was married to Roxelana's daughter. From the moment that Rustem became Grand Vizier, both he and Roxelana were able to lean on each other; and both had a vested interest in promoting Selim in place of Mustafa.

They had to wait nine years, until 1553, before Roxelana could persuade

* M. Bandier, *The History of the Imperial Estate of the Grand Seigneur*, translated from the French and published in London in 1635.

her husband to repeat the crime he had committed against Ibrahim. But once again she succeeded, despite the fact that Mustafa was 'handsome, popular and very able'. He was the hero of the troops, and no one doubted for a moment that he would succeed his father, who was now sixty. The French writer Guillaume Postel felt that Mustafa was 'marvellously well educated and prudent and of the age to reign'. Rustem, in concert with Roxelana, started a campaign of suspicion. In its allegations of treachery it was almost a carbon copy of the conspiracy which had brought about Ibrahim's murder.

Once again, Suleiman took 'legal advice', but this time of a different nature. He invented a hypothetical story of a slave who had been trusted and who had embezzled his master's money and plotted against him – a rather feeble description of his suspicions that Mustafa was trying to usurp his power. His religious preceptor told Suleiman that 'he deserved to be tortured to death'. It was a licence to murder, and on 21 September 1553, while with his troops in Asia Minor, Suleiman summoned his son to appear in his tent. Mustafa's friends warned him, but he replied scornfully that, 'if he was to lose his life, he could wish no better than to give it back to him from whom he had received it.'

In fact, Mustafa pitched his tent next to his father's, and the next morning covered the few yards of separation on horseback, according to tradition.

The Sultan's tent was enormous and luxurious, divided into sections. The earth in the entrance had been covered with rich carpets and divans, and the sloping walls were lined with golden silk; in the centre was a small silver-topped table. Mustafa saluted the guards, dismounted and signalled to the two equerries who accompanied him to remain outside, as he walked in expecting to see his father. Instead he was faced with five deaf mutes, one holding a silken bowstring – the silk being an 'honour' reserved for men of rank. The deaf mutes were also used as executioners of high dignitaries; their tongues had been slit and their eardrums pierced deliberately to fit them for the purpose. By all accounts there was a fearful struggle as Mustafa fought for his life. As the fight raged, Suleiman remained behind a curtain, watching the execution. When it was all over, and the son he had loved was dead, he emerged, 'without the slightest sign of pity or remorse'.

As soon as Suleiman returned to Constantinople, a macabre scene of protocol ensued. A letter arrived from the Divan, written in white ink on black paper, informing him of his son's death. Throwing his turban to the ground, Suleiman tore off all his jewels, had the carpets turned upside down and ordered a three-day mourning for the son he had murdered. Sheep were slaughtered in sacrifice, alms distributed to the needy. On the day of the funeral, the horses which drew the chariot carrying the body were given a preparation that caused their eyes to weep.

The way was now open to Roxelana's son, Selim.

*

The last years of the great Suleiman must have been deeply unhappy. Two years after the murder of his son, Ogier Ghiselin de Busbecq, the Ambassador of Charles V, wrote that, 'Considering his years he enjoys good health, though it may be that his bad complexion arises from some lurking malady. There is a notion current that he has an incurable ulcer or cancer on his thigh. When he is anxious to impress an ambassador, who is leaving, with a favourable idea of the state of his health, he conceals the bad complexion of his face under a coat of rouge, his notion being that foreign powers will fear him more if they think he is strong and well. I detected unmistakable signs of this practice of his; for I observed his face when he gave me a farewell audience, and found it was much altered from what it was when he received me on my arrival.'

Within five years of Mustafa's murder, Roxelana was dead. As a woman, her death attracted little notice, and Suleiman did not permit himself the luxury of showing public grief. The door into Roxelana's rooms was sealed. From then on he ate alone. Donini, secretary to the Venetian envoy, found that, 'His Majesty during many months of the year was very feeble of body, so that he lacked little of dying, being dropsical, with swollen legs, appetite gone, and face swelled and of a very bad colour. In the month of March last, he had four or five fainting fits, and he has had one since, in which his attendants doubted whether he were alive or dead, and hardly expected that he would recover from them.'

The faults in his character were now beginning to show – and they were all faults that were present in his successors. He had long since stopped attending the Divan; this greatly diminished the true authority of the monarch, who could not otherwise be expected to know all that was happening. His habit of promoting favourites – such as Ibrahim and then his son-in-law Rustem – laid the foundations of venality. When Rustem died shortly after Roxelana, he left a staggering fortune for a man who had started as a slave in the tribute school: 815 farms, 476 watermills, 1,700 slaves, 2,900 coats of mail, 8,000 turbans, 760 sabres, 600 copies of the Koran, helmets plated in gold, scores of pairs of gold-worked stirrups and two million ducats.

Suleiman's evil practice of allowing favourites to amass great wealth, together with the sale of high offices, was already spreading like a canker through the Empire; but worse still was the start of the rule of the harem, a rule in which the harem became a centre of intrigue, with nearly fatal results to the Empire. It had started at the moment when Roxelana boasted openly, 'I live with the Sultan and make him do what I wish.'

Yet Suleiman was a remarkable man. Though cruel he lived in an age of cruelty that was certainly not confined to the Ottoman Empire, but extended to a Europe dominated by equally savage examples of religious fanaticism, with heretics burned at the stake, where torture was the rule rather than the exception – possibly because in those days life itself was painful and people were less appalled by torture than today. And, though his reign was blotted by family murders, the private life of his contemporary in England, Henry VIII, was not exactly virtuous. Like so many products of the Renaissance, Suleiman could be as sensitive as he could be cruel. He wrote poetry with the intensity he applied to politics. He built with the ferocity with which he went to war. Apart from his own magnificent mosque, he and the architect Sinan (a tribute boy, by the way) built everything that *needed* to be built, from the Aqueduct of Forty Arches to the walls that still surround the old city of Jerusalem.

In war he commanded an army with discipline finer than any that could be mustered in Europe and always personally led his troops into battle – often against his most hated enemies, the Persian heretics and the infidel Hungarians. To Europe he seemed a frightening enigma, but it was during his long reign that Constantinople became a mecca for foreign embassies, and even Elizabeth I appealed to him for help 'against that idolater the King of Spain'. His treaty of perpetual amity with France in 1535 remained a vital factor in European politics for two hundred years.

He died as he would have wished – on the field of battle. He was seventy-two when he marched towards Europe for the last time against the Emperor Maximilian II. The old Sultan was too feeble to mount a horse, so he was carried on a litter; but he was not lacking in fire, for at Buda, as he marched north, he had no hesitation in ordering the execution of the local pasha 'for inefficiency'.

He died in his tent while his troops were in the midst of a fierce battle on the night of 5 September 1566. His death was kept secret for three weeks, his physician having been strangled to make sure there would be no leak until Roxelana's son, Selim, who was in Asia Minor, had time to reach Constantinople.

For days the corpse, the eyes opened, the cheeks reddened, hair tinted black, was propped up on the throne in his tent. The Grand Vizier and a few servants alone knew the secret – and they kept up the grim masquerade by insisting that the daily routine should not be broken. Meals were served, the food hidden later; messages were received and answered. Even when the battle ended and the royal tent was struck, Suleiman was seated in the royal carriage so that his stern, unsmiling features could be clearly seen (and cheered) by his troops as he headed for Constantinople.

The news of his death was revealed when the cortège reached the Forest of Belgrade near the capital. There Selim was proclaimed Sultan, and as the priests announced Suleiman's death, 'great wailings of lamentation re-echoed among the giant trees and set the leaves trembling in sympathy with an empire's grief.'

Suleiman's corpse was washed, and in accordance with tradition his hands were laid across his breast, his nose, mouth and ears were stuffed with cotton wool, and at the last moment, before the corpse was wrapped in a shroud made from a single piece of heavy silk, a priest whispered to the dead man the answers to two questions which the examining angels in Paradise would ask him.

Then he was buried, lying on his right side, the head turned towards Mecca, near the great mosque which he and Sinan had built, and the priests were commanded to recite the Koran forty times a day for forty days.

Chapter three
The reign of the favoured women

In three hundred years the first ten Ottoman sultans had built up an empire of thirty million subjects speaking twenty tongues, every inch of it won by rulers who personally led their armies from conquest to conquest; and, though they were merciless and cruel, they were statesmen of a calibre often unmatched in Europe; they were interested in the arts; they included historians, architects, poets. In short, it was probably the greatest dynasty the world has ever known.

Now, suddenly, it all changed. Greatness made way for degeneracy. Prowess in the field of battle was replaced by prowess in the harem. Statesmanship became a tool for venality. The strange fact is that these traits persisted until the twentieth century. It was not a question of a few sultans misgoverning the Empire – every ruling house spawns the occasional weakling – but this was an unbroken line of weaklings. The twenty-five sultans who followed Suleiman were, almost without exception, totally lacking in any of the qualities needed to rule.

As Professor Barnette Miller put it in her book *Beyond the Sublime Porte*, 'Between him and his immediate successors, who ceased with surprising suddenness to be either soldiers or statesmen, there was no gradation whatever. Enervated and enfeebled by seclusion and idleness, filled with *ennui*, they sought pleasure and diversion in every conceivable form of extravagance, self-indulgence, and vice.' The change was so staggering that many historians have flirted with the possibility that the Othman line was broken.

Selim had 'a face rather swollen than fat and much resembling a drunkard's', and within months of his accession court rumours had spread to every corner of the capital that Suleiman had not fathered the new Sultan. Von Hammer, the greatest authority on Ottoman history, refers to the rumour that Selim was not the son of Suleiman, and though this cannot be proved it might have been possible for an unprincipled, high-spirited woman like Roxelana to smuggle a lover into the harem.

There is another possibility – that Ibrahim was Selim's father, for Luigi Bassano, an Italian historian who served as a page in the Grand Seraglio during the early part of Suleiman's reign, insisted that Roxelana had originally been the slave of Ibrahim who presented her to the Sultan; and a slave of Roxelana's quality was not born to sweep the harem floor.

Whatever happened, 'One is tempted,' wrote the historian Lord Eversley, 'to question whether the true blood of the Othman race flowed in the veins of these twenty-five degenerates.'

Selim's first act was to banish his father's harem to Adrianople (where all out-of-work concubines were sent) and bring in his own current favourite, the Sultana Nur Banu, who had borne his first son. She arrived at the Grand Seraglio with 150 ladies-in-waiting, ready to follow Roxelana in the power-politics of the harem. Her task was made easier because Roxelana had died, so she faced no rivalry from a Queen Mother. In fact, Nur Banu bided her time until Selim died and *she* became Queen Mother, for a very good reason: Selim was almost always drunk, and took no interest in government, but he had been fortunate in inheriting Suleiman's last grand vizier, the highly talented Mahemet Sokolli, who ran the country, leading the armies into battle brilliantly. Nur Banu realized that to the people of the Empire and to Europe Sokolli provided a perfect cover for her dissolute husband. This suited the Sultan admirably; Selim never once went to war at the head of his troops. Instead, his drinking habits spread, and were soon interpreted as a licence for all to imbibe. Even judges and priests started to break the inflexible law of the Koran prohibiting alcohol. Soon a new joke was circulating in the Grand Bazaar: 'Who will stand us a drink today – the Khodja [priest] the Kadi [justice] or the Kalif?'

Constantinople's most famous poet, Hafiz, wrote an enraptured verse which announced that, 'Wine is sweeter than the kisses of young girls,' and the Mufti was asked by devout Moslems to ban the poem, 'as contrary to the injunctions of the Koran'. The Mufti refused. His verdict was that, 'When a Sultan takes to drink it is permissible for all to do the same and for poets to celebrate it.'

Barbaro, the Venetian Ambassador, has left us a picture of Selim:

'Whoever saw his face inflamed with Cyprus wine and his short figure corpulent with indulgence, could respect in him neither the warrior nor the ruler of warriors. He preferred the society of eunuchs and of women and the habits of the Serai to the camp. He wore away his days in sensual enjoyments, in drunkenness and indolence.' Selim himself summed up his life when he said that he never thought of the future, but lived only to enjoy the pleasure of each day as it passed.

The wars that raged, the battles that were won in his name, hardly interested him – except one. Selim was having some difficulty in replenishing stocks of his favourite Cyprus wine – understandably, as he could drink a bottle as quickly as some men can down a pint of beer, without drawing breath. So he was delighted when a rival of Sokolli's suggested sending an army to capture Cyprus which at that time was under the rule of Venice. Sokolli was against the war, but for the only time in his reign of eight years Selim overruled his Grand Vizier, simply because he was determined to secure regular supplies of Cyprus wine.

Selim got his wine – but only after a siege marked by the most brutal atrocities against the Christians of the island. Turkish troops who were allowed to sack Nicosia massacred thirty thousand inhabitants, and when the main fortress of Famagusta fell after heroically withstanding a siege for nearly two years, the remnants of the garrison were murdered and their valiant leader, Bragadino, was flayed alive; his skin was then stuffed with hay and exhibited to the Turkish soldiery. (It is only fair to say that at about the same time Ivan the Terrible of Russia conquered Wittenstein and had the Finnish leader roasted alive on a spear.)

The Christians were horrified by the butchery of Cyprus – the more so as the Turks had promised to spare the lives of the garrison – and Venice joined forces with Spain to form a fleet of two hundred galleys under Don John of Austria to wipe out once and for all the Turkish domination of the Mediterranean. In reply, however, the Turks gathered a much larger fleet of nearly three hundred galleys. Both were manned by galley-slaves, five prisoners to a bench pulling a single oar, each man half-naked and chained by one foot under his seat. As the vessels pulled out of the Dardanelles, iron bracelets were clapped over the wrists of each man so that, fettered hand and foot, there was no possibility of resistance as they were lashed to labour, usually with a wet rope dipped in the sea to give added pain to the weals across every man's back. To this, as one Christian captive discovered, was added another torment: 'Frequently, some jackanapes of a rascally Turkish boy amuses himself with beating the captives from bench to bench one after the other, and laughing at them. All this you must not only bear patiently from the snivelling rascal, and hold your tongue, but, if you can bring yourself to it, you must kiss his hand, or foot, and beg the dirty boy not to be angry with you.'

For days the slaves rowed into the Mediterranean until finally they met the enemy fleet in the Gulf of Lepanto in October 1571 – and the larger Turkish fleet was overwhelmingly defeated. Two hundred and sixty-six Turkish vessels were captured or sunk. Fifty thousand Turks died and fifteen thousand Christian galley-slaves were liberated.

But the victory was thrown away. Immediately after Lepanto the victors dispersed and the brilliantly led striking-force ceased to exist. Sokolli, on the other hand, immediately started to build another, larger fleet – and did so in the incredible time of eighteen months, so that when some sort of peace was patched up between Venice and Constantinople Sokolli was able to boast scornfully to the Venetian ambassador, 'In capturing a kingdom [Cyprus] we have cut off one of your arms while you, in destroying our fleet, have merely shorn our beard. A limb cut off cannot be replaced, but a beard when shorn will grow again in greater vigour than ever.'

After a reign of only eight years, Selim the Sot died in a manner not unbefitting to his life. After drinking a bottle of Cyprus wine at a draught, he decided to take a bath. As he climbed in he teetered on the marble floor, slipped and broke his skull.

As Selim's son was proclaimed Sultan Murad III in December 1574, his widow Nur Banu automatically became Queen Mother, and it was now that the in-fighting in the harem started in earnest, lasting for the hundred years which the Turks call *Kadilar Sultanati*, 'the reign of the favoured women', an era in which a procession of queen mothers and sultanas fought at first quietly but then ferociously for wealth, privilege and power.

*

As Selim's first sultana, Nur Banu had lived in a beautiful suite, its walls decorated with gold leaf, at the end of the Golden Road. Now, as Queen Mother, she made a significant change, establishing herself nearer her son's rooms at the *start* of the Golden Road, near the entrance to the harem and the Divan, so that she could easily slip into the Tower Room and listen to the Divan in session.

Murad III was not a difficult son to 'manage'. Thin, pale, of medium height, with a long red beard, he had a fondness for opium which, it was thought at the time, was responsible for his pale features; and certainly later in life, when he exchanged opium for wine, he became ruddier and much fatter. He was not particularly interested in ruling, for his twin passions were painting and clock-making. He enjoyed spending the mornings with writers, poets, painters and was largely responsible for a modest resurgence of cultural life in Constantinople. He published *The Book of Skills*, illustrated with some of his own miniatures, and encouraged others to produce books to please him.

These pursuits were of little interest to his mother, Nur Banu, who was more concerned with her one potential rival. This was her son's favourite, Sultana Baffo, the mother of Murad's only son, known in the harem as Safiye, 'The Light One', a lady whose ambitions were greater than the Queen Mother's and as great as those of Roxelana herself.

Sultana Baffo came from the noble Venetian Baffo family. All accounts say that she was tall and blonde, with 'a figure that danced as she walked'. There are conflicting accounts of how she entered the harem. Most say that she was taken captive by a Turkish sea captain, though others suggest that she was, in fact, a secret agent planted in the harem by the Venetians. She had been presented to Murad at the age of thirteen, and the Queen Mother disliked her intensely. War between the two women was declared the day Murad ascended the throne. It was a war against the background of the harem, which was now congested, with dank, dark stone corridors leading to new rooms being added almost monthly, spreading out into the woods and gardens that slanted down the hill to Seraglio Point. The buildings were of such a haphazard nature that by Murad's time the interior presented astonishing contrasts. The Sultan and sultanas lived in magnificent splendour with swimming-pools, even a lake for rowing; yet the next flight of stone stairs led to dull, impersonal cubicles where half a dozen unfavoured women slept crowded on the floor, as they waited to 'catch the Sultan's eye'.

Nur Banu had several objectives. The first was to get rid of Sokolli, the

Grand Vizier, whom she found too honest and intractable. With her ally, the Kislar Aga – at that time a particularly venal, mountainous hulk of a eunuch who had amassed a fortune through the sale of offices – she tried to devise a plot which would bring Sokolli's downfall. It was not easy. Sokolli had been the trusted servant of three sultans. It would have been difficult to accuse him of treachery. Nur Banu eventually hit on a plan which hinged on the one subject to which Murad was sensitive – money. He was a miser. Unscrupulous in selling offices, he kept the money under his bed until there was no more room, and then sank a well beneath his bed, into which 'every night he poured . . . the day's takings'. When his mother 'proved' that Sokolli had been selling offices (and thus robbing him) Murad flew into a rage and decided that Sokolli must die. The assassination was cleverly contrived so as to appear spontaneous, in full Divan, with the leading statesmen seated on the long sofa extending round three sides of the hall. Sokolli sat in the centre, the other viziers on his right and all seemed normal when a soldier whose plea had been rejected rushed upon the Grand Vizier and stabbed him through the heart. A dozen scimitars were raised to cut down the assassin, but at that moment the voice of the Sultan was heard from behind the secret grille. He absolved the soldier of the Grand Vizier's death. It was as simple as that. Only one thing was wrong. Murad planned to seize the wealth of Sokolli, only to discover after his death that Sokolli had been a comparatively poor man.

Sokolli was the last grand vizier for a hundred years who was able to wield any power. In the twelve years since the death of Suleiman, Sokolli added Cyprus, a large part of Persia, the Yemen, and recaptured the province of Tunis to the Empire. The territories which Murad, or rather his mother, ruled now extended from the heart of Hungary in the north to the Persian Gulf and the Sudan in the south; from the Caspian Sea and Persia in the east to Oran in the west. The Mediterranean was virtually an Ottoman lake.

From now on the office of the Grand Vizier passed from hand to hand. Ability was of little consequence; it was a Sultan's passing fancy that counted. Wandering in disguise around the bazaar one night Murad stopped to listen to a cook named Ferhat complaining about government mismanagement. He questioned him, found his replies and ideas intelligent and next day summoned the astonished cook to the palace, where he appointed him to replace the man he had criticized. The cook rose to be Grand Vizier.

*

The Queen Mother now turned her attention to her rival, Baffo. It was, of course, impossible to have her assassinated, so – again with the help of the Kislar Aga – she decided on a deliberate policy of supplying her son with an unending stream of concubines, younger and more beautiful than Baffo. Murad seems to have been weak, but at this time not debauched, and we have a picture of him from a document in the British Museum, one very different from that at the start of his reign, for he was now a man 'of medium stature, and so stout that he seemed to have no neck. His complexion was pink and white, and his countenance regal, large, handsome and hearty; his beard was fair, almost golden. His attire was rich and gorgeous.' He liked the good life, was fond of music (the musicians being blindfolded if the concert took place in the harem), loved parties; in short, he was just the sort of man who, though devoted to Baffo, was too weak to withstand the recurring temptation of a new and beautiful slave presented to him each Friday by his mother, particularly when it was impressed upon him, not only by his mother, but also by the politicians who surrounded him, that his devotion to Baffo (who had no more children) left the Othman dynasty with only one male heir, their only son. It was his 'duty' to father more children, if only to safeguard the line. Consequently, the harem was soon filled with 'the very flower of the slave markets of the East', and the Kislar Aga was so assiduous in procuring odalisques that we are told 'the price of this ware rose enormously in the slave markets'.

Murad became the father of 103 children; but fleeting love was one thing, devotion was another, and though Baffo no longer occupied the Sultan's bed she was still his constant companion, and when Nur Banu died in 1583, Baffo – without the hindrance of a dominating mother-in-law – ruled the harem. She was content to allow her husband his nightly pleasures, while she influenced him in public affairs.

*

During all these years of female squabbling, Constantinople was changing, and doubtless most of the citizens outside court circles knew little of the struggle for power being waged behind the Gate of Felicity. Life for them was stern, but at least Constantinople was set against a backdrop of breath-taking beauty, 'formed by Nature', as Gibbon wrote, 'for the centre and capital of a great monarchy'. Though the capital boasted no street-names, and most houses were built of wood, there were a surprising number of 'modern' amenities.

Because water played such a ritual part in the religion of Islam, there were fountains everywhere. 'Water was always deemed to be a precious gift of God,' so that wherever a spring rose a fountain followed. Aqueducts carried water to cisterns or very modern water-towers from where it was filtered and piped to the houses of wealthy people or into central tanks. The public baths were magnificent – and the water steaming hot.

The Grand Bazaar, enclosed by a wall with eighteen gates, had sixty-seven main streets; and it was not only a meeting-place, but also a super-market beyond the wildest imagination, where in nearly four thousand shops under one roof it was possible to buy anything from a camel to a pot of rose-petal jam. North of the Bosporus the brothels in the suburbs of Pera and Galata* did a thriving business till dawn, when in the nearby cafés hardened topers drank gallons of tripe soup in the firm belief that it prevented a hangover. The city boasted three hundred shops selling nothing but the favourite dish of tripe, always served with garlic, all doubtless agreeing with that seasoned traveller, Evliya Effendi, who found that, 'Tripe cannot be dressed without garlic which, though it do smell badly, is nevertheless one of God's own blessings.' Those seeking to get rid of the traces ate large helpings of warm almond cream covered with cinnamon or ginger, and if they wanted to appease irate wives they could at the next shop buy attar of roses made in Adrianople, or essence of hyacinth, the essential oil having been extracted from almond and cypress nuts.

Those with money and power dressed magnificently, often in long, flowing caftans of heavily brocaded Brusa velvet. Their homes were a series of palaces or houses, set in dense groves of cypress and plane trees along the shores of the Golden Horn.

In their homes most Turks, even of moderate means, had a negro slave

* The word Galata is derived from the Greek 'milk'; Galata was the milk market in the Byzantine Age.

who cleaned and cooked meals over a charcoal fire, fanning the red glow
with a turkey's wing. The humblest home had its harem, even if it contained only one veiled wife, and the men always ate alone, the food being
passed from the selamlik to the harem through a kind of revolving cupboard.

For the poor there were plenty of cheap vegetables for thick soups, and
plenty of onions and garlic to flavour coarse meat or tripe. Milk and
yoghourt were equally cheap. So was rice. Those who worked away from
home wrapped slices of bread with some onions into a handkerchief and
tucked it inside their blouses until lunch-time. It was a simple lunch
demanding only one condition: it had to be eaten near water for it was
forbidden to eat food without first washing.

In winter the rooms were heated with charcoal buried in wood ash in a
circular metal receptacle which kept the room warm long after the slave
had made up the night's beds – by the simple process of unfolding
mattresses on the floor.

The servant problem was non-existent, for the Constantinople slave
market was open daily, except on Fridays, from 8 a.m. to midday. Behind
an enormous wooden gate a large colonnaded courtyard was surrounded
by small chambers (and a coffee shop for would-be purchasers who liked
to dawdle). This was the slave market for 'domestic servants', mostly
negresses, whose teeth, muscles, legs were examined with the methodical
attention of a horse-trader. It was, of course, quite another matter to
purchase a beautiful Georgian or Circassian girl as a mistress, for the best
were inevitably snapped up for the Sultan, and indeed there was such a
shortage that the Circassians, so it is said, soon had to start their own slave
farms where 'they grew beautiful women as other countries might grow
wheat or cattle – for sale'. At least the slave farms produced one benefit
for posterity, for 'the avid demand for them in Istanbul encouraged
parents to preserve their girl children from the disfigurement of the widespread smallpox by inoculation'.

It was from Circassia that inoculation spread westwards to the many
European doctors living in Constantinople. However skilful the medical
men might have been, their chances of curing female patients was some-
what restricted because they were never allowed to see them. They did the
best they could – and it usually consisted of delivering a few leeches to

bleed a patient, for leeches could be applied by eunuchs or slaves in the harem. They were a government monopoly, and huge numbers were exported to Germany and Russia. The best ones came from Anatolia – 'they are said to be more eager to perform their duty' – and when the cure was ended the haemorrhage was arrested by the Turkish equivalent of a modern styptic, a coating of pounded coffee, which was not uncomfortable unless the patient had to remain in bed, for as the coffee dried and fell off the bed became covered with grit.

Most Turks at this time seem to have been reasonably happy with one wife, perhaps because the dowry was given by the bridegroom, or because divorce in those days was easy – understandably so, since many boys were married at thirteen or fourteen to girls of eleven and twelve whom they never saw before the nuptials.

But easy divorce had several curious consequences. A man could not marry a divorced woman until she had been divorced from her husband for four and a-half months. If a man divorced his wife twice, he could take her back. But if, as sometimes happened after marital tiffs, he divorced her a third time, and then realized he still loved her, she could not return to him until she had been married to someone else. This was meant as a check against abusing easy divorce but it soon produced a professional intermediary willing to marry the lady for one night. He was usually old, paid for his services, and expected not to be over-enthusiastic in the performance of his duties.

Divorces – often followed by remarriage – were common among one class in Constantinople: the men who *did* have one or more concubines. Inevitably this led to friction, scenes of jealousy, and often physical violence, particularly if the wife felt that she was being cheated of her marital rights, for though the husband could call for his concubines six nights a week every Friday was strictly reserved for his wife.

Of course, to enjoy the limited pleasures of life in sixteenth-century Constantinople, one had to be a Turk. Life for the subject races of the Empire, particularly the Christians, was subject to many stringent restrictions. Armenians had to wear deep crimson shoes, Greeks black, Hebrews pale blue. Ottoman Christians had to paint their houses black and wear black clothes. They had to dismount whenever they met a Moslem.

Christian travellers were always at the mercy of any Moslem anxious to display aggressive anti-Christian feelings, as an Englishman called Fynes Moryson, who was travelling in Turkey at this time, found to his disgust, for 'a wild-headed Turke took my hat from my head (being of the fashion of Europe not used there) and having turned it, and long beheld it, he said (to use his rude words) Lend me this vessell to ease my belly therein; and so girning flung it on the dyrtie ground, which I with patience tooke up.'

*

The few foreign diplomats faced problems of another kind, particularly the first British ambassadors appointed by Elizabeth I in the middle of Murad's reign. For though the parsimonious Elizabeth had an ambassador, who had to sidestep all the dangerous quicksands of diplomatic manoeuvre, she did not pay him a penny. Edward Barton, her second ambassador, had to beg for enough to live on, for in reality he was the nominee of the British Turkey Company, and his entire resources were derived from the income of the Company, even though he acted in the name of the Queen.

These early ambassadors like Barton were, in reality, traders, and in the first five years of the Turkey Company British ships made twenty-seven voyages between England and Constantinople, carrying woollen cloth, tin, pewter, lead and rabbit skins on the outward journey. They brought back raw silk, indigo, currants, oil, wine, mohair, and the forerunner of today's camel-hair cloth, called chamblette. They also carried a commodity which delighted Elizabethan England – angora wool of a brilliant whiteness from the city of that name (the modern Ankara). Even in those days it was costly, for the Turks found that if the wool were cut off the goats it became coarse, but if pulled out it was 'as soft and fine as silk'. (Pulling out hairs was a painful business for the goats, but some humanitarian Turks deadened it by washing the goats with a mixture of chalk and ashes.) There was also another highly prized export – the droppings of Stamboul dogs, used in the British tanning industry.

Edward Barton finally persuaded Elizabeth to send gifts for the Sultan. Without doubt the most arduous task a diplomat could face was an audience of the Sultan, as Barton discovered when he delivered Queen Elizabeth's gift of '12 goodly pieces of gilt plate, 36 garments of fine English cloth of al colors, 20 garments of cloth of gold, 10 garments of sattin, 6 pieces of fine Holland, and certaine other things of good value'.

On the day in which he had been granted an audience, Barton, magnificently attired in cloth-of-gold and cloth-of-silver, crossed the Golden Horn from the Embassy in Pera. He was attended by 'seven men in costly suits of satin', and thirty members of his staff in a dark-russet livery. As Barton stepped ashore near Seraglio Point a British merchantman fired all her guns in salute. Two pashas and forty heralds waited with horses to greet Barton, who then rode in state into the first court of the Seraglio, dismounting before the ornate second-court gate with its 'candle-snuffer' turrets. Meeting the Sultan was a long-drawn-out process. A guard of honour lined the route to the Divan. Rows of courtiers bowed ceremoniously as Barton passed between them. In the Divan the British Ambassador handed the Queen's letters to the Grand Vizier before lunch was served. It consisted of a hundred dishes of food set out on long carpets, dishes ranging from 'mutton boiled and rosted, Rice diversely dressed', to 'fritters of the finest fashion'. Everyone squatted on the floor to eat, washing the food down with rosewater and sugar squirted into cups with unerring aim from a goatskin slung over a waiter's back. The meal was eaten with 'great sobriete and silence' – until the guests got up, when there was 'some undignified scrambling for scraps among the black slaves'.

The Sultan was in the throne-room of the third court behind the Gate of Felicity, but before Barton could be allowed to look upon his exalted person he had to be suitably clothed. A special gown of cloth-of-gold was placed over his other fine garments and then the presentation of the gifts started. It took a hundred men to carry them in procession to the Sultan – still invisible to Barton, as he waited outside the gate, surrounded by an exotic crowd of eunuchs, dwarfs and mutes.

As the last servant passed inside the throne-room with the last roll of cloth, Barton followed. According to custom (based on a fear of assassination) two pashas grasped the folds of his long sleeves, pinioned his arms and marched him into the presence.

Murad was alone except for a pasha 'who stood near him with bowed head and downcast eyes'. The Sultan was dressed in cloth-of-silver and seated on a golden throne presented by his Egyptian vassals and made by melting down eighty thousand gold ducats. It was surrounded by a carpet of green satin embroidered with silver and pearls. Still in the grip of the pashas, Barton bowed and kissed Murad's bejewelled hand. Then he was unceremoniously dragged backwards to the door and the bizarre audience was at an end, and Barton was free to make his way back to his caïque, escorted to the water's edge by two thousand horsemen. This was an era of gifts bestowed and received, but the court at Constantinople must have been impressed with the magnitude of British presents (in contrast to Venice which sent four Parmesan cheeses), for when Murad died Elizabeth was apprised of the fact in a letter addressed to 'The most chaste among the women of the world'.

Queen Elizabeth had also sent gifts to the Sultana Baffo. They consisted of 'a jewel of her majesties picture, set with some rubies and diamants, 3 great pieces of gilt plate, 10 garments of cloth of gold, a very fine case of glass bottles silver and gilt, with 2 pieces of fine Holland'.

Baffo was delighted when she received them and asked, via the Kislar Aga, what Elizabeth would like in return. Barton suggested a princely royal costume because of its rarity, and Baffo sent it immediately, with a quaint note. 'I send your Majesty so honourable and sweet a salutation of peace,' she wrote, 'that al the flock of Nightingales with their melody cannot attaine to the like, much lesse this simple letter of mine. The singular love which we have conceived one toward the other is like to a garden of pleasant birds ... I will alwayes be a sollicitour to the most mighty Emperour for your Majesties affaires, that your Majesty at all times may be fully satisfied.'

Barton must have been an astute diplomat, and he had long since arranged a secret code between his Embassy and London. For the Sultan he used the number 105; for Queen Elizabeth it was 9. And so, when Murad III died in January 1595 – eight years before Elizabeth – Barton added a postscript to his fortnightly despatch: '105 is extreame sick, some say deade and his sonne sent for.'

Murad had, in fact, died of a kidney complaint and an epileptic fit in the middle of the night four days before Barton wrote to the Queen. Death was hastened by his debauchery, for, as the Venetian envoy reported, he 'lived on solid meats, thick soups and sheeps' marrow and other aphrodisiacs, for he lay immersed in lust.' He was fifty and had reigned for twenty years. Twenty of his sons and twenty-seven daughters survived him, and seven of his wives were pregnant when he died.

*

The new Sultan, Mahomet III, was twenty-nine, a big man with a black beard and a huge pair of fearsome moustaches, plus a streak of abnormal cruelty. A description of him in a British Museum manuscript describes how his father had virtually banished him to a distant province because of his ungovernable temper, and tells of his bouts of maniacal rages and cruelty, 'causing sometime upon malice, sometime upon humour, women's breasts to be seared off with hote irons.'

As soon as he was apprised of his father's death Mahomet arrived at the Grand Seraglio in an admiral's galley. It was shortly after nine o'clock on a drizzling January morning. In gratitude for his safe journey he freed the galley slaves; he also despatched an order to Aleppo for half a million hyacinth bulbs to plant a garden where he landed, before attending the funeral of his father. All Constantinople lined the streets as Mahomet, in a purple robe, followed the body of the old Sultan in its cypress coffin covered with cloth-of-gold and a belt of diamonds as it was carried to St Sophia. Palms were borne over him by the captains of his personal guard, and the men of the court, all dressed in black, wore unusually small black turbans as a sign of mourning.

The corpse was hardly in its grave before Mahomet went to see Baffo. It was twelve years since he had last met his mother. What happened at that fatal meeting between mother and son has naturally never been told, but most historians agree that it was the dominant mother with her lust for power who insisted to her weak-minded son that he must invoke the law of fratricide. Mahomet agreed, though from the grief he displayed (a rare emotion among Ottoman rulers) it must have been with a torn heart that he faced the prospect of the ghoulish evening that lay ahead. Baffo had insisted there was no time to lose, so that night the new Sultan commanded his nineteen brothers to come and kiss his hand. The eldest was only eleven and they were 'very fair and pretty boys'.

As they trooped into the throne-room, Mahomet told them they had nothing to fear, he wished them no harm, but he felt that they should be immediately circumcised.

The surgeons were waiting in adjoining rooms. And so were the deaf mutes. Each boy was circumcised within a few minutes of his royal audience then taken to the next room and dextrously strangled by the high priests of that peculiarly Turkish institution, the silken bowstring. The next morning the corpses were laid out in nineteen small coffins and the Sultan went, according to custom, to inspect the grisly parade before the bodies were taken to be buried with their father.

This terrible deed was permitted by law – the *Zanān-nāmeh* – passed by Mahomet the Conqueror in an attempt to avoid the perils of disputed succession. It read that, 'The majority of legists have declared that those of my illustrious children and grandchildren who shall ascend the throne shall have the right to execute their brothers, in order to insure the peace of the world; they are to act comfortably.' It was, however, one thing to 'have the right', but quite another for a mother to encourage her son to exercise it so brutally, or for a son to agree.

On the other hand, Mahomet had a sense of royal dignity. When he received the official notification of his brothers' deaths (as usual in white ink on black paper) he immediately ordered a state funeral which all persons of rank were bidden to attend.

The day after the funeral Mahomet set about spring-cleaning his own house – and that meant sending his father's concubines to the Old Seraglio (Adrianople was now out of fashion) to join their sisters in monastic seclusion for life. Murad had been so prolific that, 'All the carriages, coaches, mules and horses of the court were employed for this purpose.' With the exception of the seven pregnant widows, who were tied up in sacks and flung into the Bosporus, the women went to the Old Seraglio in a dismal procession lasting all day. At least there the mothers of the nineteen strangled boys could weep in peace, an emotion so strictly denied in the Grand Seraglio that it carried the penalty of instant death.

Baffo, like Messalina, now deliberately started to corrupt her own son, realizing that the easiest way to retain power was to decorate her son's harem as attractively as possible and to change the decoration weekly. According to Fynes Moryson (the British traveller whose hat had been employed for such an embarrassing purpose), Mahomet at the time of his succession 'was said to have sworne never to take any Concubine, nor to know any other woman than his own Sultana.' This was apparently because of his grief at the murder of his brothers; but before long, according to Moryson, 'He received fifty virgins presented to him, and within a few months . . . had five hundred Concubines for his owne saddle.'

Baffo was now all-powerful. During the eight years of her son's vacuous reign, she prevented a war with her native Venice, using a Jewish woman called Chiarezza, who regularly brought jewels to the harem for sale, to carry her messages to the Venetian Ambassador, and her secret letters to Catherine de Medici in Venice. Only once was she unable to control her son – when war flared up with Hungary. Baffo felt strongly that if her son were out of her sight she might be out of his mind. But in 1593, with Transylvania and Wallachia in rebellion, Austria and Hungary, under the Emperor Maximilian, marched on the Empire. Before Constantinople realized what had happened, the enemy had crossed the Danube and routed the Turks from several vital strong-points. Urgent action was needed and Mahomet was urged to unfurl the standard of the Prophet and lead his troops. After a great deal of hesitation, he did so – for the only time in his life and in defiance of his mother.

'Lead' is a comparative term. Mahomet took no part whatsoever in the direction of the war, leaving his Grand Vizier in command, though the Sultan was present on the edge of the battlefield, surrounded by his personal bodyguard. The armies clashed in the three-day battle of Cerestes on the Plain of Hungary, and on the first two days the Austrians swept all before them. Mahomet panicked and suggested an immediate retreat. It was only the courage and ability of a renegade Italian turned Moslem, called Cicala, that saved Turkey. On the third day he led a daring cavalry charge and completely turned the scales. Thirty thousand Austrians and Hungarians perished, and Maximilian was compelled to flee for his life. All the lost territory was regained and Mahomet was able to return to Constantinople, and a hero's welcome.

Now Baffo's influence was greater than ever. She appointed the grand viziers – at a price. She extended the sales of offices from government posts to the judiciary and army commands. Officials who wished to retain their posts could only do so by payments to Baffo. Inevitably the entire government system became more and more infected with bribery and corruption, for every official realized the temporary nature of the office for which he had paid, and so had to recoup swiftly by plunder before some unknown rival bought his way into Baffo's favours. When one grand vizier was given a grant to build naval vessels he embezzled a fortune by showing the Sultan (from a safe distance) some old dismantled hulks in the Constantinople dockyard as new naval construction.

Mahomet died at the age of fifty-two, unmourned by the court, which was delighted to see the last of a ruler, 'wholly given to a sensual and voluptuous life, the marks whereof he continually carried about him, with a foul, swollen, unwieldy and overgrown body.' He was the last sultan ever to be trusted with liberty during the lifetime of a predecessor. And his nineteen brothers were the last to be strangled under the law of fratricide. (This did not prevent some future heirs to the Sultan from living in terror of the bowstring, often with reason.)

Not long afterwards Baffo was strangled in her bed; her death did not mark the end of the harem rule, but another influence dominated the lives of the princes who followed Mahomet. It was a fate in many ways more grim than death itself. To make certain they would never become involved in plots against the reigning Sultan, any possible heirs were immured in a building in the Grand Seraglio. It was called the *Kafes*. Its literal translation is 'The Cage'.

Chapter four
The years of the Cage

The *Kafes* was not a barred cage in the accepted sense of the word, but it was most certainly bolted. It consisted of a two-storeyed grey building tucked away behind a high wall in the heart of the Grand Seraglio, almost opposite the rooms of the First Sultana. It had handsome courtyards and gardens, and its tiled walls were among the most beautiful in the Seraglio. There was, however, one sinister note. There were no windows on the ground floor, though those on the second floor looked out to sea.

For the next two centuries heirs to the throne were immured, sometimes from the age of two, until they were either called to the throne, or their miserable lives were mercifully ended with the bowstring. One heir was to remain nearly fifty years without ever leaving the building, and when he emerged to be proclaimed Sultan he had all but lost the power of speech. The princes' only companions were deaf mutes unable to give news of the outside world, and a modest harem of concubines, the only living creatures to whom they could talk. Once inside, the odalisques suffered the fate of their masters. They never left the Cage unless one carelessly became pregnant, in which case she was immediately drowned. This happened very rarely for great care was taken to make these women barren – either by the removal of their ovaries or by the use of pessaries (made up by the Seraglio doctors from a bewildering assortment of ingredients, including musk, amber, aloes, cardamom, ginger, pepper and cloves).

Sultan Ahmed I, who succeeded Mahomet in 1603, founded the cages because he rebelled against the barbaric custom of fratricide; perhaps he was even proud of discovering such a humane method of guarding his brothers' lives. But it is not difficult to imagine the debasing effects of years of solitary confinement on men who were expected to take up the reins of office at a moment's notice after half a lifetime in which their minds and bodies had vegetated. As N. M. Penzer, a leading authority on the harem, wrote, 'The *Kafes* has been the scene of more wanton cruelty, misery and bloodshed than any palace room in the whole of Europe. To its institution are due the weakness, vices and imbecility of so many of the Sultans and, to a large extent, the gradual decay and fall of the Ottoman Empire.'

Ahmed was responsible for another innovation of a rather different kind during his reign of fourteen years before he died of consumption at the age of twenty-eight. This was the introduction of tobacco, and it caused tremendous opposition amongst religious leaders. The Sheik-ul-Islam – the highest religious authority – prohibited it, saying, 'It is contrary to the Koran. Smoking is a hideous and abominable practice which no true believer should adopt.' And that, apparently, was that – until someone discovered that the Sheik had not done his homework, for tobacco had never been mentioned in the Koran. The learned Sheik had to recant, and tobacco was cultivated in Turkey on an enormous scale.

*

During Ahmed's reign Mustafa, who succeeded him, spent more than ten years in the Cage, providing the first terrible evidence of its effect on human beings, as each succeeding sultan seemed more mad, avaricious, debauched and besotted than his predecessor. By the time Mustafa I became Sultan he was completely demented. He appointed two favourite pages – scarcely out of their infancy – to be Governors of Cairo and Damascus. He dismissed a high-ranking officer so that he could offer the post to a peasant who gave him a drink of water when hunting. He clapped the French Ambassador in the Castle of the Seven Towers on the flimsiest pretext. After three months he was deposed – very politely. A five-day hunting-trip was arranged for his enjoyment, and when he returned he was no longer Sultan. He went back to the Cage. His nephew, Osman II, who succeeded him in 1618 (less than a year before the first negro slaves reached Virginia), was even madder. His favourite pastime was archery, but he only enjoyed the sport when using live targets. Prisoners of war were considered fair game for the Sultan, but when there was an insufficient supply Osman insisted on using his own pages. After four years of misrule – or, rather, no rule at all – the Janissaries decided he must go.

'Young Osman' – so called because he had not yet grown a beard –

tried to flee, but when the Janissaries heard of his plans they raced into the first court unarmed and picked up logs of wood from the firewood pile as they dashed to the Gate of Felicity and into the sacred precincts of the Sultan's private third court. There they discovered the room in the harem where Osman was hiding behind a heavily barred door. They broke it down, then dragged him to the prison of the Seven Towers – an Ottoman Bastille – on the outskirts of the capital. Osman was a heavily built man, and with the added strength that often comes to the insane he fought for his life, killing six of his attackers before he was cut down by a sabre thrust. It was the first regicide in Ottoman history.

But who was to succeed him? Incredibly, it was decided to give the luckless, insane Mustafa another chance, but this was easier said than done. While one party had been searching for Osman, another had been looking for Mustafa. When he refused to open the door of the Cage, several men climbed on to the roof, pierced it, and through the hole could see Mustafa sitting on a cushion with two odalisques. He was 'grinning vacantly'.

A man was let down on a rope, but Mustafa refused point-blank to allow him to open the door. So the plotters tied Mustafa to the end of the rope and hauled him up through the roof. They hoped to put him on a horse and show him to the crowds in the first court, but he was too weak, because during the disturbances the palace servants had forgotten to feed him. Instead, Mustafa was carried to the throne-room and shown to the public in a sitting position.

His second term as Sultan was a total failure, and lasted only one year and four months, after which he was quietly strangled.

*

The Ottoman Empire was now sinking fast. Sir Thomas Roe, the British Ambassador appointed by James I at that time, wrote in one of his despatches,

All the territory of the Grand Seignior is dispeopled for want of pasture and by reason of violent oppression – so much so that, in the best parts of Greece and Anatolia, a man may ride three or four, or sometimes six, days and not find a village to feed him or his horse, whereby the revenue is so lessened that there is not wherewithal to pay the soldiers and to maintain the Court. It may be patched up for a while out of the Treasury, and by exactions which are now onerous upon the merchants and labouring men to satisfy the harpies.

I can say no more than that the disease works internally that must ruin this Empire; we daily expect more changes and effusion of blood. The wisest men refuse to sit at the helm, and fools will soon run themselves and others upon the rocks.

*

No wonder Roe likened the Ottoman Empire to, 'an old body, crazed through many vices that remain where youth and strength is decayed.' Indeed, the prestige of the Empire had so declined that Europe was beginning to lose its fear of the force which had terrified it in the days of Suleiman the Magnificent. But the Christians were torn with dissension and in no position to take advantage of the decay in an empire of alien religion which had so grossly persecuted them. The German states were involved in religious wars; Spain had been in decline since the death of Philip II, and was almost as decadent as Turkey; Russia was in the throes of revolt; England was looking inwards at her constitutional problems. Yet, if any Christian power had been able to attack the race and religion they despised, the Ottoman Empire would have been unable to resist.

And now, at this juncture, there came on the scene a sultan of totally different calibre from his immediate predecessors. Murad IV was only ten when proclaimed Sultan in 1623 – and that meant that at least the Cage had not had time to break his spirit. Murad's far-seeing mother, Kiusem, ruled during his youth. She chose his grand viziers wisely and took one other extraordinary step for a doting mother: she encouraged the young prince towards homosexuality, in the belief that she would be spared the dangerous consequences of interference by harem favourites. For a time it worked, but when Murad came of age and assumed power in 1632 that part of his life was quickly forgotten.

Murad was a big man in every sense of the word, a monster of cruelty yet the last brave sultan to reign, a man with savage black eyes glaring out of a face half-hidden by his dark brown hair and long beard. Dressed almost always in blue silk, he could out-ride any man in the Empire. In an age when archery was a national sport, and archers were popular heroes with followings as devoted as those of the athletes of ancient Greece or today's footballers, Murad would challenge any one of them and could fire an arrow 1,500 feet from a post at one end of the Hippodrome to a column at the other end. He was an expert with the javelin, the sword and the musket. He was unbeatable as a wrestler and was always ready to fight the leading wrestler of the day in open combat. It was said that none could prise open the thick fingers of his clenched fist.

From the first moment of his power he faced a crisis with the Janissaries, who, over the years had relaxed their discipline. The oath of celibacy had been rescinded, and their sons had started joining – a major change from Suleiman's days when it was composed solely of tribute boys and Christian slaves captured in battle – boys whose original identity had completely vanished. As one degenerate sultan followed another the Janissaries became more outrageous in their demands; now they overturned their kettles – a traditional sign of unrest – demanding of the new Sultan the life of the Grand Vizier and sixteen high officials. Murad had to yield, but he felt deeply the humiliation and immediately resolved on revenge. Quietly he gathered round him a band of loyal troops, and when the Janissaries least expected it seized their leaders, strangled them – and had more than six hundred executed in their quarters.

Murad quickly found a simple panacea for the ills of the country. He cut off the head of any man who came under even the slightest suspicion. In 1637, he executed twenty-five thousand subjects in the name of justice, many by his own hand. His maxim was, 'Vengeance never grows decrepit though she may grow grey.' He executed the Grand Mufti because he was dissatisfied with the state of the roads. He beheaded his chief musician for playing a Persian air. He prohibited the use of opium and forbade smoking in public. Like the famous Harun-al-Rashid, he liked to patrol the taverns in disguise by night, and if he caught anyone smoking he declared himself and executed the offender on the spot. When he caught one of his gardeners and his wife smoking, he had their legs amputated and exhibited them in public while they bled to death.

Inevitably the savage, relentless temper soon got out of hand and was used against imaginary grievances. When a Venetian called Zanetti built an extra room on top of his house, Murad was convinced he had done so in order to spy on the harem ladies and hanged the man in his shirt. When a French interpreter arranged a clandestine meeting with a Turkish woman, Murad had the luckless man impaled. He would spend hours sitting in the Alai kiosk at the most westerly corner of the Seraglio wall, exercising the royal prerogative of taking ten innocent lives a day, as he practised his powers with the arquebus on passers-by who were too near the palace walls. On one occasion he drowned a party of women when he chanced to come across them in a meadow and took exception to the noise they were making. He ordered the batteries to open fire and sink a boat-load of women in the Bosporus when their craft came too near the Seraglio walls. 'When he rode forth, any unfortunate wretch who displeased him by crossing or impeding the road was instantly put to death, and frequently fell pierced by an arrow from the gloomy despot's own bow.'

Wherever the Sultan went he was followed by his chief executioner, Kara Ali, whose belt bulged with nails and gimlets, clubs for breaking hands and feet, and canisters containing different kinds of powder for blinding.

On less grim occasions, Murad was fond of teasing the ladies of the harem. According to Sir George Courthop, who visited Constantinople, the Sultan had 'a pond made all of porphyry stone, that is in the middle of a grove all beset with trees, on which he hangeth carpets: that none can see into it, or dare approach near it. Here he putteth in his Concubines stark naked and shooteth at them with certain pellets that stick upon them without any damage to their bodies. And sometimes he lets the water in such abundance upon them (for he can let what quantity of water he will in) that being above their heights they all bob up and down for life; and when his pleasure is satisfied with the sport, he lets down the water, and calls the Eunuchs who wait upon his women, to fetch them out if alive.'

To make matters worse in a city already in the depths of misery, one of the periodic bouts of plague swept Constantinople in 1637, taking five hundred lives a day. Abel Cook, an English merchant there at the time, wrote home despairingly, 'It is not safe to walk abroad in the streets by day, let alone by night. The dogs are so ravenous from lack of food, that it is dangerous to go near them. People sell and eat their dead . . . the distress is beyond belief, you cannot conceive anything like it. I beg of you to ask for prayers to be said for us in all your churches, for we Christians are in a dreadful plight. Even a rat is welcome food.'

The Sultan took it all in his stride. He executed fifty men for permitting a famine which no one could have foreseen. And, as for the plague, all he said was, 'This summer God is punishing the rogues. Perhaps by winter he will come to the honest men.'

And yet, with all his ferocious cruelty, Murad was at least cast in the mould of the first Ottoman sultans, and in 1638 he made his greatest expedition of war against the Persians, to take Baghdad which, by tradition, could only be captured by a sovereign in person. Suleiman had first won the city for the Empire, but his successors had lost it. On 8 March 1638, the Imperial Standard was planted on the heights of Scutari on the Asian shore of the Bosporus and a vast army prepared to set off on a journey of 110 days.

Departing for such a prolonged war demanded the maximum of comfort; and unlike Suleiman, who preferred a monastic life when on active service, Murad insisted on a retinue of sixteen camp-followers from the harem who accompanied him in several coaches, guarded by eunuchs.*

Scutari was resplendent with Asiatic pomp, and now all was ready for the long march, the army being increased along the route by quotas of troops drawn from the regions through which they passed, a vast colourful cavalcade resembling nothing so much as a mighty river, with tributary streams adding to its strength until finally nothing could resist the vast tide of half a million men.

On 16 November 1638, the Ottoman standards were unfurled before Baghdad, and Murad laid siege to the capital. It was desperately defended, but Murad himself gave his troops the impetus needed for victory. He worked in the trenches with them, he helped to site and point the cannon, and though he paid regular visits to his tented harem he spent most nights with his saddle as a pillow. When during a sortie one gigantic Persian soldier challenged the bravest Turk to single-handed combat, Murad never hesitated and 'clove his foe from skull to chin with a sabre stroke'. By the end of the year the city had fallen and Murad ordered a general massacre of the garrison. It was carried out in one day of butchery when all but three hundred of the garrison of thirty thousand were slaughtered. There was worse to come. When a powder magazine accidentally blew up killing some Turkish troops, an incensed Murad ordered another thirty

* Murad was not alone in demanding feminine company when at war. Exactly fifty years previously, six hundred women were discovered on the vessels of the Spanish Armada before it sailed for England.

thousand to be killed, this time the innocent citizens, mostly women and children.

Murad had a flair for publicity and was determined that his victory should be celebrated in Constantinople on a scale the citizens would long remember. When he was within a few days' march of the capital he sent his instructions ahead by carrier pigeons,* and by the time he returned in triumph to Constantinople he made his way to the Grand Seraglio, 'with splendour and magnificence which no tongue can tell'. Riding a Nogai charger he wore the chain armour in which he had fought – an exquisitely made suit of interwoven steel and gold links with a leopard skin held across his shoulders by a clasp of diamonds, and in his turban a triple aigrette of diamonds. Seven led horses with jewelled caparisons followed him, together with twenty-two of the noblest Persians on foot, wearing chains of gold. So great was the excitement that men even scrambled on the rooftops to catch a sight of the hero and the victorious army 'bending under their booty'. In the Bosporus every vessel fired constant salutes, 'so that the sea seemed in a blaze.' It was the last time a sultan returned to his capital as a conquering hero, but Murad had retaken Baghdad and, though he was ferociously cruel and drowned his Empire in blood, it can at least be said that, with all his misdeeds, he tolerated only his own crimes, and temporarily checked his country's decline.

His last command, uttered as he lay dying from a fever aggravated by a bout of drinking, in February 1640, was typical. He ordered the execution of his brother Ibrahim, his successor (he was himself childless). It seems likely that Murad wished to go down in history as the last great sultan of the race of Othman, rather than hand over the Empire to an incapable successor, but in this last wish he was thwarted by the Queen Mother, Kiusem, mother of both brothers, who realized that if Ibrahim died her power would vanish. She sent a false message back to Murad that Ibrahim had been strangled, whereupon Murad 'grinned a horrible and ghastly smile and then expired'.

*

Ibrahim, who was twenty-four, had been immured in the Cage since he was two. He had lived through the reigns of Mustafa, Osman and Murad.

* Used in war from the time of the Saracens. Rich Turks going on the pilgrimage to Mecca also frequently used pigeons to carry back accounts of their progress.

He knew nothing of politics or war and had existed for twenty-two years in mortal terror of the bowstring, so that when the soldiers came to announce his succession he refused point-blank to believe them, convinced that he was about to be strangled. With the help of his sterile concubines, he dragged all the furniture across his room and barricaded the door, defying all pleas and even attempts to batter it down. Finally the Grand Vizier hit on the only way to dispel Ibrahim's terror. He brought the body of Murad to the courtyard of the Cage and begged Ibrahim to look at it from the upstairs window. For a moment Ibrahim 'stood transfixed with a feeling of mingled joy and fear', before tumbling down the stairs and dancing round his brother's corpse, screaming with insane delight, 'The butcher of the Empire is dead at last.'

Once on the throne, Ibrahim proved to be the most detestable and debauched of all the Ottoman sultans. A picture of him shows the bleared countenance of a drunkard, his turban tipped crazily to one side. From the moment of his accession he seemed to have but one thought in mind – to make up for lost time. A man who regarded sex almost as a duty which had to be practised daily, his excesses were such that even the harem murmured in protest, to say nothing of the government.

His power-mad mother, Kiusem, was no novice in the art of harem rule, for she had been mother to three sultans. Quickly she adopted the by now well-known tactics of providing distraction in the form of a steady stream of virgins. There was another reason for these tactics. Despite his cravings, Ibrahim suffered from protracted fits of impotence, and as he was the last living member of the Othman race his mother was anxious for him to produce an heir – which he did after two years on the throne, when the first of his ten children was born.

By chance the first-born was conceived shortly after Kiusem had introduced Ibrahim to a 'magician' called Cinci Huseyin, who boasted of knowing several magical formulas guaranteed to encourage fertility. When the magic coincided with the birth, Cinci was loaded with gifts, given an important theological post and made a wealthy man.

Ibrahim's impotence, which recurred regularly during his life, was caused by a curious sexual streak in his nature – an insatiable passion for women beyond his reach. With few exceptions the women of the harem bored him, so that he found it difficult to make love to slave girls who had no option but to agree. He apparently needed the impetus of a challenge before bedding a girl.

His mother could not help him, but someone else could. This was Sechir Para, 'Sweet Lump of Sugar', one of his sultanas and a deadly rival to Kiusem, who hated her; for 'Sugar' not only shared Ibrahim's bed (successfully) but she was a born procuress who realized that she could maintain a stronger hold over her royal lover if she were able to find him attractive girls outside the harem. Ibrahim provided her with a jewel-studded coach in which she visited places like the public baths to search out attractive girls, and this quirk in Ibrahim's nature might never have been known had not 'Sugar' set eyes on the Mufti's daughter when bath-ing. She reported to the Sultan that, 'I have seen the most beautiful girl in all Constantinople.'

Ibrahim's reaction was immediate; he had to possess her whatever the cost. But even Ibrahim realized that he would never be allowed even to meet the daughter of such an exalted religious leader as the Mufti. There was only one way and Ibrahim took it. He sent for the Mufti and, to his astonishment – and horror – he asked for his daughter's hand in marriage. Such a thing had never been heard of in the history of a dynasty of rulers born from slaves. The Mufti knew of the excesses in the harem – indeed, they were common gossip – but he also knew that if he did not tread warily he would be in grave danger of losing his head. He replied that nothing would more honour his name than for his daughter to become the wife of the Sultan; but, he added, the Sultan must know that it was against the canons of Moslem law for a religious leader 'to impose upon the affections of a child'. He would, he promised, do all in his power to per-suade her to accept such an honour, yet 'if she proved refractory, it would not become his power to force her'.

It does not require much imagination to picture the dire warnings the Mufti gave his daughter before she answered the Sultan's proposal with a polite but frigid refusal. Furious, Ibrahim asked 'Sugar' to follow the girl to the baths and try to make her change her mind. When her pleas failed Ibrahim had the girl watched and one morning abducted her. The terrified virgin was now introduced to some of the bizarre practices of the harem, by now a hotbed of unnatural vices. (There was one room which Ibrahim had lined with mirrors to stimulate him, and where, 'One of his little games was to strip all his women naked and make them pretend to be mares while he would run amongst them acting the part of stallion as long as his strength lasted.'

The Mufti's daughter must have been a girl of courage for we are told that after Ibrahim had enjoyed her for several days, even though she was in tears, he sent her back to her father 'with Scorn and Contempt'. From that moment Ibrahim had an implacable enemy in the Mufti who vowed never to rest until the Sultan was killed.

Ibrahim now proceeded – with the help of his mother, Kiusem – to alienate the members of his government. When Kiusem complained that there was not enough wood for the harem fires, Ibrahim arraigned the Grand Vizier on a capital charge and he was later executed. When some of his eunuchs on a pilgrimage to Mecca were captured by pirates who put into Crete for shelter, Ibrahim launched a mad war against the island which belonged to the Republic of Venice with which Turkey had a treaty of peace. The war culminated in the historic siege of Candia, its chief fortress, which resisted the Turks for nearly twenty-five years.

His extravagances were those of a demented man. He adorned his beard with diamonds. He had a morbid craving for ambergris, drenching his beard, caftans, even his curtains with this heady perfume. When one of his concubines told him the story of a king who always dressed in sables, Ibrahim decided to become a 'sable king' with sables on all his clothing, and the walls and curtains of his favourite room. He even had cats with sable coats. But sables on such a scale were hard to come by – until Ibrahim summoned the Divan and ordered a general collection of sables from every corner of the Empire.

All this, however, was nothing compared with the dreadful series of events leading up to wholesale murder in the harem in the middle of his eight-year reign. The chain of tragedy started when 'Sugar' told the Sultan of a rumour that a concubine had been discovered in a compromising situation with a man. Such a thing seemed impossible, and 'Sugar' may well have picked up a rumour at second hand, for she could add no details, certainly not the name of the girl; but Ibrahim did not need proof.

There had indeed been cases of girls becoming involved in affairs of some kind; no one – not even the eagle-eyed Kislar Aga – could check all harem scandals. Lesbianism, naturally, was rife, but there had also been cases in which concubines, bored by the deadly existence of waiting for a despot's favours, formed deep attachments and even sexual liaisons with eunuchs, either the white ones captured in battle (and castrated outside the city as the Koran did not permit castration) or the black eunuchs who were bought as slaves from the upper reaches of the Nile and the area south of Lake Chad. Not all these eunuchs were completely castrated. Most black eunuchs had both penis and testicles cut off; but some eunuchs had only their testicles removed, either by dragging or crushing until the seminal glands were permanently injured. Some had only the penis removed, retaining all the sexual urge without being able to perform the act. Penzer, in his book on the harem, says that, 'It is quite incorrect to imagine that a castrated male loses all desires immediately. Not only is he often attracted strongly to women, but, strange as it may seem, evokes affection in return, and in the history of the harem many marriages of eunuchs have taken place. Such venereal promptings are naturally regulated by the state of the prostate.' A eunuch in touch with the world outside the harem of Ibrahim would find it quite a simple matter to smuggle in erotic aids which were much in vogue at the time, and with which a eunuch would sometimes play the part of a lesbian, 'which by its very novelty might well help to satisfy the cravings of a bored and neglected woman'. And, as Juvenal wrote, 'Some women always delight in soft eunuchs and tender kisses and in the absence of beard and the fact that the use of abortives is unnecessary.'

Whether or not one of these unfortunate creatures did form a liaison with a concubine of Ibrahim's harem will never be known, but according to several sources, the Sultan believed. The Kislar Aga tried to discover the girl's identity, resorting to torture of some of the girls. But no name was revealed – perhaps because the ill-used concubines banded together in self-defence, perhaps because no such girl or incident existed. For three days Ibrahim stalked around the harem 'in a mood of fury and black anger'. When his son Mahomet, who was too young for the Cage, made some jocular remark that displeased him, the enraged Sultan drew his jewelled dagger and stabbed his son in the face. The wound was not fatal, but it left him with a scar for life.

Finally Ibrahim decided to act. Like the headmaster of a school where the culprit has refused to step out and confess, he decided to punish the entire 'school'. But no one, not even the Kislar Aga, could have imagined the form the punishment would take. Ibrahim decided that, with the exception of 'Sugar', every one of his 280 concubines should die by drowning.

The girls in the harem were murdered in batches, tied up in sacks weighted with stones and carried to the Water Gate where each batch was loaded on a small boat, with a larger boat tied to it so the eunuchs could pull the frailer craft away from the shore and then, by a dextrous jerking of the rope, make the women in the sacks topple off.

All but one of the odalisques were drowned. Her sack was not sufficiently well tied and she managed to wriggle free. Floating to the surface, she cried for help, and was picked up by a passing boat bound for France. She was able to give the details of the massacre to the crew before eventually reaching Paris.

Long before that, ugly rumours swept the city, particularly after a kind of proof which came in a ghoulish postscript. One of Constantinople's three hundred divers was lowered from a boat to inspect a wreck in the Bosporus. Though he had no mask, he was able, like all the divers of those days, to see even the most minute objects on the sea bed, for the divers filled their mouths with oil and when they reached the sea bed spat it out, 'the drops [being] transformed underwater into as many looking glasses through which they can spy even such minute objects as a needle'.

The diver told of seeing 'a great number of bowing sacks, each containing the body of a dead woman standing upright on the weighted end and swaying to and fro with the current'.

In a matter of days the story was common gossip in the capital, and now the Mufti was given the opportunity for revenge. He and his followers were determined to dethrone Ibrahim and replace him with his seven-year-old son, Mahomet. But it had to be done carefully, so first of all they approached the powerful Queen Mother and put their charge to her. It read formally, 'The Padishah has ruined the Ottoman world by pillage and tyranny. Women wield sovereignty. The Treasury cannot satiate their expense. The subjects are ruined. The armies of the infidels are besieging towns on the frontiers. Their fleets blockade the Dardanelles.'

Kiusem argued, but finally gave her consent to the deposition. The Sheik-ul-Islam and the Mufti next held a public meeting in St Sophia before a vast congress which accepted their demands without one voice of dissent. The way was now open. The Janissaries marched to the Gate of Felicity and demanded to see Ibrahim in person. Briefly they announced the decision of the government. It seems that Ibrahim took the decision calmly. In any event, there was nothing he could do about it and he was taken back to the Cage where he had lived so long before his accession.

This was not enough for the Mufti, who wanted the life of the man who had ravished his daughter; but, as he was a religious leader, any plot had to be 'legal'. It did not take much engineering. With Ibrahim in the Cage, the religious leaders confronted the Mufti (doubtless by arrangement), and put to him a simple question, 'Is it lawful to dethrone and put to death a Padishah who confers all the posts of dignity in the Empire not on those who are worthy of them, but on those who have bought them for money?' In one of the world's most laconic judgements on a matter of life and death, the Mufti replied with one word: 'Yes.'

Incredibly, Ibrahim, who for so many years in the Cage had lived in terror of the arrival of the deaf mutes, now seems to have convinced himself that it would be only a matter of time before he was restored to the throne, so when a deputation arrived at the Cage there was no thought of barricading the door as he had done eight years previously. Indeed, he hailed the deputation with excitement. But this time it *was* the bowstring.

Despite one important victory, in which the Turks beat the Cossacks to recapture the important city of Azov, Ibrahim's reign had been disastrous. The unfinished war in Crete was draining the country. All the abuses which Murad had checked (however cruelly) flourished again; the resources of the State were frittered away by the rule of the harem. Understandably, the Government wanted more than the blood of the Sultan. It was essential that the harem rule be ended forever – and that meant death for Kiusem.

It was a grisly, undignified murder, totally at variance with the normal ceremonious Turkish forms of death for people of rank. Kiusem had been forewarned. She fled from her room along the Golden Road and hid in a small room by the Carriage Gate behind the Divan. A search was made in the Seraglio, and the toothless old woman of sixty-two was finally found cringing in a chest under a pile of dirty clothing. There was no ceremony this time. Kiusem was dragged out, her rings, earrings and bracelets torn off, her robes ripped off in shreds. Only when she was naked – a scene never before witnessed in the Seraglio – was she dragged by the feet to one of the gates. She fought to the end, before she was strangled with a curtain cord, the blood from her nose and ears staining the clothes of her murderers.

'Sugar' was luckier, for a time. She was one of the few sultanas who married after the death of her husband, but when her second husband died she became Constantinople's most exclusive procuress, a calling for which she had received an admirable training. She was known everywhere as La Sultana Sporca – the Filthy Sultana. She specialized in buying young girls, training them in singing, dancing and the arts of coquetry, then hiring them out to the young gallants of the town or to rich pashas. For her, as she grew older, a more refined death was reserved, by one of her many enemies. She was poisoned in the traditional Turkish manner with a cup of coffee in which chopped hair and ground glass had been mixed, destroying the intestines during a long and painful death.

One can detect almost a note of glee in the Bank of Genoa's report that *'Le stata assassine aquella Sultana che si chiami la Sporca, che le fu una vecchia meterola'* – 'That wicked old woman, the Filthy Sultana, has been assassinated.'

Chapter five
The rule of the Viziers

For the next century and a half – an era marked by historic milestones in the relations between Turkey and Europe – the sultans of the Ottoman Empire were merely nonentities. It was as though an old man had become so satiated by his excesses that all he asked was to end his days quietly while others did the work. The sultans still maintained their courts with exaggerated splendour unmatched in Europe (with Louis XIV, the Sun King of France, running them a close second). They still had their whims, ranging from one ruler's passion for the chase to another's craving for tulips, but for the most part their depravity was limited and unexceptional.

Mahomet IV, who now succeeded to the throne in 1648, inherited a great statesman to guide him as Grand Vizier. This was the first of the famous Kiuprili family, chosen by his mother as Mahomet was under age. The Kiuprilis – father, son, brother – guided the Empire's destinies for half a century. While the grand viziers were of such high calibre, one sultan after another was content to leave the fate of the country in their hands.

There was a savage twist of irony to the situation, for despite the qualities of the grand viziers (give or take the odd black sheep) this was a time in which the Ottomans faced one crushing defeat after another, an era in which all fears of their military prowess vanished as limb after limb was lopped off the Empire.

The first of the Kiuprili grand viziers was an Albanian called Mahomet who started his working life as a kitchen boy in the Sultan's palace, and on the advice of the Sultan Mahomet's mother, the Queen Mother Tarkhan, became Grand Vizier in 1656 at the ripe old age of seventy. To the pashas of the Divan the appointment was regarded as little more than another royal joke, for Kiuprili, so they said, was in his dotage and could

neither read nor write. Never were the pundits proved more wrong.
Kiuprili had already ruled wisely as governor in turn of Damascus, Tripoli
and Jerusalem, and he only consented to become Grand Vizier after the
Queen Mother had solemnly sworn on behalf of Mahomet, who was still
too young to assume power, that his every act would be ratified without
examination and that he would be free to appoint all offices in the Government. It seems that Kiuprili was well aware of the folly of putting one's
trust in princes (or their mothers), for he had the conditions confirmed by
the Mufti.

Once this was done he became 'more of a Regent than a Vizier', and
set about putting the Ottoman house in order. Like Murad, the pugnaci-
ous Kiuprili had to purge the Turkish system by a relentless war on wrong-
doers. Officials, judges, army generals all suffered. In five years thirty-
five thousand people were executed. Soulfikar, Constantinople's chief
executioner, admitted that he personally strangled five thousand people in
this period; but at least corruption and injustice were halted. A navy was
rebuilt. The army became once again a disciplined force, so that several
lost provinces were restored, and Kiuprili was actually preparing to lead
an army into Hungary when he fell mortally ill.

The Sultan was hunting near Adrianople, but he rushed back to
Constantinople. The Grand Vizier lived simply in a comparatively modest
palace with only a small harem, but the Sultan made his way there and,
heartbroken, told Kiuprili that he would willingly give him ten years of his
life if he could, and when he asked the old man for his advice Kiuprili had
no hesitation in giving it. He urged the Sultan never to listen to the advice
of women; never to choose a minister who was too wealthy; to keep the
Treasury filled; and to keep the army on the move. As the Grand Vizier
lay dying, the Sultan asked him who should succeed him. 'I know none',
replied Kiuprili, 'more suited than my son Ahmed.'

And so Ahmed at twenty-six – six years older than the Sultan – became
Grand Vizier and ruled the country firmly for the next fifteen years with,
if possible, more astuteness and dignity than his father. All who met him
placed him in the first rank of statesmen, a man of 'most engaging
manners, dignified and modest. He spoke with reserve and without verbi-
age.'

Though the strictest of Moslems, Kiuprili tolerated all other religions, expressly forbidding violence towards them. To the Christians of Constantinople, he granted permission to rebuild their ancient churches, and when some underling pointed out that, according to an old law, this could only be done with the same wood and stones of the original church, Kiuprili retorted, 'They are fools who invented that formula and greater fools still are they who follow it. These people desire to repair their temple; if it is so dilapidated that to repair it is impossible, let them build a new one All that we need care about is, that they do it at their own expense, and not with money of the Mussulmans; and provided that they pay their tribute regularly, the rest does not concern us.'

He was the first statesman in the Ottoman Empire to lay down the principle of free trade. When he was asked to regulate sales, he replied, 'The Koran says nothing on the subject. Sale and purchase should be left to the free will of both parties.'

*

Even when Mahomet came of age, he never interfered with his Grand Vizier. Though, like all sultans, he had his quirks, they did not impinge on affairs of state. Hunting had been his all-consuming passion since the age of eight. 'The Mighty Hunter' maintained a force of eight hundred falconers in charge of the hunting birds which were always adorned round the neck with either a diamond or some other precious stone, their hoods being embroidered with pearls. The Sultan took no heed of the weather when hunting around Adrianople, and on one night over a score of falconers died from exposure. The rest 'were in a fair way to follow them'. (When the Grand Falconer mildly remonstrated, the Sultan's only retort was to order him to take better care of the dogs.) On another occasion Mahomet assembled thirty thousand peasants from different parts of the Empire to act as beaters during a gigantic hunting-party. The weather was cold and stormy, washing away the beaters' makeshift camps. Thirty died of exposure. The Sultan looked at the bodies and merely remarked, 'These men would doubtless have rebelled against me. They have received their punishment in anticipation.'

Mahomet also admired the arts, and took a keen interest in the historians compiling the annals of his reign – particularly those writing eulogistic accounts of every bird or beast he slaughtered. Among his favourites was the Turkish historian Abdi, who had to tread warily, for the Sultan had a sardonic touch of humour. When one evening Mahomet asked what he had written about his reign that day, Abdi incautiously replied that nothing had happened. Without a moment's hesitation the Sultan threw a hunting-spear at the author, wounding him slightly. '*Now* thou has something to write about,' he cried.

Though the Sultan was uninterested in politics, he still believed in maintaining the opulence of his court, wherever it happened to be, as Dr John Covel, Vice-Chancellor of Cambridge University, discovered when he chanced to be in Adrianople during the circumcision ceremony of the Sultan's son. The young prince rode to his father's tent, outriders sheltering him from a hot sun with large fans of bustards' feathers, while others ran ahead sprinkling the road with water to lay the dust. The crowds were kept at a distance by men with blown-up bladders daubed in tar from which, as Covel noted, 'the spruce Turks fly as from the Divel'.

A procession followed in which a hundred slaves each carried a thirty-foot-high pole, not unlike a maypole, decorated with paper ornaments and wax fruits and flowers; these were planted in front of the royal tent. In accordance with tradition a score of urchins too poor to participate in a proper ceremony (and who would normally have been at the mercy of a barber with a rusty razor) were circumcised with the prince and, again according to custom, received a modest pension for the rest of their lives. The actual operation was performed in a few seconds by Mahomet's chief surgeon, an Italian, with 'the aid of a razor, tweezers and small box-wood stick'. According to Covel, the Italian received a fee of £6,000, handed to him in a silver bowl, after which the day ended with a public fête with sideshows and sports.

The Sultan sometimes did not visit Constantinople for months at a time, but the Seraglio was, of course, the centre of government, and the thousands of officials (and sycophants) who lived or worked there must have had gargantuan appetites, for around this time a French traveller, Aubry de la Motraye, compiled a list of the Seraglio's annual meat supplies: 60,000 head of mutton, 20,000 of veal, 200,000 fowls, 100,000 pigeons, 3,000 turkeys. The quantity of other foods needed for the Seraglio was equally astonishing. One manuscript lists the deliveries to the palace store-rooms in 1660 as, 'three thousand pounds of vermicelli, twenty-five hundred bushels of chick-peas and the same amount of lentils, twenty-five bushels of eggplant, six hundred hundredweight of onions, twelve barrels of starch, sixty thousand pounds of honey, forty thousand pounds of yellow wax, six thousand loaves of sugar, nine hundred and eighteen pounds of pepper, two thousand pounds of cloves and nutmeg, two hundred and ninety-seven pounds of ginger, two hundred and six pounds of saffron, twelve thousand pounds of salt, seven hundred and eighty camel-loads of ice, five jars of olive oil, seventy barrels of vinegar, twenty large barrels of lemon juice, thirty barrels of verjuice, six hundred and ninety-three pounds of henna, twenty-four hundred and seventy-five pounds of sal volatile, and eighty-two pounds of amber'.

Some of these provisions were eaten by the foreign ambassadors who, like Barton, years previously, always had to plough their way through vast meals before a royal audience. When the Venetian ambassador, Giorgio Battista Donado, had his first audience of the Sultan Mahomet, he sat down to 130 courses served on green celadon porcelain, which was reputed to neutralize poisons. There was now an added refinement, a sort of private joke of which the Ambassador, fortunately for his pride, was in ignorance; for Mahomet was not particularly fond of Christians and lost no opportunity of saying so – in the language of the country. This had produced a rigidly observed private conversation between himself and his Grand Vizier whenever he received a Christian.

As the Grand Vizier announced to the Sultan the arrival of Donado, Mahomet replied, 'Feed and clothe the dog and bring him in to me.' After lunch the Grand Vizier duly reported, 'The infidel is fed and clothed and he now craves to lick the dust beneath Your Majesty's throne.' 'Then let the hound enter,' was the Sultan's laconic reply, at which the smiling Ambassador, with a sense of quiet triumph at being received, was allowed to kiss hands with the ruler.

The picture that emerges of Mahomet is of a man not unhappy, indeed rather jovial, and, according to some historians, a homosexual. His manner changed when he was at Adrianople, away from royal chores, for he hated Constantinople violently. Firstly it kept him away from the chase, and secondly it reminded him of rival claimants to his throne – his two brothers, both born of the same mother as himself, the Queen Mother Tarkhan. His fear of plots became such an obsession that Mahomet finally tried to murder the two young princes. The Queen Mother, aware of the danger, hid the boys each night in a room that could only be reached through her bedroom. Even so the Sultan crept into her room with a dagger in his hand. Two pages watched terrified, not daring to speak, but one touched the Queen Mother who jumped off her divan, clung to the Sultan, begging him to kill her before touching her children. Tarkhan undoubtedly saved the two boys' lives, though the two pages were put to death the following morning.

*

Ahmed Kiuprili's statesmanship had done much to stabilize internal affairs, but when it came to war he was not so fortunate. Though he managed to end the 25-year-old siege of Candia, and annex Crete for the Empire, he lost two battles of great historical significance. In 1663, he marched against Austria at the head of 120,000 men with 123 guns, crossing the Danube and striking north, finally meeting the Austro-Hungarian army near the convent of St Gotthard. The Ottomans had overwhelming superiority, on paper; but they were resoundingly thrashed, largely by the heavy Austrian cavalry under the dashing Prince Charles of Lorraine, already on the way to becoming a living legend; ten thousand Turks were killed, thirty thousand fled in terror. It was the first great defeat of the Ottomans by the Austrians.

Nine years later he marched against the Polish army led by their future king, Sobieski. For the first time the voice of the Czar of Russia was heard when, with the King of Poland, he protested at 'Turkish intervention'. Kiuprili's retort was proud, but unfortunate. 'Such is the strength of Islam,' he said, 'that the union of Russians and Poles matters not to us.'

But it did. The Turks were defeated in several major battles, and even when the war petered out after four years the signs were there for all Europe to see: Turkish arms were no longer invincible.

Ahmed Kiuprili died a few days after the peace treaty was signed and it seemed obvious that his brother Zadé, who had displayed all the Kiuprili qualities, should succeed him, but for the only time in his reign Sultan Mahomet interfered. Exercising his royal prerogative, he chose his son-in-law, a boon companion of the chase and, according to some sources, a close friend. (He was reputed to be bi-sexual.) The appointment of Kara ('Black') Mustafa was a fatal choice, for he was not only bloodthirsty but corrupt. Years of disaster for the Empire culminated in Kara Mustafa's siege of Vienna in 1683, despite the fact that no one really wanted the war – least of all the Sultan. But Kara Mustafa wielded immense influence over his master and, to help persuade him, actually produced forged letters in support of his position from one official who violently opposed the war, until finally the Sultan agreed to the venture.

By May of 1683 Kara Mustafa gathered an army variously estimated at more than 200,000 and a few days before the march the Sultan – anxious to accommodate his friend of the hunting-field – agreed to hold a spectacular demonstration, including a 'personal appearance', to popularize the war. It was perhaps the most bizarre spectacle that even Constantinople had ever seen.

The troops were encamped in tents of green, red, white and orange on the Asian side of the Bosporus. On one flank stood the Sultan's own huge screened camp, the centre-piece a vast tent of three compartments – his private quarters, a throne-room, a hall of justice. Every conceivable luxury had been provided, from Turkish baths with specially piped water to a page-boy 'of the most pleasant visage', whose task (officially, that is) was to rub the Sultan's feet when they were cold. Kara Mustafa's nearby camp was almost as opulent. A member of the Venetian embassy called Benetti saw it all, even catching a glimpse of the Sultan's favourite sultana setting off from the palace across the Bosporus shielded by a double line of black eunuchs with hangings of green silk above the level of her head, while the boat was steered by a man who scrupulously averted his eyes. Once ashore, the sultana was driven to the camp in a carriage adorned with silverwork and drawn by four horses harnessed abreast.

The Sultan arrived in a procession headed by an emir carrying the green standard of the Prophet. Then, as Benetti recorded it, came judicial officers 'wearing turbans of such a size that a man's arms could hardly embrace them'. A pack of wolf-hounds made a bizarre appearance, for they wore gold-embroidered coats and red spiked collars, and their paws and tails were dyed red and yellow. Horsemen nursing hunting-leopards on their saddles followed them, together with two plumed camels, one carrying the Koran in a green case, the other a shred of cloth once worn by the Prophet. A hundred Janissaries banged and clattered their kettles and cauldrons, a hundred of the Sultan's archers wore helmets of beaten gold flashing in the sun; a hundred men in tiger and panther skins were followed by a hundred pikemen in mail – an innovation in the Army – their fretting, frothing, prancing horses armoured with metal plates on flank, shoulder and rump, their beaten-gold headpieces giving them a curious mask-like appearance. Even their bridles jingled with gold plaques.

Then came the Grand Vizier, preceded by a mounted band of kettle-drums, cymbals and trumpeters – military bands originated in Turkey – and he in turn was followed by the palace pages in shining mail, their caps covered with gold discs. Immediately behind them rode Mahomet in a white toga with frogging of diamonds, a fur-lined hood slung across his shoulders and a diamond spray in his turban. The Mighty Hunter did not cut a very dashing figure, for Benetti found that, 'The man himself was a sad contrast to his magnificent trappings as he rode along with bent shoulders, his peaked nose, thin beard, scraggy neck and undistinguished features relieved only by the fine black eyes that were the heirloom of the imperial house.'

Six coachloads of harem favourites, their carriages drawn by white ponies, wound up the procession with twenty camels loaded with house-hold equipment. In and out of the procession darted the dervishes, naked except for their green aprons fringed with ebony beads, encouraging religious fervour among the troops by the doubtful method of blowing discordant blasts on cow horns. As an 'added attraction' slave dealers exhibited their choicest wares in the hope of a quick sale, while more than two hundred lunatics were brought out of captivity for the amusement of the crowds. Strung together with silver chains, they were led by their keepers who carried flasks of medicine to dose the unruly who did not respond to a box on the ears. Some were naked, some wept, others laughed and swore as their keepers thrashed the wretched creatures (beating being, at the time, a recognized 'cure' for insanity).

It never entered anybody's head that such an auspicious prelude to the war could be marred; but Kara Mustafa had reckoned without divine interference. The day before the Army was due to march, a savage storm swept the mighty camp; the tents were levelled for miles around and the Sultan's quarters were reduced to a soggy field of mud and slush. Worst of all – to the superstitious Turks anyway – a gust of wind blew off the

Sultan's turban. It was a dreaded omen as the sword of Islam marched out, the soldiers in their plumes and bright colours stretching in columns for miles, to the scene of its greatest disaster.

And yet by rights von Stahrenburg's puny garrison of eleven thousand behind the walls of Vienna should have been easily defeated; the defences had been neglected; the Emperor had fled to the safety of Bavaria; the Polish army was nearly eight weeks' march away. The Turks had overwhelming superiority, and by now they had flintlocks heavier than European models and capable of a greater range. In archery they were second to none and their hollow steel-tipped arrows could pierce armour at a hundred yards. The 'sappers', who excelled at mining defences, were held in terrified respect, and with heavy cannon the Turks had partly overcome the problem of mobility by using 'camel artillery' in place of lumbering oxen. And, above all, the Turkish soldier fought with the fervour of religion and the promise, devoutly believed, that a man who died on the battlefield had earned himself an immediate passport to Heaven.

Nothing, it seemed, could save the day against the terrifying reality of Ottoman arms. So what went wrong when, on 15 July 1683, Kara Mustafa laid siege to the city?

The greed of the Grand Vizier, an avaricious and venal man who had amassed immense riches but was still not satisfied, was to deprive the Sultan of his victory. Kara Mustafa wanted Vienna and its riches for himself; but he faced one problem. If the city were taken by assault, most of the booty would go to the troops. If on the other hand the city could be persuaded to capitulate or be starved into surrender, he could seize its wealth as representative of the Sultan. So he delayed the attack, with fatal results. He allowed Sobieski time to march his army from Poland and for Prince Charles of Lorraine to bring up more reinforcements. At the end of August a soldier from Sobieski's army swam the Danube with letters of hope carried in a bladder round his neck, and on 6 September – seven weeks after Vienna had been invested – rockets from the relieving forces announced to the beleaguered garrison that help was at hand in the form of eighty thousand troops.

Sobieski and Charles of Lorraine's first task was to gain the heights above Vienna. That night Sobieski addressed his troops. 'We have to save today not a single city but the whole of Christianity,' he cried, 'of which the city of Vienna is the bulwark. The war is a holy one. The infidels see you now above their heads, and with hopes blasted and courage depressed are escaping among the valleys destined to be their graves. I have but one command to give – Follow me! The time is come for the young to win his spurs.'

On a beautiful September morning, with autumn mists clinging to the valleys and giving promise of a warm day, Sobieski and Charles of Lorraine attacked. Kara Mustafa, confident in his superior numbers, had already ordered the massacre of thirty thousand prisoners, picked up on the way to Vienna.

Never in his wildest dreams could Kara Mustafa have imagined the rout that followed as Sobieski and Prince Charles attacked and the Turkish line faltered, crumpled, then broke. Even the Janissaries were annihilated, and the entire Turkish camp fell to the Christians. The immense booty included three hundred guns, nine thousand ammunition wagons, twenty-five thousand tents. The panic-stricken Turks fled blindly. Dozens of pashas and generals were killed, though Kara Mustafa, his right eye bandaged, managed to escape with his treasure and the banner of the Prophet.

Around six o'clock Sobieski, who had not eaten all day, made his way into Kara Mustafa's sumptuous pavilion, the main tent of purest Chinese silk and gold brocade studded with gems and scarlet tassels. To the astonished Sobieski it seemed incredible – room after opulent room, silver tableware, costly furniture, and even a courtyard with its fountain, containing tame rabbits, several breeds of cats and a parrot.

Back in Adrianople Kara Mustafa pleaded such a powerful case that, for the moment, the Sultan absolved him of all blame. Mustafa, however, had made a fatal mistake on the march home, executing the Pasha of Buda, who would have been a hostile witness at any enquiries. The Pasha was married to the Sultan's sister, a particularly resourceful woman, who was determined that her brother should know the truth. Afraid of travelling from Buda to Constantinople openly, she slipped out of the harem in disguise and reached Constantinople where the Divan and Janissaries confirmed her story. Mahomet had no option but to change his mind, though very much against his will. Kara Mustafa, called upon to deliver up his seals of office, asked brusquely, 'Am I to die?' When the executioner stepped forward with the bowstring, Kara Mustafa asked for time to wash and pray, then, kneeling, he put the noose round his neck himself. All he said was, 'As God pleases.' His head was stuffed with straw and placed by the Gate of the Divan.

It was 25 December 1683 – though the significance of the date may have been lost on the Turks. This was the day that marked the last Ottoman attempt to increase the Empire by attack. From now on the Turks would be almost always on the defensive.

*

Other powers were quick to attack. The Pope launched a crusade. The oligarchs of the Republic of Venice fitted out a fleet with the help of the Pope and the Knights of Malta. A Venetian army invaded Bosnia and Albania and captured Athens, while the Austrians defeated the Turks in Croatia, freeing the country after 151 years of Turkish rule. The Prince of Lorraine captured the fortress of Buda, Turkish for 145 years. Inevitably Turkish heads had to roll, but at least on this occasion the royal head did *not* roll. Zadé Kiuprili, Ahmed's brother, was by now Grand Vizier, and insisted on deposing Mahomet after thirty-nine years of useless rule, but he spared his life. His brother, Suleiman, 'of long, lean pale visage', who had spent forty-five years in the Cage, became Sultan, and Mahomet occupied his comfortable prison for the rest of his life.

The last notable Kiuprili, in fact, regained considerable territory in two years before being killed in the thick of battle at Salankemen when, once again, the Turks and Austrians were locked in war. After that, one disaster followed another; Ahmed II followed Suleiman II to the throne but died of a broken heart four years later. His successor, Mustafa II, who had spent nearly thirty-one years in the Cage, insisted on leading his armies against Hungary.

It was a hopeless venture. The Hungarians, led by Prince Eugène of Savoy, met the Turks at Zenton on the River Theiss some sixty miles above the point where it parts company from the Danube. Here the Sultan had erected a bridge of pontoons for his troops to cross. Eugène waited until the Sultan and his artillery were on one bank and the infantry on the other. Then he attacked. As the Sultan looked on helplessly, twenty-six thousand Turks of the infantry were killed and another ten thousand drowned trying to swim to safety. The Grand Vizier and four viziers were killed.

It was now that the major European countries realized for the first time the dangers of leaving Turkey open to attack by their rivals anxious to seize Constantinople with its unrivalled strategic position. Each country wanted a neutral Turkey: Britain to safeguard her route to India; France and Italy to safeguard the Mediterranean; Russia to prevent expansion by the other powers. In the last years of the seventeenth century, Britain and Holland offered to mediate in a peace based on the principle of *uti possidetis* – that Austria, Venice and Poland should agree to terms based on retaining territory wrested from the Turks. The peace conference was held at Carlowitz on the Danube in 1699 and lasted seventy-two days. Its most humiliating provisions for the Ottoman Empire were that Austria kept two-thirds of Hungary and Russia gained all the area north of the Sea of Azov, together with Azov itself.

The re-drawn boundaries must have caused much anguish in Constantinople, but it was not the lines on a map that made the Treaty of Carlowitz a milestone in relations between Turkey and Europe. The significance of the treaty lay deeper. Carlowitz rejected not only all Ottoman pretensions to a career of conquest, but recognized that the status of the Empire was a matter of deep concern to all major European powers even though they might not be at war with Turkey. It was, however, to take the Ottoman Empire another fifty years before the full significance of Carlowitz sank in, and in these years the fortunes of the Empire seesawed.

*

Even in these years of tumult, one thing remained obstinately unchanged: the Grand Seraglio and its wild extravagances. Behind the Gate of Felicity the wars slowly dismembering the Empire passed almost unnoticed. Ahmed III, who ascended the throne in 1703, four years after the peace of Carlowitz, devoted most of his twenty-eight-year reign to wild extravagances. When his daughter married, 1,500 cooks prepared a special feast and the Sultan devised novel 'sugar gardens' about eighteen feet long, which were set in tents where the guests could nibble bits of the garden as a change from watching jugglers or listening to concerts by more than two thousand musicians.

Ahmed's greatest love was the tulip,* which grew profusely on the Mongolian steppes. By now tulips were more refined, for in the middle of the sixteenth century an Amsterdam merchant took the first bulbs to Holland and later developed hundreds of varieties of cultivated tulips. Ahmed imported 1,200 different bulbs for the Seraglio gardens. The rare blooms were catalogued and no man could sell tulips outside the capital on pain of exile. Popular blooms were given poetical names, and a French merchant, Jean-Claude Flachat, felt that the Turks valued human life 'less than a horse or a fine tulip'. When one ambassador lost a bulb intended as a gift for Ahmed, the Grand Vizier sent a town crier through the streets of Constantinople offering a huge reward.

Each April Ahmed held a tulip fête, whenever possible in bright moonlight. On miles of specially made shelves in the Seraglio gardens, vases of tulips were placed alternately with glass globes filled with different coloured water, and lamps of coloured glass. Guests were forbidden to dress in colours that did not harmonize. From the trees hung dozens of cages of canaries. In the midst sat Ahmed, receiving court officials, while on one night only the ladies of the harem organized a charity bazaar, with the odalisques acting as saleswomen, for the Sultan – the only patron, of course.

Ahmed's tulip mania soon began to interfere with state business, and the cost of his fêtes proved such a drain on the national resources that he was deposed in 1730, and when his successor became Sultan Mahmud I he took the hint and curbed the wild extravagances of the 'Tulip Age'.

Anyway, Mahmud's tastes were more concerned with frolicking in the harem, as Monsieur Flachat, the French businessman who became an intimate friend of the Kislar Aga, noted. According to Flachat the Sultan liked to play peeping tom among the girls. Hidden behind a grille, he watched them arrive in the ornate baths of the harem in their white chemises. Mahmud, however, had had all the stitches removed and the material glued together. When the doors were closed and the usual head of steam developed he 'watched as the heat and moisture did their work. Some . . . laughed as the dress fell away in pieces, but others were very angry.' This may be apocryphal, but it is the sort of story the Sultan might

* The name tulip is derived from the Turkish nickname *tulbend*, which means turban.

retail to his chief black eunuch from whom Flachat heard it.

Osman was as ineffectual as Mahmud whom he succeeded in 1754, though his tastes were strangely different. A stout, dark, brooding man, who was fifty-four when he reached the throne, his chief passion in life was food. Presumably unimpressed by the fare offered by the palace chefs he would, each evening after dark, shed his regal gowns and don clothing of humbler cut, before setting off to scour the city's eating-houses, later buying a few choice morsels of food in the market to take home in case he was hungry during the night. Though his other passion was building, Osman was not extravagant. In the three years of his reign, he dismissed all the musicians he had inherited – he loathed music – and was the despair of the harem for he had little use for women.

*

Outside the Seraglio, most of the country was in a pitiful state. Bocaretto, an Italian travelling there at the time, wrote that, 'Unless one has seen it, one could scarcely believe human beings could live in such filth. Every day there is some fresh tragedy. The other morning I saw a pyramid of human heads on the left side of the principal entrance to the Imperial Palace. At the Seven Towers, a number of prisoners, among them several Christians, were thrown the other day over the parapet of the Tower which is annexed to the Torture Chamber, and which stands at the corner of the square in which political executions usually take place. You can see from the road, naked and still living men, caught on long spikes, where they will have to remain until death delivers them.'

*

The climax of this era was now almost at hand, brought about by one of the stupidest of all the stupid Ottoman wars when Osman's successor, Mustafa III, came to the throne in 1757 and rashly decided to pit his strength against the Russians, setting off on the northward march burdened with a staggering load of supplies. Senior generals and pashas each had the right to fifty camel loads of personal effects (though this was nothing compared with the Russians, now moving south, for the Russian generals were each allowed three hundred cartloads of personal possessions and provisions).

The war lasted five years, during which the two armies, like 'two brainless monsters met each other on many a bloody field and disported them-

The Second Court of the Grand Seraglio. On the right are the kitchens; the centre path leads to the Gate of Felicity; the crowds are moving towards the Divan behind which are the roofs of the harem

2 The Grand Bazaar in Constantinople. It looks virtually the same today

3 Suleiman the Magnificent in old age, with his sword-bearer

Roxelana as a western painter imagined her

5 Suleiman the Magnificent

6 Mahomet III

9 A birth in the harem

7 Mustafa I

8 Sultan Ibrahim

Turkish marriage procession at the Hippodrome

11 Abdul Hamid I ('the Reformer')

12 Aimée Dubecq de Rivery

13 *below* Mahmoud II in his state caïque

14 Etchi Bashi, or Chief Cook of the Janissaries

selves in scenes of unspeakable carnage and purposeless ruin'. Not until shortly after Mustafa's death did the war end with the Treaty of Kainardji in 1774. For Turkey it was a disaster, for she virtually lost control of the Crimea, while other states became vassals of the Russian Czarina. And there was one thing more in the Treaty, a clause hardly noticed at the time but which was to have dangerous significance in the years to come. 'Turkey,' it ran, 'promises to protect constantly the Christian religion and churches and allow the ministers of Russia at Constantinople to make representations on their behalf.' Thus, at a stroke, a Moslem province was torn from the Empire and Russia won the right to intervene on behalf of the Christian population in Turkey.

After centuries in which Christian Europe had waged war *against* Moslem Turkey, Europe now faced a supremely ironic situation. From now on, nations must be prepared to fight *for* the Ottoman Empire, to bolster it, to protect it, to see that it did not die, if only to stop rival powers seizing Constantinople, which the Emperor Constantine, on the night before it fell to the Turks, hailed as 'The queen of cities which had subdued nearly all the lands under the sun.'

Part 2

'The sick man of Europe'

Chapter six
The French Sultana

No great empire declines for one reason alone, and the Ottoman Empire's downhill course was certainly not caused only by the debauchery of its sultans, though they were largely responsible for the internal decay which slowly ate into the efficiency and honesty of Suleiman the Magnificent's system of government by slaves educated in his tribute school. As the 'rules' were relaxed by succeeding sultans – as nepotism crept in – the government could no longer depend on them absolutely. Much the same thing happened with the Janissaries once they were allowed to marry. Corrupt and pampered, they ceased to be real soldiers but employed their strength to render even the good sultans useless, until in the end the army, which had been a major factor in winning the Ottoman Empire, became a major cause of its decline.

There were many other reasons – the high price of high office; the cankers of bribery and corruption, which sapped all energy; even the Empire's size, which made administration difficult in hostile regions among alien races, particularly as the Turks had never really succeeded in the art of ruling their subject peoples; but the Ottoman Empire was essentially a military one, its primary aim the conquest of non-Turkish lands, and so, as Kiuprili had advised the Sultan on his deathbed, the Army had to be kept on the move. This might have been comparatively easy in the early days when nomadic tribesmen took command of the Byzantine Empire, but as the decadence of Byzantium sapped the strength of a race of fighters the Empire was faced with the growth of Russia, with brilliant leaders in Britain, Hungary, Poland and Austria, all with new weapons, disciplined troops, who went to war with such a hatred of 'the infidel Turk' that they fought with the zeal of a Holy Crusade. Together they formed a European bulwark no single empire could withstand.

Yet, despite the signs of decay – visible to all Europe – the Ottoman

Empire in Europe at the beginning of the nineteenth century included Greece, Crete, Servia, Bosnia, Herzegovina and what is today Bulgaria and Albania, together with half of what was then Montenegro. South of the Danube, Moldavia and Wallachia and part of Bessarabia were tributary states. In all, the Turkish dominions in Europe covered 238,000 square miles. But it was not size alone that kept the Empire alive, it was a deeper feeling. To paraphrase Scott Fitzgerald, Europe was a land, Russia was a people, but the Ottoman Empire possessed the quality of an idea.

Year after year a province would be lopped off, but even so the Empire lumbered on, the Turks blissfully convinced that it would last for ever, perhaps instinctively feeling, as their able diplomat Fuad Pasha felt when he wryly remarked to a Western colleague, 'Our state is the strongest state. For you are trying to cause its collapse from the outside, and we from the inside, but still it does not collapse.'

*

Towards the end of the eighteenth century, 59-year-old Abdul Hamid I, who had been Sultan for eleven years, received a gift which delighted and rejuvenated him, for it consisted of a golden-haired French girl with a witty, upturned nose below large blue eyes, and a perfectly formed Cupid's bow of a mouth above a determined chin. She had been captured by Algerian corsairs while returning from a convent in France to Martinique where her parents of good Norman stock lived. The pirates had taken her to the Bey of Algiers, who offered her as a present to the Sultan. Her name was Aimée Dubucq de Rivery, and her closest friend was her dark-haired, amusing cousin, also from Martinique. Though the two would never meet again, both girls were destined to become the power behind the thrones of great rulers.

Aimée spent the rest of her life in the harem, first as the 'wife' of Abdul Hamid, then as the friend of Sultan Selim, and finally as the Queen Mother of Sultan Mahmud, 'The Reformer'. Her dark-haired cousin was Joséphine Bonaparte.

Aimée must have been a remarkably resilient girl, for when she was forced to exchange the strict and decorous life of the convent (where she had been made to wear a calico robe each time she took a bath) for the imperial harem where the odalisques spent long hours 'lolling in Turkish baths, naked and sleek, ladling perfumed water over each other', she appears to have quickly realized that it was useless to struggle against her lot.

The odalisques in the harem paid her the supreme compliment of christening her Naksh, 'The Beautiful One'. Aimée had the French eye for style and always dressed in Turkish costume, in velvet or fur caftans and pantaloons, with a pillbox hat tilted to one side on her head, and her fair hair falling to her waist, covered with brilliant sequins which looked as though they had been carelessly thrown on the hair to glitter amongst the gold, but which were, in fact, attached by thin chains.

Before long the French convent girl was escorted along the Golden Road to Abdul Hamid's bed. Within a year, in 1783, she gave birth to a son, Mahmud, to the delight of the ageing Abdul Hamid, who had only one other son, Mustafa.

The ceremony of having a baby in the harem must have been something of an ordeal to a strict Catholic like Aimée. She had to watch as the swaddling clothes were protected against the Evil Eye by an amulet and a sprinkling of sesame seeds. The Koran in a silk bag was placed on top of the bundle. As the birth approached, a midwife brought in the customary walnut birth-chair, with a seat which had a piece shaped like a horseshoe cut out near its front.

Here poor Aimée sat, gripping the solid arms, as the midwife chanted 'Allah is most great' until the boy was born. Then she was tucked into a bed covered with rich shawls, with an onion, a clove of garlic, some blue beads, a Koran, to guard her against the Evil Eye. The baby was washed, the umbilical cord cut, and three sesame seeds placed on its navel before it was bound and swaddled.

The worst was now over, and on the sixth day, dressed like a bride, Aimée received her harem friends in state, though it was not until the fortieth day after the birth that she and her son took part in a joint ceremony, when the midwife washed the young baby in the lavish harem bath, with music playing in the background and aloe wood burning in a censer, as the poor boy* was smeared all over with a broken duck-egg, 'to accustom it to water, like a duck.'

*

* Who would later be kept from crying by soothing drinks of poppy-head water, or by a 'dummy' of marzipan tied in a cloth for him to suck.

However difficult the birth might have been, it not only delighted the Sultan but made Aimée's position secure, for from that moment Mustafa's mother was forgotten, and Aimée became the Sultan's unquestioned favourite. Abdul Hamid was so excited that he ordered a huge tulip-festival, and for a centrepiece in the Seraglio grounds he commanded a kiosk to be made entirely of spun sugar, decorated with palms, the traditional emblem of fertility. Cages of nightingales hung from the trees or encircled the splashing fountains. Afterwards there were wrestling matches at the Hippodrome, which Aimée watched unseen from a latticed window. Five hundred sheep were ritually slaughtered and given to the poor.

There is little doubt that Aimée was deeply attached to the Sultan, who was a man cultivated enough to stop once and for all the wretched practice of immuring possible heirs in the Cage; he treated his nephew Selim, heir to the throne,* as a son, and allowed him complete liberty. Selim was about the same age as Aimée, and when Abdul Hamid died in 1789, and Selim III was proclaimed Sultan, he was already a passionate devotee of her French 'liberalism'. The widowed Aimée's influence was obvious in many ways, and nothing could shake their love for 'that great country'.

They must have been shaken when, within three months of Selim's accession, the Paris mob stormed the Bastille. It is possible that this event, coupled with the fear of a mutiny by the Janissaries, prompted Selim to form a 'New Army', a separate body of troops loyal to him alone and disciplined along French lines. The Janissaries murmured, but for the moment held back as French artillery officers trained the new army – young Napoleon volunteered but was turned down; as French naval officers reorganized the Turkish navy; as French engineers started the famous Top Hané cannon foundry; as French military manuals were translated for Turkish troops. Selim even sanctioned Turkey's first weekly newspaper *Le Moniteur de l'Orient*, with Aimée no doubt its most avid reader.

*

The relationship between Selim and Aimée provides a fascinating question, to which no historian has been able to find an answer. They had

* The eldest living male, not the eldest son, was always the heir.

known each other well since Aimée first entered the harem to become the sultana of an ageing husband who had allowed Selim every liberty, permitting him even to learn the precious art of French politics from Aimée (veiled and under the strictest supervision, no doubt). They were both in their twenties, physically attractive, and shared a love of literature. Selim was 'of a pallid delicacy . . . one of those sighing princes, whose vellum-toned features have a feminine cast'. Lamartine described him as 'a lonely, dreamy prince, sensitive and shy, with almond eyes, a long, serious face'. He spent hours listening as Aimée read to him. Aimée, a full-blooded Frenchwoman in the prime of life, was consigned to a life of chastity. Selim was totally uninterested in his harem, and died childless. It seems impossible that after Abdul Hamid's death they did not become lovers. And there was another curious fact. Why did the mother of Mustafa, the heir, virtually disappear from the scene during Selim's reign? Since Selim was the only man in the way of her son's accession, one would have expected her to have plotted against him; yet history tells only of Aimée's selfless influence. It is pleasing to hope that the innocent golden-haired French girl who became a slave was not only a loyal wife and a devoted mother, but (as some recompense for her misfortunes) was also the passionate mistress of a good-looking intellectual who adored her to the exclusion of every beautiful woman who could have been his at the snap of a finger.

*

And yet poor Selim did not have much luck in his reign. As the French stormed the Bastille, Catherine the Great of Russia was doing everything in her power to cause unrest in the Ottoman Empire, and in 1790 decided to attack Ismail, a vital fortress on the Danube forty miles from the Black Sea, and defended by a garrison of forty thousand men. Potemkin, the Russian Commander-in-Chief (and Catherine's lover), sent for General Suvarov and gave him a laconic order, 'You will capture Ismail, whatever the cost.'

Suvarov was a military genius of the first order, a brusque, tough soldier who shared all the hardships of his troops and who was idolized by them. His favourite maxim was 'Forward and strike!' He had little time for musketry. 'The ball is a fool,' he said, 'the bayonet a hero.' Six days after arriving outside Ismail, he ordered the attack – in his usual jocular manner.

'My brothers,' he cried, 'no quarter. Provisions are scarce.' The city was taken after a terrible slaughter. Thirty-four thousand Turks were killed in weather so bitterly cold that none could be buried. Holes were hacked through the Danube ice and it took six days to drag the corpses into the river. Suvarov, who could be as laconic as Potemkin, announced victory with the despatch, 'The Russian flag floats on the ramparts of Ismail.' And when the news reached St Petersburg it was left to the Empress Catherine to put Britain, which tried to mediate, in her place by telling the British Ambassador, with a sarcastic smile, 'I hope that those who wish to drive me out of St Petersburg will allow me to retire to Constantinople.'

Selim's empire was now in a decline which seemed impossible to check. But at least to Aimée and Selim there was always France to fall back on. Selim was among the first rulers in Europe to recognize the Republic. After some heart-searching, Selim made history by appointing the first Turkish ambassador to France in 1797, though Aimée had been horrified by the executions of Louis XVI and Marie Antoinette. But Napoleon was now married to Joséphine so the cousins could write to each other, and Napoleon welcomed the new ambassador warmly, though secretly, 'he had long had his eye on Constantinople as the greatest strategic prize Europe could offer'. Still, there seemed no reason why the firm friendship between the two countries should not continue for decades, particularly as it was backed not only by the presence in Turkey of French military experts, but by the influence of Napoleon's wife in France and his cousin-by-marriage in a Turkish harem.

Napoleon was also a near neighbour of Turkey since his invasion of Italy ended the long reign of the Republic of Venice and he annexed the Ionian Islands – 'more interesting to us than all Italy put together'. This, too, must have reassured Aimée and Selim, blissfully unaware that Napoleon had written to the Directory, 'It is of no use to us to try to maintain the Turkish Empire; we shall witness its fall in our time.'

The state of Selim's empire more than justified this view. The power of Constantinople – the central power – was virtually paralysed. The pashas of huge, distant provinces were independent rulers in all but name. Egypt was so much under the rule of the Mamelukes – as corrupt as the Turkish Janissaries – that Selim had no authority in Cairo.

In July 1798 the blow fell; Napoleon at the head of forty thousand men had landed in Egypt, a province of the Ottoman Empire. Selim had no option but to go to war against France.

The blow was not lessened when it became apparent that it was not aimed against Turkey, but at England. Napoleon's 'orders' (doubtless drawn up by himself) were 'to clear the English from all their Oriental possessions which he will be able to reach and notably destroy all their stations in the Red Sea'; while to his generals he boasted, 'I shall turn the British Empire upside down.' It was, in fact, not yet an empire, but a series of trading-posts and strongpoints, and Napoleon knew that an Egypt in French hands would deny Britain a valuable bulwark to defend India, as well as a trade route far speedier than the long haul round the Cape.

Everybody knows the story of Nelson's victory at the Nile, and how at a stroke Napoleon's army in Egypt was cut off from French soil; it also gave heart to Selim in Constantinople, who knew that France did not have the ships to send out a large-scale rescue-force. He entered into an alliance with Britain.

*

During these years Aimée's son Mahmud had been carefully and skilfully educated by his mother and the finest tutors from France. He was growing up into a handsome and talented young man, and though he was not the heir Aimée faced a constant problem in finding trustworthy guards to watch over the boy, for Mustafa's mother still regarded him as a danger to her son's accession, and on several occasions tried to have him poisoned. If Aimée had not had the foresight to install a professional toxicologist in the Seraglio, Mahmud would have died. And he nearly did die when the unresolved quarrel between Selim and the Janissaries broke into tragic and open revolt in the summer of 1807.

The main body of the Janissaries was with the army fighting on the Danube. Selim foolishly felt he was strong enough to increase his New Army by trying to draft some of the youngest and best Janissaries into it. The Janissaries still in the Constantinople garrison overturned their kettles, refused the Sultan's food, and finally sent a deputation to the Mufti, asking, 'What punishment is deserved by one who has established the new military force?' After a few days, in which the undercurrents of hate, plot and counterplot seethed, the Mufti gave his reply, 'Death, and that according to the Koran, since the Divan has introduced among Moslems the manners of infidelity, and manifested an intention to suppress the Janissaries, who are the true defenders of the law and the prophets.'

The Janissaries now passed a resolution that Selim must be deposed, but Selim had been forewarned. He made for the safety of the Cage, found his half-brother Mustafa, the heir, announced his abdication and made obeisance to him as Sultan Mustafa IV. As the astonished Mustafa listened, Selim attempted to commit suicide by taking poison. Just in time Mustafa smashed the cup; and when the Janissaries reached the Grand Seraglio Mustafa was already on the throne, and Selim had 'retired with dignity to the Cage'.

That might have been a comparatively happy ending to the reign of Selim, had he not had friends who tried to restore him to power. They were led by the Pasha of the province of Rustchuk, called Bairactar, who owed his position to Selim, but was away fighting when the Sultan abdicated. Bairactar immediately marched back to Constantinople with forty thousand troops and by dawn on 28 July 1808 was camped on the plain within a mile or two of the capital.

With a small band of trusted followers Bairactar secretly entered the city, made for the main gate of the Seraglio and demanded entrance to see Selim. He was refused. Bairactar and his men tried to batter down the door, but the noise warned the newly appointed Sultan Mustafa and he realized immediately that the only way to safeguard his life was to murder both Selim and Aimée's son, Mahmud, leaving him the last of the Othman race. As Bairactar tried to force open the main gate Mustafa gave orders for them both to be strangled, and went to the Cage to witness Selim's murder.

As the deaf mutes reached Selim with the bowstring, he managed to send a warning to Aimée and then fought a delaying action. Drawing his dagger, he rushed on the deaf mutes, stabbing two to death before one managed to place the bowstring round his neck. His action saved Mahmud. Aimée grabbed him and together they escaped, but only by seconds. As the murderers raced down the Golden Road, one of Aimée's slaves, a formidable Georgian woman known in the harem as 'The Strong' blocked their way. She alone could do nothing, but she waited until the last moment before hurling a brazier of red-hot coals in the assailants' faces. It gave Mahmud a few precious extra seconds. He crept through a chimney and into a disused bathroom furnace, and there lay hidden under a pile of old clothes while the murderers searched the next room.

Bairactar by now had hammered down the Gate of Felicity. The grounds, the kiosks, the courtyards, were deserted. Everyone from ministers to cooks seemed to have fled as Bairactar called for Selim. Finally, as he approached a heavily curtained door, Mustafa's voice was heard from behind crying, 'Hand over Sultan Selim to the Pasha of Rustchuk if he wants the swine's carcase!' Then he kicked Selim's body out of the room into the bright sunlight of the courtyard.

Bairactar threw himself on the corpse, weeping bitterly, until Ramis Pasha, one of his captains, cried, 'Is it for the Pasha of Rustchuk to weep like a woman? Let us avenge Sultan Selim.' Bursting open the traditional heavy leather curtain that shrouded the door, Bairactar found Mustafa seated on a throne. Without a moment's hesitation he dragged him on to the floor.

But as Bairactar and his men prepared to kill Mustafa, there was a dramatic interruption. Mahmud appeared, his clothes in tatters, his face blackened with soot; but in this, almost the first moment of his thirty-one-year reign, Aimée's son displayed all the dignity that was to earn him the title of 'The Reformer'. His first order on his accession was to consign Mustafa to the Cage.

As Bairactar knelt and kissed the hem of the new Sultan's filthy robe, Mahmud lifted him and told him not to press for revenge. He would, he promised, avenge himself at the right time not only on Mustafa, but on the Janissaries who were the root cause of all that had happened.

Before dusk that night the cannon of the Grand Seraglio boomed out the news to the people of Constantinople that Mahmud II was Sultan of the Ottoman Empire.

*

It was years before Mahmud could subdue the Janissaries, for soon after he became Sultan part of Constantinople was burned to the ground during several days of civil war when the Janissaries mutinied again. Mahmud

had appointed Bairactar Grand Vizier; unfortunately, he had celebrated
his appointment with a fatal error, allowing all but four thousand of his
troops to return to their homes, and those who remained were insufficient
to contain the Janissaries.

Bairactar liked good living; he ate and drank well, he appreciated the
fruits of office, including a harem, and he was fast asleep with an odalisque
after a splendid banquet when the Janissaries struck. Forming a cordon
round the Grand Vizier's palace, they set fire to all the adjacent houses
and waited until the flames reached the Grand Vizier's opulent home. It
was not until the walls were crashing about him that his concubine awoke
Bairactar.

Instead of cutting his way through the Janissaries, the Grand Vizier
preferred to retreat to a strong square tower at the rear of his palace which
he used as a store-room for arms and ammunition, hoping that its stone
walls would withstand the fire until help arrived. And help was coming –
in the form of Ramis Pasha, who had so recently told his master not to
weep at the death of Selim. Ramis's troops raced to the rescue as the
flames smothered the entire area from the Seraglio to the Grand Vizier's
palace. They almost arrived in time, for the strong old tower was still
standing – until a stray spark or bullet hit its powder magazine with a
roar, and the whole mass of masonry exploded. Bairactar's burned body
was found in the smoking ruins by the delighted Janissaries.

As the civil war raged for several days it was clear to Mahmud that his
life was in danger and there was only one course open to him: he ordered
the strangulation of Mustafa in the Cage, knowing that by making himself
the last surviving male of the Othman race he was secured from intrigues
against his life.

Mahmud now faced his most humiliating moment. He was forced to
yield to every demand of the Janissaries. He was compelled to put his
name to an edict repealing Selim's reforms. All the old abuses crept back.
For the next three or four years the Janissaries virtually ruled the Empire,
appointing and dismissing grand viziers as they pleased. All that the
'Reformer' could do was to wait for the right moment to crush these
enemies of his dynasty.

*

Mahmud was a fine-looking man. Charles MacFarlane, an Englishman who saw him several times, remembered 'his robust, vigorous frame, his magnificent breadth of chest, his most striking countenance, proud, haughty and handsome, and his large jet-black, peculiar eyes which looked you through and through and which were never quiet'. Aided no doubt by Aimée, he was a liberal and, like Selim, a passionate lover of France. He preferred chairs to cushions, used a gold knife and fork instead of his fingers. He also learned to drink too much, insisting on champagne with every meal; any after-effects were mitigated by pills of opium covered with several coats of gilt which dissolved at different times. Almost as soon as he mounted the throne he reduced the number of odalisques, for he had fallen in love with a buxom bath-house attendant called Besma, who bore him six children. He was, of course, influenced by Aimée, by now the Queen Mother, who loved luxury and display. She had her own mirrored carriage, the exterior a bewildering mixture of diamond-shaped pieces of glass and mother of pearl. Aimée revelled in precious stones, but often added a bizarre refinement: instead of wearing her jewellery she would appear plainly adorned, but followed by a slave carrying her gems on a tray. Even when she crossed the Bosporus in her painted caïque rowed by twelve slaves, it was followed by a shoal of jewelled fish attached by chains so that they seemed to be escorting her.

Mahmud, inspired by Aimée to westernize his country, soon instituted startling reforms. He was the first Ottoman sultan to found a medical school (with French doctors, of course). He sent groups of students to study in Paris, London, Vienna. He created a quarantine system to combat the annual outbreaks of plague, which killed 150,000 people in 1812, and which had decimated the population of Constantinople for centuries. When a visitor from London mentioned casually that Britain had taken a census (which in 1802 showed the population of London to be 864,000), he too had a census taken, which gave the population of Constantinople as 630,000; he founded a newspaper and an Official Gazette on the lines of the French *Journal Officiel*. He minted coins, and built the first bridge across the Golden Horn. To the dismay of the many old-fashioned Turks, he even reformed the national dress. Overnight the romantic ballooning pantaloons, the sable-trimmed caftans, the two-foot-high turbans vanished, to be replaced, for all officials, by tight black trousers, the 'Stambouline' – a dreary black frock coat – and the fez, the red headdress that originated in Morocco.*

Even Stratford Canning at the British Embassy, later to become Britain's greatest ambassador to Turkey, was staggered. 'Every person who has been absent,' he wrote, 'and has now returned, notices the change, which has been most extraordinary. Very few years more, and not a turban will exist . . . employees of every description now wear the red cap, Cossack trousers, black boots, and a plain red or blue cloak buttoned under the chin. No gold embroidery, no jewels, no pelisses.'

The reforms in dress outraged the diehards, in much the same way as the Russians felt the innovations of Peter the Great had 'cleft the soul of Muscovy'. A dervish grabbed the reins of Mahmud's horse and shrieked, 'Infidel Sultan, God will demand an accounting for your blasphemy. You are destroying Islam.' Yet Mahmud persevered. He fought for the doctrine of Ottoman equality, saying, 'I distinguish among my subjects Moslems in the mosque, Christians in the church, Jews in the synagogue, but there is no difference among them in any other way.'

*

Despite Mahmud's liberal attitudes, the Empire suffered drastic shrinkage during his reign. The Russians gained complete control of several provinces, together with large stretches of the right bank of the Danube, and they might have advanced much deeper into Ottoman territory had not Napoleon invaded Russia in 1812, forcing the Czar Alexander to withdraw his armies from the Danube. At least Mahmud was lucky in that no great power could afford to allow Constantinople to fall into the hands of a rival, for they all felt as the German General von Moltke (who had helped Selim to organize the New Army) when he said, 'The partition of Turkey is a problem like the division of a diamond ring. Who is to obtain Constantinople, the single costly stone?' England was terrified that a Russian victory over Turkey would endanger her lifeline to India; Austria was fearful that if Russia became stronger she would overwhelm her; so deep were the fears and suspicions that the Congress of Vienna in 1815 expressly made it clear that Turkey must never pass into the hands of one power.

So, for the time being – and with Napoleon soon out of harm's way on

* Some of Mahmud's reforms bordered on the absurd, such as a decree regulating the length of moustaches.

St Helena – Mahmud confronted no problems from the West. But within his own borders he faced humiliation in two provinces, Greece and Egypt. The Greeks, more than any other subject race, had cause for revolt. This hatred of the Ottoman burst into the open in 1821. 'Nowhere throughout the Ottoman Empire were the results of its rule more degrading and intolerable than in Greece. Life, property and honour were without security.' This did not apply to Greeks in Constantinople, who enjoyed wealth and privilege, and whose religion had been protected since the days of Mahomet the Conqueror, but in Greece itself it was very different. Here the oppressed peasants outnumbered the twenty thousand or so Moslems spread thinly over a large area, and as the uprising spread like wildfire from the Morea, where it started, the Greeks murdered almost every Moslem – men, women, children. Soon major towns like Navarino and Tripolitza were in Greek hands. As each fortress fell, the Greeks guaranteed the lives of the Moslems but rarely honoured the pledges. At Tripolitza the Greeks murdered eight thousand people, including women and children, and as Finlay wryly remarks in his *History of Greece*, 'Greek historians have recoiled from telling of these barbarities, while they have been loud in denouncing those of the Turks.'

The reaction in Constantinople to these massacres was a demand for instant revenge. Massacre might have been an accepted weapon in Turkish military strategy, but when a subject race indulged in such a luxury it became barbarous. The leading Greeks in Constantinople were executed, including the Greek Patriarch, Gregorios, who was hanged (on Easter Day) at the gate of the episcopal residence, though he could not possibly have been involved in the rebellion. Four other bishops were also hanged, while thousands of ordinary Greeks were murdered. The Sultan made no move to stop the excesses, which lasted on both sides for nearly four years, with the Turks usually getting the worst of it as the Greeks formed a fleet, set up a provisional government and thrust further north to the Gulf of Corinth, Thessaly, and even liberated the then squalid, third-rate town of Athens.

At first European statesmen tended to take little notice of the Greek battle for independence, feeling much as Metternich did when writing in 1821, 'It matters not much if over there beyond our frontiers three or four hundred thousand people get hung, strangled or impaled.' But slowly the attitude began to change. To thousands of students and thinking men, the glories of ancient Greece invested the modern Greek fight for freedom with far greater lustre than that of the struggle for emancipation in other countries which they could hardly find on a map.

It was this more than anything else that finally awoke Europe to the 'tragic case of Greece', and sent men like Byron charging into the fray.

After four years, Mahmud realized he could never subdue Greece without help, so he called on the great vassal state of Egypt, one of the Empire's most thriving provinces, ruled by a remarkable man who had been thrown up into power in the débâcle following the battle of the Nile, Mehemet Ali. The son of an Albanian Moslem fisherman, he had been saved from drowning during the battle when he was picked up by Nelson's barge. He was a military genius who could not read or write, and boasted that the only books he read were men's faces.

After the rout of Napoleon's army, Mehemet Ali found himself fighting against British forces, and celebrated one victory by marching into Cairo through an avenue of British heads stuck on pikes. He had eliminated the Mamelukes by inviting five hundred of their leaders to a sumptuous meal in the Citadel of Cairo, and as the last guest wiped the last crumb from his lips Mehemet Ali ordered the door to be locked. All but one, who managed to escape, were coldly murdered.

From that moment Mehemet Ali was undisputed master of Egypt. Mahmud called for his help. Mehemet agreed, but was powerful enough to demand conditions: he had already become Pasha of Egypt. He would fight for the Sultan, in theory his master, if Mahmud extended his Pashalic to include Syria, Damascus and Crete. Mahmud had no choice but to agree, and Mehemet sent his troops into the attack. The Greeks, who had long since become accustomed to dealing with the unruly, undisciplined Turks, were powerless against the European-trained troops of Egypt. City after city liberated from the Turks fell to the Egyptians, and eventually much of Greece was restored to the Empire. At this moment Britain stepped in. Public opinion was outraged at the Turkish barbarities, while George Canning, then Foreign Secretary, felt that the continued fighting might encourage Russia to attack a weakened Turkey. And that was the last thing Britain wanted to see. In 1826 Canning sent the Duke of Wellington to St Petersburg to discuss the matter with the Czar, and by July of the following year Britain, Russia and France agreed to make a formal offer to Turkey to mediate in the war. They also signed an additional secret clause agreeing that, if the Sultan did not agree, the European powers might find it necessary to intervene with force.

The Sultan refused point-blank to permit foreign nations to interfere in what he regarded as a domestic problem. The Greeks, said Mahmud, had no causes for complaint and, indeed, he added, 'They have been loaded with benefits by the present Sultan.'

At this a three-power naval fleet, under the British Admiral Sir Edward Codrington took up war stations outside the Bay of Navarino to prevent any Turkish or Egyptian vessel using the port.

Codrington was ordered not to fire the first shot, but once the Turks had opened fire a naval battle was inevitable, and the Turco-Egyptian fleet was virtually destroyed. Of their 82 vessels only 29 remained afloat. The enemy lost 6,000 men, compared with allied losses of 172. It was the biggest Turkish disaster since Lepanto and all communication between Mehemet Ali's troops and Egypt was cut. Greece held command of the sea in the archipelago, and Greek independence was assured.

*

Despite the unending struggles that faced Mahmud, whose only ambition was to be left in peace to reform his country, he did finally erase forever the Janissaries, the men whom Stratford Canning felt 'had become the masters of the government, the butchers of their sovereigns and a source of terror to all but the enemies of their country'.

Mahmud had had to wait eighteen years for the day which has gone down in Turkish history as 'The Auspicious Event'. In June 1826 he called a meeting of the Divan, for he was determined that any action he took would be within the bounds of law. The ideal solution would be to provoke the Janissaries into revolt, and this is what he set out to do.

To the assembled political and religious leaders, Mahmud explained that while the Janissaries had been beaten time after time by the Greek insurgents the Egyptians fighting for Turkey had proved that troops trained on the European model were superior to any in the Empire. Carefully avoiding any suggestion of abolishing the Janissaries, Mahmud merely proposed that their fighting qualities would be improved by incorporating into them a quarter of the New Army which had been formed by Selim. The Divan agreed and gave him formal powers to act. Mahmud reassured those who feared a revolt, though he did not feel it necessary to announce that he had built up a personal army of fourteen thousand artillerymen, drilled, trained and led by an officer of unscrupulous devotion, who was soon to earn the nickname Kara Djehennem, or 'Black Hell'.

Mahmud now issued the edict. The Janissaries growled and upset their kettles, which suited the Sultan perfectly; on 14 June they assembled in the Hippodrome to cries of 'Death to the Giaour [Christian] Sultan'. Determined to behave correctly the Sultan sent four officers under a flag of truce to offer pardon if the Janissaries would immediately disperse. Not only was the offer spurned, as he expected, but the four officers were put to death before the Janissaries marched in a body to the First Court of the Grand Seraglio, doubtless expecting to overawe the Sultan.

The leaders gathered, as they always had done, at one point associated with sedition, a plane tree so huge that eight men with outstretched arms could not gird it.

Then Mahmud appeared in front of them on a white horse caparisoned in cloth-of-gold and with gold harness, though the ruler wore a plain uniform, his only concession to tradition being a diamond aigrette in his fez. In person he unfurled the green standard of the Prophet and called on all true believers to rally round their Sultan. The Janissaries pressed forward.

Now 'Black Hell's moment had come. As Mahmud watched, his troops opened fire. Grapeshot cut lanes of dying men in the struggling columns of Janissaries as they fled back to the Hippodrome. But 'Black Hell' had troops covering the Hippodrome too. Hundreds were shot down as the survivors stumbled in panic to the safety of their barracks, bolted the doors, and prepared for the expected attack.

But the assault by troops, the classic next step in Turkish siege warfare, never materialized. Instead 'Black Hell' brought up his cannon before the barracks. 'Orders were given to set fire to the edifices and consume them, together with all their unhappy inmates; and the dreadful command was faithfully performed.' For several hours the barracks were remorselessly pummelled by shellfire while Mahmud waited in a small square room over the main gate of the Seraglio for news. When the buildings started to blaze,

the Janissaries who tried to escape death by burning were shot or cut down.
There was one last macabre battle – against those who managed to flee to
the great Cistern of the Thousand and One Columns,* near St Sophia, a
vast underground 'lake' more than three hundred feet long, which since
the age of Byzantium had held enough water to supply the entire population of Constantinople through a two-week drought. Splashing in the
murky water, lit only by beams filtering through from holes in the roof, a
hundred or so die-hard Janissaries fought to the last man. In a ferocious
hand-to-hand fight both sides plunged through water up to their shoulders,
slipped, drowned, for most of the time hardly able to distinguish friend
from foe.

In all, at least ten thousand men were killed that day – some historians
put the figure as high as twenty thousand – and those corpses not burned
in the fires or drowned in the Cistern were tossed into the Bosporus, where
for many months the corpses floated and 'fish in Constantinople was
uneatable'.

*

By the time Mahmud died in 1839, the Empire had lost Greece, Egypt (in
all but name), and was involved in wars with France, England and Russia.
Yet he left the Empire stronger than he found it, for despite the overwhelming difficulties he faced, he at least made himself master in his own
house. True, it was a smaller house but, in a way, that was an advantage
for he was able to control it more easily.

And there was one thing more. Whatever his faults, it was the son of
Aimée who had taken the Ottoman Empire by the scruff of its neck and
forcibly tugged it from the enervating grip of the medieval age.

Long before this, the French mother who had so inspired him died in
the harem where she lived for thirty-three years, and as Aimée's life slipped
away the grief-stricken Mahmud made what was, for a devout Moslem
ruler of a Moslem empire, a decision of courage and love.

A storm was tearing at the creaking wooden houses of the city, but two
guards managed to cross the Golden Horn to Pera and made their way to
the convent of St Antoine. The Convent Superior, Father Chrysostom,
was in his cell when a violent knocking disturbed his prayers. The guards

* In fact, the roof was supported by 336 exquisite marble columns in twelve
rows of twenty-eight columns each. It is still in excellent repair.

presented him with a message bearing the imperial cypher, and Father Chrysostom walked down the steep hill to Galata and boarded a royal caïque with twelve oars. At the other side of the Golden Horn he was led through deserted gardens into a richly furnished room with silken hangings and splendid carpets. In the middle, on a bed, lay a dying woman. A Greek doctor was by her side. Two black slaves made statues by the door. And there was Mahmud, overwhelmed with grief. The good Father noted that he 'appeared to be about forty years of age; his height was above the ordinary; his brow high and noble; his expression commanding. His beard was black, and gave his face an impressive, grave beauty.'

All this the Father took in almost at a glance as Mahmud signalled to the Greek doctor and the slaves to withdraw; then Mahmud approached the bed and, kneeling, said to his mother, 'You wished to die in the religion of your fathers; let your wish be fulfilled.'

Father Chrysostom listened to Aimée's confession, prayed with her for an hour and gave her Absolution, while in a corner of the room the 'Christian Sultan', as he was nicknamed by those opposing his reforms, called on Allah to help him bear his loss. So Aimée died in the faith to which she had been born. Father Chrysostom was escorted back to the convent by the same guards but he waved aside the questions of the Brothers intrigued by his midnight excursion in a storm, and spent the night in prayer for the soul of Aimée Dubucq de Rivery, of Martinique, the Queen Mother of the Ottoman Empire.

Chapter seven
The road to the Crimea

Abdul Mejid was sixteen when his father Mahmud the Reformer died in 1839, two years after Victoria ascended the British throne. His mother Besma, the one-time bath attendant, had always been convinced that too much drink had hastened her husband's death. Consequently, in the spirit of a reproving, teetotal Victorian mother, she warned her son against the evils of drink (in vain, alas) and sought to protect him by destroying the remaining stocks of Mahmud's champagne, brandy and wine. At least fifty thousand bottles were smashed against the city walls and flowed into the Bosporus, together with all the decanters and glasses collected by Aimée.

Unfortunately Besma, a simple country girl, did not realize that sexual excesses were just as dangerous as over-indulgence in alcohol, and she cheerfully encouraged her son to pleasure the ladies of the harem as often as he liked – or could; for Abdul Mejid was 'frail, narrow-chested, dull-eyed, sickly-looking, mild and gentle'; even so, any boy in his teens would have been hard put not to try to gratify the bevy of beautiful girls proudly produced by an adoring mother. Inevitably Mejid 'was enfeebled early in his reign by excessive indulgence in the harem' and – equally inevitably – when he became impotent at an early age he took to the bottle.

Abdul Mejid was not a vicious or dissolute man, he had none of the earlier traces of hereditary insanity; but the chores of government were not for him. He was determined to enjoy his good fortune. He did not, however, appreciate the surroundings of the Grand Seraglio. As he grew up he found the warren of passages, courtyards and kiosks that had grown haphazardly over the centuries gloomy; and no doubt the presence of so many earnest officials going about their business irritated a man to whom the daily grind of office work was anathema. So he decided to separate – by the width of the Golden Horn – his private life from the centre of government, and started to build himself a family home on the shores of the Bosporus.

This was the Palace of Dolmabache, 'The Filled-up Garden', sited on land reclaimed from a bay by sixteen thousand Christian slaves in the time of Suleiman, and which Barbarossa, his admiral, used to say produced the finest cabbages in the Ottoman Empire. Abdul Mejid employed an Armenian architect called Balian, giving him a free hand and unlimited money, making only one stipulation: 'It must surpass any other palace of any potentate anywhere in the world.' In size, if not in taste, it certainly did. Its marble terrace stretched half a mile along the edge of the Bosporus; the palace itself was rococo gone mad. More than fourteen tons of gold leaf were used in the decoration. The throne-room was 150 feet long, the roof supported by gilded Corinthian columns in groups of four, reflecting the world's largest mirrors, while the ballroom, the largest in the world, had a central chandelier weighing more than four tons. Musicians played from four galleries near the high ceiling – where there were also fan-shaped latticed windows for the harem to watch the festivities below. The main staircase, which curved like two snakes, had banisters supported by hundreds of crystal balustrades. Mejid's bed was of solid silver; his marble-floored bathroom had bath and basins in transparent alabaster, sculptured with flowers and stalactites, and with silver taps in the shape of swans. Nor did he forget Besma, who on becoming Queen Mother changed her name to Pertevalé, and who had a bedroom in which gold leaf was even used on her bow-fronted wardrobe and on her chairs. The three hundred rooms included twenty-five ornate salons – and, tucked away, comfortably out of sight, a series of monastic cells where the concubines slept three to a room on mats until their services were required.

The great height of the central portion provided problems for the masons, but instead of using ladders they constructed inclined planes from the ground to platforms on the scaffolding large enough for a mule to ascend.

News of the great project soon reached Europe, whose rulers each tried to outdo their rivals with house-warming gifts, so that much of the furniture consisted of a bewildering assortment of styles – grandfather clocks from Victoria, Bohemian glass from Francis Joseph, Buhl tables (with his picture on the top) from Napoleon, white bear-skin rugs from the Czar.

By the time it was finished Abdul Mejid had spent a fortune, and now the Grand Seraglio, the scene of so many dramas, became government offices and its harem still another refuge for out-of-work odalisques whose sultan had died.

After the serious approach to life of the Reformer, Abdul Mejid's ostentation and sheer delight in spending money caused relief in Constantinople, particularly among those lucky enough to be invited to his receptions, for which he imported European actors, ballet dancers, conjurors who had already become famous in the West. He built a beautiful theatre in which – like a pantomime in reverse – the leading lady would be a pretty page who would fall in love with an equally handsome boy. No women were allowed to act, for modesty was so strict that some country women still carried it 'to such an extreme of delicacy that, when they feed their poultry, if there be cocks among them, they will not appear without veils'.

The extravagant court life was soon echoed in Constantinople itself, particularly when Abdul Mejid started permitting the favoured members of his harem to go into shops and choose, instead of waiting in their carriages for the goods to be brought out. No sultana could resist spending with this added inducement, particularly when the Sultan ordered them, 'as a sign of progress', to refurbish their wardrobes. The covered market in Constantinople was now 'filled to supply the wants of the glittering personages who figure in the Arabian Nights Entertainments'. Those buying small items were presented with embroidered handkerchiefs in which to carry them (baskets being considered vulgar). An English visitor, Mr Tugay, found that, 'No spot in the world – neither the Parisian Boulevards, nor our own Regent Street – can boast of such an accumulation of valuable wares from afar as the Great Bazaar of Constantinople.' They included one new item: bottles of hair bleach, very much in demand by the ladies, for Abdul Mejid had a passion for 'blue-eyed, delicate beauties with golden hair'.

Europeans in Istanbul had what was in effect their own shop in Pera – Stampa, where you could buy all the items nostalgic of England and home; everything from a bottle of Tennant's pale ale or Harvey's sauce to a Stilton cheese or Windsor soap. Stampa was not British, but he spoke good English and his son had been educated in London, so that Stampa was more than a place to buy something. It was a meeting-place, and if you wanted the name of a merchant or the departure time of a steamer Stampa would have the information at his fingertips, or if by chance he did not, 'His clever son is a walking Bradshaw.'

*

Far north of the marble magnificence of Dolmabache stood a palace as large, as opulent as the home of Abdul Mejid, and in it ruled a despot as all-powerful as the Sultan. The place was the Winter Palace stretching along the Neva at St Petersburg. The man was the Czar Nicholas I.

Russia and Turkey had much in common in 1853. The splendid fêtes and balls at the Royal Court at St Petersburg were so magnificent that the French artist Horace Vernet felt 'one could literally trample on diamonds'. Yet the veneer of court life masked – as it did in Constantinople – the most wretched poverty among Russia's fifty million people, who were treated as badly as the peasants in Turkey, despite the fact that leading Russians were more sophisticated than the Turks. One English traveller watched aghast as his cosmopolitan host knocked a servant to the floor during dinner for passing the wrong dish. The country was as backward as Turkey, and if the Turks believed that the Sultan was God's Vice-Regent, many Russian peasants were firmly convinced that the Czar went to heaven once a week to hold a conference with God.

Every hotel in St Petersburg was alive with vermin – even the Winter Palace, possibly because cows providing milk for the Czar's family were kept on the top floor of the palace, near the Maids of Honour.

Nicholas was no sybarite like Abdul Mejid, but regarded himself as a soldier; he startled Queen Victoria when staying with her by sending for straw from the stables for his portable canvas mattress. Victoria called him the 'Mighty Potentate', and his autocratic, almost insolent look of disdain was aggravated by a slight defect in one eye giving him a stare so terrifying that Victoria found, 'The expression of the *eyes* is formidable and unlike anything I ever saw before.'

The Czar had decided that it was time to add lustre to his crown by conquest, and the obvious area for attack was the Ottoman Empire. It was easy to pick a quarrel with Constantinople by re-enforcing Russia's rights to guard the Holy Sepulchre in Jerusalem – a right by treaty for eighty years, but rarely enforced.

Yet Nicholas had to tread warily; he needed the support of England, the only other stable throne in Europe after the 'revolution of contempt' in which Louis Philippe had lost the throne of France and the Emperor of Austria had fled for his life.

In an extraordinary, and foolish, series of conversations with Sir Hamilton Seymour, the British Ambassador to St Petersburg, Nicholas tried to sound out British opinion and to disarm any English opposition. Summoning Seymour to the Palace for a private conversation, Nicholas blandly told him that the Ottoman Empire was in such a poor way that it might not be a bad idea for Britain and Russia to carve up its European possessions and share them out. 'The affairs of Turkey are in a very disorganized condition . . .' said the Czar. 'We have on our hands a sick man – a very sick man. It will, I tell you frankly, be a great misfortune if one of these days he should slip away from us before all necessary arrangements were made.'

The British Ambassador might well have thought this the end of the matter, but a few days later, at a private dinner, the Czar buttonholed him and this time outlined his views at great length, carefully attempting to give the impression that he had no territorial ambitions. He ended his peroration:

Now, I desire to speak to you as a friend, and as a gentleman. If England and I arrive at an understanding in this matter, as regards the rest it little matters to me. It is indifferent to me what others do or think. Frankly, then, I tell you plainly that, if England thinks of establishing herself one of these days at Constantinople, I will not allow it. For my part, I am equally disposed to take the engagement not to establish myself there – as proprietor, that is to say.

Within a few days the Emperor was repeating to Seymour that, 'The sick man is dying, and we can never allow such an event to take us by surprise. We must come to some understanding.' On the very next day, no doubt as an encouragement to Britain, he added that if the Ottoman Empire *did* fall, and Britain took Egypt, 'I shall have no objection to offer. I could say the same thing of Candia [Crete]. That island might suit you, and I do not see why it should not become an English possession.'

To this astonishing offer of the Czar's, Seymour replied that he did not think the possession of Egypt interested Britain, since all that his country wanted was a safe route to India. Seymour's astonishment can hardly have diminished when the Emperor replied,

Well, induce your Government to write again upon this subject – to write more fully and do so without hesitation. I have confidence in the British Government. It is not an engagement or convention which I ask of them; it is a free inter-change of ideas in case of need – the word of a gentleman–that is enough between us.

What was the Czar doing? What was he thinking of? Did he really imagine the British could be taken in by such guileless nonsense, by such patent fibs? Seymour immediately rumbled the 'gentlemanly' suggestions and gave his own views bluntly to Lord John Russell, then Foreign Minister:

The Sovereign who insists with such pertinacity upon the impending fall of a neighbouring State must have settled in his own mind that the hour, if not *of* the dissolution, at all events *for* the dissolution, must be at hand.

No doubt Seymour's attitude encouraged the British Government to decline – courteously but extremely firmly – to enter into any secret agreement with the Czar on the 'Eastern Question'.*

Nicholas was furious. He had been quite confident of reaching an agreement with the English, and soon he was talking of 'that cad Palmer-ston' and 'those Turkish dogs', and insisting on Russia's right to guardian-ship of the Holy Places, together with a further and more provoking demand: 'A Russian protectorate in matters of religion over members of the Greek Church throughout the Ottoman Empire.'

It was now that Stratford Canning, the life-long friend of Turkey, returned to the scene. After being ambassador to Constantinople, Canning had retired to England only a year previously, where he had been rewarded with a peerage. Now Britain sent him back – as Lord Stratford de Redcliffe – and as the threat of war loomed he was told to use Britain's influence to neutralize the alarming position that was developing; for the danger was that Nicholas had now gone too far to withdraw – if he wanted to withdraw.

Stratford was a curious man. An old Etonian, he had spent most of his

* Though Britain disclaimed any wish to acquire Ottoman territory, it was not long before she would acquire Egypt, the Sudan and Cyprus.

working life in Turkey and he had exercised enormous influence over Abdul Mejid. Eversley, who regarded him as the most distinguished diplomat ever employed by the British Government, also felt that he was one of those men who 'took much responsibility upon themselves, and dictated rather than followed the policy of their Governments'. He was tall, dignified and impeccably honest. The Turks trusted him implicitly, and they were highly impressed with his steadfast refusal to deal with any Turkish statesman 'whose hands were known to be stained with blood'. He loved Turkey; and he loved England. His two missions in life were simple: to compel Turkey to reform, and to serve his country. Tragically, in both of these he failed; perhaps because of a third obsession: that he felt it his duty, as Eversley put it, 'to oppose the schemes of Russia at every turn'. It was a bigoted hatred, stemming from a snub when the Czar Nicholas refused in 1833 to receive him as ambassador to his court. His bigotry had not much mattered in the past, though it had embarrassed his government more than once, but at least Stratford had given Britain a powerful voice in the Turkish court. The Turks worshipped him, christening him 'The Great Elchis', the Great Ambassador.

As the threat of war grew nearer, it became clear that the sanctimonious Russian excuses of 'saving the Christians' masked the Czar's main reason for going to war. This might be a 'Holy War' in the censored Russian newspapers but it was, in fact, a war for Constantinople, and Britain could not afford to let the Ottoman capital fall into Russian hands, since this would cut her life-line to India. The political reasons in England were disguised, too. A generation had passed since the Napoleonic wars, and a war spirit was aroused in which the hatred of the French had been replaced – in the minds of the adventurous who knew nothing of war – by a fear of the Russian Czar.

Austria and France were equally afraid of Russia. France saw a danger of her superiority in the Mediterranean vanishing if the Russians took Constantinople. Austria feared a land attack if the Russians became all-powerful. Therefore, Europe made one last desperate bid for peace. All the European powers except Russia met in Vienna and produced a formula for settling the religious differences between Russia and Turkey. It was reasonable, and gave Nicholas a chance to back down without losing face. Delightedly, he agreed to the terms. The European powers commended the agreement to the Turks, and Britain instructed its ambassador 'to use all his efforts to obtain its consent'. Stratford's influence over the Sultan was so powerful that Britain knew he could persuade Abdul Mejid to agree. But could Stratford be trusted? Lord Aberdeen, the British Prime Minister, had such doubts that he sent a note to the Foreign Ministry warning that, 'I have prepared the Queen for the possibility of Stratford's resignation.' Lord Clarendon, by then Foreign Minister, complained bluntly that, 'It is a misfortune that the government cannot feel sure of Stratford acting with us for a peaceful solution.' But there was an insuperable problem to recalling him. 'We have no one fit to take his place.'

Their worst fears were soon confirmed. Stratford, with his almost paranoiac hatred of Russia and his belief that the Turks were being humiliated, was unable to face up to his duty. Officially, he performed his task of asking the Turks to agree; but the Turks knew their man, and the very manner in which he spoke the words left no doubt in their minds that he disagreed with his government. Flatly the Turks rejected the Vienna proposals, and so, as Eversley summed up, 'He was undoubtedly the main cause of the war which soon ensued between Great Britain and Russia.'

To the rapturous Turks, Stratford was still the Great Elchis, for though he was largely responsible for the deaths of thousands of his fellow country-men he pushed the Turks into a war in which they played only a minor role but which, thanks to Britain and France, gave the tottering Empire a respite of twenty years.

Chapter eight

The madman of Dolmabache

The three-year Crimean War hardly touched the life of the Turks. The battles that have gone into history – Balaclava, Inkerman, Sevastopol – were virtually unknown to most of them. When the princes of the royal harem visited the mosques on feast days, anything that might remind them of war was hastily removed from the routes along which their carriages would rattle.

Many Turks did fight, and many died, half-starved, their pay months in arrears, but they almost preferred the fighting and misery to the horrifying spectacle of unveiled women like Florence Nightingale nursing wounded soldiers in Scutari. 'It aroused a bitter resentment'; and when Abdul Mejid made a dutiful tour of the battlefields the Turkish troops were profoundly shocked to see their Sultan riding with foreign generals, saluting red-faced infidel troops whose bare and hairy knees showed beneath their kilts.

Hostilities ended in 1856 with the Treaty of Paris by which Turkish territory was left virtually untouched. Russia abandoned her 'religious' claims; the Black Sea was opened to merchant vessels, but forbidden to warships. The most significant clauses, however, were those in which Europe in effect promised not to meddle in the internal affairs of Turkey. To Stratford, who believed that the rights of Christians in Turkey would only be guaranteed by reforms imposed by outsiders, it was the bitterest blow of his life. 'I would rather have cut off my right hand than have signed that treaty,' he said.

*

The Crimean War may have stopped the Russians from invading Constantinople, but the doors of the capital were now wide open to an even more unscrupulous invader of a totally different sort: the European moneylender. In the last five years before he died, Abdul Mejid became the first sultan of the Ottoman Empire to fall into the clutches of the financiers of Western Europe. Using the war with Russia as a pretext, he borrowed vast sums, ostensibly to modernize his armies. But the Dolmabache ran up a fair-sized housekeeping bill and a large slice of the money went into one of Abdul Mejid's pockets and out of the other as he indulged in wild spending sprees, building new annexes, commanding the ladies of the harem to order new modern dresses. When one of his daughters was married he spent forty million francs on her trousseau and the wedding breakfast (which lasted a week). By the time Abdul Mejid died and was succeeded by his brother Abdul Aziz in 1861, the Ottoman Empire had managed to achieve the double distinction of being not only morally bankrupt but almost financially bankrupt as well. The downward course was enthusiastically pursued by the newcomer to the throne, a vast hulk of a man weighing 230 pounds, whose first task when he took up residence in the Dolmabache palace was to order an eight-foot-long bed, wide enough to accommodate not only his bulky frame, but also that of one of his concubines, the number of which he increased to nine hundred, guarded by three thousand black eunuchs.

Abdul Aziz was big in every way. He loved food, one of his favourite meals being a dozen fried eggs at a sitting. He did not, however, always finish the dish, for he had an irritating habit of throwing his lunch at any courtier who displeased him, in particular anyone who refused him money for some new project, from a new palace to lions and tigers imported from Africa and India.

Still, to look at he was every inch a sultan, with a full face and large staring eyes, and a beard streaked with grey even when young. Physically he was probably the finest of his race for four hundred years, 'but this was about all that could be said of him. His mind was vacuous.' He promised reforms and economies, but nothing came of them, and though in his reign of fifteen years he suffered no wars, his insane extravagance soon raised the Turkish debt to foreign bankers to nearly £200 million sterling.

*

By the sixties Abdul Aziz faced another problem: the mounting demand among the Turks themselves for reforms, for by 1865 (the same year Lincoln was assassinated), 'The Society of New Ottomans' had been secretly formed in Constantinople. It had only 245 members to begin with, but they were led by a liberal writer called Namik Kemal, and two of the royal princes were among those who attended its secret meetings. The aim was simple: to transform the despotic rule of the sultans into a constitutional monarchy, and the Society based its programme on the Italian secret society, the Carbonari. This was the forerunner of the 'Young Turks', and the Society grew rapidly. The members were not reckless revolutionaries; they did not at this stage envisage westernization, but endeavoured to open the way to reform without precipitating fatal reaction. Among the sympathizers was a great patriot destined to change the entire pattern of Turkish history. His name was Midhat Pasha. Midhat, whose family came from Bulgaria, had received an old-fashioned education. At the age of ten he knew the Koran by heart. He learned French, rose steadily in government circles and a few years previously had taken six months' leave to visit Europe. He had already achieved respect as a provincial governor, and was a convinced believer in constitutional government. A shrewd and ambitious statesman, he could see clearly that the only hope of arresting the downward course of the penniless Empire under its new, half-mad Sultan was to institute reforms from within.

When news of the secret society reached the ears of Abdul Aziz, he was horrified, and was only dissuaded at the last moment from hanging the ringleaders. He immediately commanded that the Society should be disbanded, but his edict had no effect, for too many Turks in high places were beginning to feel a sense of shame at the antics of their ruler. Officially the Society ceased to exist, but unofficially its influence became even wider, and branch offices were soon founded in all major cities, while Turkish exiles indulged in propaganda in Europe.

Most foreign residents in Turkey knew of its activities. In his diary in 1864, an American missionary called Van Lennep remarked that, 'There is a party, chiefly composed of young men educated in Europe, who may be denominated "Young Turkey", whose object . . . is to introduce a general and radical reform into all branches of the administration.'

Midhat Pasha had immense influence among thinking Turks; his name was synonymous with progress, and soon Abdul Aziz realized that the danger of revolt was very real. A firm believer in the maxim that money was the root of all success, he determined on a startling measure. He would be the first sultan of the Ottoman Empire to visit Europe. Louis Napoleon had already invited him to Paris, and though his first inclination had been to refuse, he now changed his mind. A European tour would have a two-fold object: he hoped that by the Young Turks it would be taken as a sign that Turkey was no longer an empire whose frontiers were closed to the liberal ideas of Europe; and secondly his presence in Europe would undoubtedly help to solve the problem of the interest owed on the £200 million. To the simple mind of Abdul Aziz it must have seemed delight-fully easy for, after all, this was the era of 'high finance', the very year when the United States bought Alaska for just over $7 million. It never occurred to the Sultan that it might be difficult to raise a new loan and use the money to pay off the interest on the previous loans.

*

Abdul Aziz paid his state visits to Paris and London in 1867, and achieved exactly the opposite of what he intended. Before his departure he was hailed as the most enlightened son the line of Othman had ever produced. But the luxurious splendour he found in France and Britain left an indelible mark on a mind already feeble, and caused such delusions of grandeur during the years that followed that even his own government officials rose against him.

In Paris, the halcyon days of the Second Empire were drawing to a close, but the Great Exhibition had drawn kings and their consorts from every corner of Europe. There had never been such a galaxy of crowned heads in the capital at the same time, but none excited the imagination of the French more than the Sultan who, so one newspaper revealed, always travelled in a solid-gold coach with a retinue of concubines, and a trail of elephants led by negro slaves chained in gold. In fact, when the Sultan did arrive at the Gare de Lyon, the sight of a portly gentleman in a plain frock-coat must have been something of a disappointment.

He was fêted with the wildest extravagance by Louis Napoleon, who transformed the Élysée Palace into a fairyland of the Arabian Nights in his honour, but the visit was not a success because the Sultan felt grossly insulted when Louis Napoleon, harking back to Aimée and the Empress

Joséphine, had the temerity to suggest that the two rulers were related through their Creole grandmothers. To make matters worse, the Sultan failed to raise a loan in Paris.

In England, he had a much better time. True, the reception was not so gaudy when Aziz crossed the Channel with his nephews Murad and Abdul Hamid, for Queen Victoria had only agreed to come out of retirement and meet him after weeks of argument. But once she did agree (hoping in her diary that 'the Sultan is not likely to come again') she invited him to Windsor, and the Government did everything in its power to delight the visitor – though far more subtly than the French had done.

The streets were lined with cheering crowds, for though the Crimean War was already history, Britain still remembered her gallant ally. From the moment that Aziz was hustled into the latest train that covered the distance from Dover to London in the astonishing time of only two hours, and then escorted to Buckingham Palace by a clattering escort of the Household Cavalry, he received a deep and lasting impression of the wealth of the country. And he responded with a splendid gesture: when invited to dine in the Guildhall, he arrived on a white charger, his uniform scintillating with medals, and with the traditional aigrette of diamonds on his fez.

Alas, the climax of the visit was not so happy – a naval review at Spithead in squally weather. The Sultan was so seasick that Victoria noted in her diary, 'The Sultan feels very uncomfortable at sea. He was constantly retiring below and can have seen very little, which was a pity, as it was a very fine sight.'

The effect of the visit on the Sultan's megalomaniac personality was to plunge him into even greater extravagance when he returned home. The annual cost of running the Dolmabache Palace was soon running at £2 million – a lot of money in those days. He had a staff of five thousand servants, entertained on the most lavish scale in Ottoman history, with three hundred or more guests dining at his table most evenings. He had four hundred musicians, two hundred men looking after his menagerie, three hundred in the kitchens, four hundred grooms. Each morning, when he rose and donned his bright red dressing-gown and white skull-cap (his normal dress until lunch-time), a bevy of palace servants attended to his every whim – from the slave whose task was to put the royal backgammon board in its proper place to the *ternakji*, the page whose duty it was to trim the royal nails.

The splendours of Europe had so impressed him that he now engaged in a royal spending spree beyond the imagination of any of his forebears. From Paris he ordered a solid gold dinner-service, encrusted with rubies and emeralds. He had the walls of one palace panelled in mother of pearl. From Britain he bought dozens of pianos – in the hope of having them played in the palace gardens strapped to men's backs so the music could follow him on his every stroll. He bought something else from Britain – locomotives, though there were no tracks on which they could run, and several ironclads, though there were no sailors to man them.

The ladies of the harem spent as never before. Pertevalé – the one-time Besma, whose name had been changed when she became Queen Mother – thought nothing of buying fifty dresses of Brusa silk a day, and then giving most of them to slaves. She called it 'spreading happiness around me'.

In fact, the Sultan was becoming more and more insane. He 're-wrote' all Turkish schoolbooks, deleting every Turkish defeat, the chapter on the French Revolution and every reference to Christianity. In the palace he behaved like a mad martinet, sometimes forcing his courtiers to grovel on their knees and kiss his feet before addressing him. When a minor government servant called Aziz brought him a letter, the Sultan was so furious that anyone should dare to bear the same name as himself that he ordered everyone in the government called Aziz to change his name. During his bouts of madness he would wave away any documents written in black ink. The entire Ottoman Government, a creaking institution at best, would be brought to a halt until everything was copied in red.

In the evenings he had two favourite pastimes. One was playing soldiers – with real soldiers. As he watched from a lattice grille, detachments of troops fought mock wars in the cellars, fighting throughout the night, the survivors emerging, grimy and smoke-blackened, with the dawn. At other times he played with hens and cocks in the grandiose splendour of the palace reception rooms. Officials had to remain stoically expressionless as the Sultan chased the fluttering birds from room to room until he caught one, when, with an insane laugh, he would hang the

Ottoman Empire's highest medals for gallantry around its neck. And the palace servants had to make certain that no cock or hen ever appeared later without its Order.

At times he was seized with dark suspicions. When he believed that his court was trying to poison him, he lived for days on hard-boiled eggs, and these had to be cooked by the Queen Mother and served to him wrapped in a parcel of black crêpe sealed with her own seal. At other times he had a dread of fire, and then he would have nothing made of wood in the same room and read at night by a candle placed in a bucket of water.

Abdul Aziz had only one consolation, his favourite Circassian slave, a sixteen-year-old girl of rare beauty called Mihri Hanoum, whom he first heard singing one evening in the palace gardens. Soon he was spending every evening – and much of every day, too – in her arms. In all, he gratified Mihri's whims to the tune of one million pounds.

As the money in the coffers dwindled – and as the old Sultan became increasingly deranged – the discontent in Turkey grew, and took the form of more meetings of the proscribed Young Turks party, which was growing bolder and more vociferous and looked to Midhat as its only hope. Finally, after two thousand theological students stopped the Sultan's son, and demanded the removal of a pro-Russian grand vizier, Aziz, in a panic, shut himself up in the harem for several days and nights, spent in the arms of his Circassian favourite. At last he was persuaded that, if he wanted to prevent a revolution, he must recall Midhat from a post in the provinces where he had been discreetly 'banished', and appoint him Grand Vizier. In doing so, he sealed his own fate.

*

The empire was ripe for revolt. The misery of the majority of the people had been exacerbated by two bad harvests. There was bound to be an explosion.

On 21 April 1876 the Bulgarians, long seething with disaffection, broke into open revolt. Bulgaria had been part of the Ottoman Empire since 1396. Its language, like that of Russia, was Slavic. It belonged to the Orthodox Church, and even before the Crimean War a committee had been formed in Odessa to press for reforms in the field of religion. For decades the bishops sent by Constantinople to Bulgaria had been Greeks. Often they did not know a word of Bulgarian, so that when the indefatigable Lady Mary Wortley Montagu travelled through the province she thought the churches and their congregations were Greek.

All attempts to substitute a Slavic for a Greek liturgy failed, and it did not take Russia, sympathetic to the Bulgars and always anxious for an excuse to stir up trouble, long to encourage an uprising. It started in the mountains around the town of Batak. It is doubtful whether the half-deranged Sultan could have even pinpointed Batak on the map. To him it was that part of the Empire which included the famous rose gardens of Varna, which provided his harem with attar of roses. The uprising itself was easily quelled by troops sent from Constantinople, but the matter did not end there, for the Turks decided to make an example of the entire area. Circassian troops, who received no pay but fought for loot, had been stationed in the district and were now let loose to exact a merciless revenge. In normal times that, as far as the rest of the world was concerned, would have been the end of the affair. However, it happened that, for the first time in Ottoman history, a respected foreign correspondent of the London *Daily News* happened to be in Constantinople. J. A. MacGahan, an American, had already achieved fame by riding across central Asia to report on the Russian war there. Now he set off for Batak, accompanied by Eugene Schuyler, the American Consul-General in Turkey.

In their way, the reports of MacGahan proved a turning-point in Ottoman history, for until now stories of the bestiality and brutality of the Turks had always been comfortably regarded as exaggerated rumours. But now the authenticated descriptions of indiscriminate murder and rape could not be ignored. Sixty villages had been burned. Twelve hundred people, mostly women and children, were burned alive in a church at Batak. In all twelve thousand were murdered – and Achmed Aga, the leader of the Ottoman troops, was personally decorated by the Sultan for what was considered to be a normal method of repressing a rebellion.

On the morning of 7 August, England was stunned and horrified when MacGahan's first despatch appeared in the *Daily News*. Describing the moment he approached Batak, he wrote:

I counted from the saddle a hundred skulls, picked and licked clean: all of women and children. We entered the town. On every side were skulls and skeletons charred among the ruins, or lying entire where they fell in their clothing. They were skeletons of girls and women with long brown hair hanging to their skulls. We approached the church. There these remains were more frequent, until the ground was literally covered with skeletons, skulls and putrefying bodies in clothing. Between the church and the school there were heaps. The stench was fearful. We entered the churchyard. The sight was more dreadful. The whole churchyard for three feet deep was festering with dead bodies partly covered – hands, legs, arms and heads projected in ghastly confusion. I saw many little hands, heads and feet of children of three years of age, and girls with heads covered with beautiful hair. The church was still worse. The floor was covered with rotting bodies quite uncovered. I never imagined anything so fearful. There were three thousand bodies in the churchyard and church . . . In the school, a fine building, two hundred women and children had been burnt alive. All over the town there were the same scenes . . . The man who did all this, Achmed Aga, has been promoted and is still Governor of the district. No crime invented by Turkish ferocity was left uncommitted.

A week later his second despatch appeared:

I fear I am no longer impartial, and I certainly am no longer cool . . . I have already investigated enough to feel convinced that, except from a purely statistical point of view, further investigation would be unnecessary . . . When you are met in the outset of your investigation with the admission that sixty or seventy villages have been burned, that some fifteen thousand people have been slaughtered, of whom a large part were women and children, you begin to feel that it is useless to go any further. We asked about the skulls and bones we had seen up on the hill upon first arriving in the village when the dogs had barked at us. These we were told were the bones of about two hundred young girls, who had first been captured and particularly reserved for a worse fate than death. They had been kept till the last; they had been in the hands of their captors for several days – for the burning and pillaging had not all been accomplished in a single day – and during this time they had suffered all that it was possible that poor, weak, trembling girls could suffer at the hands of brutal savages. Then when the town had been pillaged and burned, when all their friends had been slaughtered, these poor young things, whose very wrongs should have insured their safety, whose very outrages should have insured their protection, were taken, in the broad light of day, beneath the smiling canopy of heaven, and coolly beheaded, then thrown in a heap there and left to rot.

Repercussions of horror rippled across the world. The British Government sent Walter Baring of the British Embassy in Constantinople to see whether or not the newspaper reports were exaggerated, and he described what had taken place as 'perhaps the most heinous crime that has stained the history of the present century'.

Though there was nothing that Britain could do, the sense of revulsion against the Turkish empire mounted despite discreditable efforts by Disraeli to pooh-pooh MacGahan's despatches as 'picturesque journalism'. He had to reckon with Gladstone, however, who had retired the previous year, and now set about writing a violently anti-Turkish pamphlet on the Bulgarian atrocities: branding the Turks as the 'great anti-human specimen of humanity'.

The atrocities caused enough bad feeling in Europe, but there was another reason for the wave of anti-Turkish emotion, and one which hit harder nearer home, and produced repercussions of another kind. Because of his extravagances Abdul Aziz had cancelled all the interest due to European bond-holders in the Ottoman state bonds, causing fury in every European capital – except, significantly, St Petersburg, from where the Czar officially congratulated the Sultan on 'a wise and precautionary measure'.

*

In Constantinople Midhat Pasha now realized that only one course was open, however dangerous. The Sultan must be deposed, despite the fact that his nephew Murad, the heir, was weak, vacillating, already besotted by his favourite drink of champagne laced with brandy, a tipple he had first tasted during the state visit to Paris with his uncle. A physical wreck, fuddled with drink, he lived in seclusion, in perpetual terror of the bowstring. But Midhat needed a successor. And so the drunken prince became, to the Turkish people at large, 'Murad the Reformer'.

Now Midhat was ready for the *coup* to depose Aziz. To help him he called in Hussein Avni, the bluff and honest Minister of War, and just before midnight on 29 May 1876 these two middle-aged men, far removed from the accepted notion of revolutionaries, put their plan into action. One small group including the War Minister set off in a caïque from Constantinople to cross the Bosporus and reach the white palace of Dolmabache. The wind was howling as the War Minister landed on the marble waterfront. Soldiers had already thrown a cordon round the gates, and Aziz was in his huge gilded bed (with his Circassian) when the first shots sounded from the wet and windy gardens. The few loyal guards were quickly overcome and the conspirators made for the palace.

Hussein Avni forced his way into the vast throne-room to face a crowd of hysterical eunuchs, headed by the grotesque figure of the Kislar Aga, a huge Nubian in a white nightshirt. As they shouted and screamed, a figure appeared at the head of the stairs and there was a deadly silence.

It was Abdul Aziz, in a pink nightshirt, one hand wielding an unsheathed sword, the other holding Mihri, the Circassian, sobbing as she clung to him in terror.

His first inclination was to resist. But then he was presented with a declaration signed by the Sheik-Ul-Islam, the highest spiritual and judicial leader in the Empire, and to Aziz this was Kismet – fate, the 'appointed time' decreed by Allah which was (so it was believed at the time) written in invisible ink on the forehead of every man.*

At this moment a fearful apparition appeared at the top of the stairs. It was Pertevalé, the Queen Mother. In an instant, the lessons of decorum learned during fifty years in the harem vanished and she became a bath attendant again. Huge, her hair tousled, her face unveiled, she charged towards the War Minister, clawing at his face with her painted nails, finally flooring him with a well-placed kick in the stomach.

In Constantinople, another scene bordering on farce was being played out. When, just before dawn, Midhat received a signal that the Sultan was deposed – it was the single boom of a gun – he went to tell Murad that he was now Sultan of the Ottoman Empire.

It was easier said than done. Murad was awakened. Half-drunk, he was almost dragged from his bed, and his first thought was that the moment of the bowstring had arrived at last. In vain Midhat urged him to dress and follow him, told the Prince of the increasing disorders in the city, warned him of the danger that the Russians might seize the opportunity to march on a leaderless country. Terrified and whimpering, Murad's only response was to beg for his life. Finally Midhat told Murad that if he did not accept the throne, he would go straight to his younger brother,

* If Midhat, and not the War Minister, had confronted the Sultan, it is possible that Aziz might have fought to the death, for he hated Midhat and never forgave him for once appearing before him wearing spectacles.

Abdul Hamid. That was enough, for the two brothers hated each other. Like a frightened schoolboy Murad allowed himself to be led to the caïque that would carry him to Dolmabache.

The two craft bearing the old and the new sultans passed each other in the Bosporus, and the wailing of Aziz's women could plainly be heard. Before dawn the deposed leader was installed in the Old Seraglio, and the people of Constantinople woke to the sound of a 101-gun salute in honour of Murad V.

Curiously, the people of Britain knew about the *coup* as quickly as the people of Constantinople. A British journalist, suspecting that a crisis was imminent, had devised a code, and during the night obtained permission to cable a telegram of an urgent and private nature. It read, 'The doctors have found it necessary to bleed "poor Jane" [Abdul Aziz]. "Grand-mamma" [the Queen Mother] is with her. "Cousin John" [Murad] has taken charge of the business.'

*

An extraordinary sequence of violent events now took place. Five days after he had been deposed Abdul Aziz was found dead, blood dripping from wounds in his wrists. He had been sitting with Pertevalé, the Queen Mother and Mihri, who was expecting a baby, in the harem of his new quarters. Both Mihri and the Queen Mother (as the latter testified later) were worried about the man they loved. Abdul Aziz's face was sunken and haggard. He told them to leave him as he wanted to sleep and, almost as an afterthought, asked for a pair of Persian scissors with which to trim his beard. Within hours, Mihri found him dead. He had severed his arteries to commit suicide.

Or had he? The ritual of trimming a beard was so elaborate – every hair had to be preserved – and so wrapped in protocol that it seemed unthinkable for a man of Aziz's character to cut his own beard. The Queen Mother, however, was adamant that she herself had handed the scissors to her son, though with fifty years' experience in the harem she must have been highly suspicious at the odd request from a ruler steeped in tradition. Even the British Ambassador was suspicious. No one will ever know for sure whether or not Aziz was murdered, but to Midhat, desperately trying to promote the image of Murad, it was vital that suspicions of foul play be laid to rest.

Nineteen doctors, the most eminent in the city and largely drawn from the foreign embassies, were called in to establish the true cause of death. They agreed that it was suicide.

Within a few days the dead Sultan's Circassian slave died in childbirth. As one Turkish newspaper put it, 'In giving birth to a second prince – the terrible emotions she had suffered from the death of the Sultan having prematurely carried off this young and beautiful princess.'

Mihri's funeral blocked the streets of the capital. The twin elements of tragedy and beauty brought tens of thousands to line the route as her coffin of polished wood, encrusted with mother of pearl and covered with garlands of fresh roses, was carried to Scutari cemetery by pashas, beys, officers and eunuchs.

The violence had not ended. Mihri had a brother, Hassan, a young officer known as a crack pistol-shot. Like his sister he had also been devoted to Aziz, and he decided to revenge their deaths by taking the life of the War Minister.

To pluck up courage he drugged himself with marijuana, stuck two pistols in his boots, two more in his pockets and burst into a cabinet meeting. With his first two shots he killed the War Minister and Foreign Minister. Troops and police who tried to arrest him were gunned down. In all, seven people were killed and eight wounded in the bloody twenty minutes before he was overpowered. The next morning he was hanged in public before a large crowd. To the end he insisted that his sole motive was revenge on the man who had deposed Abdul Aziz.

Already feeble-minded after years immured in the Cage, this torrent of violence was more than the new Sultan Murad's unhinged mind could take. A specialist from Vienna and the court physician both declared him incurably insane. So, after only three months on the throne he, in turn, was deposed at the instigation of Midhat, and put away in another palace, and his brother Abdul Hamid II came to power.

Chapter nine
The city of intrigue

Abdul Hamid II was thirty-four when he became Sultan in 1876, and he was the last supreme despot of the Ottoman Empire. Born in 1842, the second son of Abdul Mejid, his mother was an Armenian professional dancer before entering the harem. She died when Abdul Hamid was only seven.

Thin and ugly, his dark, suspicious eyes were set in a sallow face above an enormous hooked nose, a cruel mouth and the straggling beard, in his case black, which every prince was required to grow when he became Sultan. 'His face differed profoundly from the fresh, powerful, fleshy faces of his ancestors'; his knee-length stambouli coat 'covered his slight figure without elegance', while his fez 'appeared abnormally large above the pale narrow face'.

Professor Armenius Vambery, a scholar from Hungary who knew Abdul Hamid better than any other European, wrote that, 'I never met with a man the salient features of whose character were so contradictory, so uneven and disproportionate, as with Sultan Abdul Hamid. Benevolence and wickedness, generosity and meanness, cowardice and valour, shrewdness and ignorance, moderation and excess and many, many other qualities have alternately found expression in his acts and words. If there was a predominant feature in his character it was his timidity, the constant wavering and the apprehension of having committed a wrong step, which left an indelible mark upon all his doings. This unfortunate quality, the disastrous effect of harem education, frustrated his best intentions; it blunted his otherwise splendid mental capacities and made his reign a misfortune to his country.'

Perhaps Abdul Hamid's greatest tragedy was that he seemed incapable of adjusting to the altered attitude of Europe towards an empire which it had once feared, but which now it regarded as a weak pawn. Perhaps, too,

Abdul Hamid was unable to grasp the magnitude of change within the country itself.

Even Constantinople itself was changing. The first telegraph lines were functioning. The first petrol and oil had been imported. The first steam engine had been set up in the capital. The French Lycée had opened in Galata and was bringing Turk and foreigner together. The influence of the West had spread in other ways. The flowing oriental robes, with their splendid colours, had long since gone, and much of the life of oriental magnificence had also vanished, as it so often does, with progress. And, as the new Sultan vacillated between yesterday and tomorrow, Constantinople, sunk in a morass, lost its colour, its spice of life, and reverted to a city of the dark ages; it became a city of suspicion and intrigue.

To the people, at least, Abdul Hamid seemed (at first) a serious, hopeful ruler when, within a week of his accession, he was girded with the sword of Osman. On the morning of the ceremony the Sultan took the classic milk-bath that preceded many religious occasions, while 100,000 men, women and children crowded the banks of the Bosporus and the Golden Horn to catch a glimpse of the new Sultan's procession by sea from Dolmabache to Eyub, the most venerated of Istanbul's four hundred mosques.

It was a windless day of dazzling sunshine reflected in millions of points of light on the bright blue sea which, more than any other city in the world, seemed to come right into every Constantinople home; a sea without even a pebble shore, the slime of a river, the black waters of a canal; the sea which was as much a main street in Constantinople as the Grand Canal of Venice.

Behind the waterfront the streets were crowded with a dozen different Asiatic races (to say nothing of a sprinkling of Europeans in billycock hats) intent on enjoying the holiday. By now the wives of pashas and other notables had been allowed some measure of emancipation, and though they were still veiled many wore small thin yashmaks made of an almost transparent silken gauze. Some arrived packed in bullock carts; others in light open carriages, imported from Vienna, the smarter ones with a coachman, escorted by a fierce-looking Nubian eunuch on horseback carrying a drawn sword.

The men had arrived long before. For hours they squatted in the streets waiting, smoking almost without pause, the richer men content to puff only the upper part of each pipe, the *kaimak* or 'cream', while the poor smoked the tobacco they knocked out. As the heat of the day mounted, the sellers of melon and sherbet did a roaring trade. Children sucked Turkish delight (wrapped in painted paper). Veiled ladies who had to contain their thirst chewed mastich, a chewing-gum carried in little filigree boxes and supposed to keep the gums healthy. At every corner there were mounds of fruit – grapes, pears, plums, pomegranates, together with a special fruit drink called *khoshab* – 'Agreeable Water' – concocted from local peaches and other fruit flavoured with musk and amber.*

For those with heartier appetites oysters caught with iron rakes that morning were fried in the street; together with pilaffs, stuffed cucumbers and at least two dishes still highly esteemed today – haggis, cooked by the roadside on portable stoves, and the ever-popular tripe.

Shortly before noon the white and gold imperial caïque, manned with fourteen pairs of oars, set off up the Golden Horn, with the Sultan sitting under a crimson canopy while the hundreds of foreign ships dipped their flags in salute. Near Eyub the Sultan mounted a white charger bridled in gold, and passed through the Gate of Adrianople, wound his way under the overhanging eaves of timber dwellings, through the narrow streets, made narrower by the double file of troops in their gold-embroidered uniforms.

As the Sultan reached the mosque, built by Mahomet the Conqueror and lying north-west of the city, beyond the walls of Heraclius, the normally drab Constantinople was transformed into a scene of splendour. Soldiers and marines – the Albanians in their tall, plumed hats, the Circassians, the Spahis in gold and blue, the *bostangis* proudest of all in gold-edged uniforms and scarlet cloaks – lined the sunlit courtyard, its tiled walls in bold patterns blazing with colour, yet never jarring. In the shade of an enormous plane tree, by a fountain, the Sultan dismounted. The standard-bearers carried the green banner of the Prophet inside the cool interior of the mosque, the walls of plain dressed stone, the

* Made by pouring rosewater on refined sugar, removing the scum, adding spring-water and fruit, boiling it, straining through a fine sieve, adding more fruit and a drop of musk or amber and imbibing it with a sandalwood or pearwood spoon.

white marble dome resting on simple pillars. The banner was followed by the Sheik-Ul-Islam, in his white and gold cashmere robes; and then Abdul Hamid entered. With quiet dignity – and according to a rigid protocol from ancient times – he slowly walked the prescribed seven paces towards the chief of the howling dervishes who, since the time of Osman, had been privileged to gird the sabre on every new sultan. The dervish kissed his left shoulder. The Sultan, in his first act as ruler, took three steps towards the Grand Vizier who, in the name of the people, kissed the hem of his garment.

In the centre of the mosque stood a white marble tomb covered with a thin plating of fretwork silver, as delicate as a piece of lace. Inside were the ashes of the Prophet's standard-bearer, and in front of it, on a table covered with crimson velvet, lay the sword itself, its blue sheath almost hidden by precious stones, its gold hilt covered with turquoises and rubies.

For exactly seventeen minutes the inside of the mosque hummed with muted prayers; then the muezzin, from the top of the minaret, proclaimed to the people of Constantinople that the Commander of the Faithful was inside. Within a few seconds the Sultan was handed the belt, then the sword itself, and the ceremony was all but over.

As the Sultan clasped the hilt with one small, brown hand, the mosque lay in an almost uncanny stillness, broken only by the fluttering of doves nesting in the courtyard. Then from the floor crammed with kneeling figures, came the sounds of more mumbled prayer, echoed and thrown back from the high dome as the procession returned to the harsh sunlight of the court. Abdul Hamid mounted his white horse, 'his face', according to one historian, 'marked with lines of thought, a profound expression of melancholy'. Slowly he proceeded back to the streets, to be acclaimed by tumultuous crowds as God's Vice-Regent on Earth.

The political and financial crises did not spoil the event. The Turks were prepared to give the new ruler the chance to prove that the change would be for the better, particularly with the increasingly popular Midhat Pasha very much in evidence with his reforms. Bulgaria was conveniently forgotten in the general rejoicing. To the man in the street on that sunny day, Abdul Hamid was (quite apart from being extremely close to God) a ruler who would take his duties seriously. Not one in the vast crowds which spent the night roistering at the Hippodrome would have believed that the young Sultan would become (in the words of Eversley), 'the most mean, cunning, untrustworthy and cruel intriguer in the long dynasty of Othman'.

This was the very day on which Gladstone published his pamphlet on the Bulgarian massacres; perhaps it was as well, too, that the new Sultan did not know of that pamphlet's reception in the Court of St Petersburg, where General Ignatiev gleefully told the Czar, 'The Bulgarian massacres have brought Russia what she had never had before – the support of British public opinion.'

*

In Europe, something had to be done. The horrors in Bulgaria were on every man's lips. The Czar was thirsting for blood. Every politician knew that Turkey was in revolt. Montenegro and Servia had both declared they 'would perish sooner than continue under Turkish misrule'. Bosnia and Herzegovina were in the flames of revolt against the rapacity of the Turkish pashas. Bulgaria was gasping out its last breath of life. And to Europe – particularly Britain, fearful for its lifeline through the newly-opened Suez Canal to India – this presaged the gravest danger of all: an opportunity, 'in the cause of Christianity', for the Czar to march again on the Ottoman Empire and seize the immense power that would come with control of the Bosporus.

Britain therefore needed a good excuse to interfere with the internal affairs of Turkey as a means of warding off the Czar's threats of war. It was to hand. As a signatory to the Treaty of Paris, Britain felt she could not be indifferent to Turkish 'crimes' against Christian subjects, and so, barely two months after Abdul Hamid had been girded with the sacred sword, she persuaded the European powers to meet in Constantinople and suggest Turkish administrative changes to protect her Christian subjects.

Abdul Hamid, whatever his faults, was a loyal Ottoman. He was furious at what he regarded as an impertinent interference in home affairs. So was Midhat Pasha, who was intelligent enough to realize that, since he had been instrumental in deposing Abdul Hamid's two predecessors, he could expect some help and gratitude from the present incumbent. He was right, for the moment.

The European conference, with Lord Salisbury, Secretary of State for India, representing Britain, and General Ignatiev the Czar, arrived in

Constantinople, ready to open proceedings on 23 December 1876. As they sat down with Turkish delegates in the Hall of the Admiralty overlooking the Golden Horn, they heard a salute of 101 guns. When the last boom had echoed, the senior Turkish delegate stood up, and announced, 'Gentlemen, the cannon you have heard is the signal for the promulgation by the Sultan of a constitution guaranteeing the rights of all the subjects of the empire without distinction. In the presence of this great event, I feel that our task is superfluous.'

In fact, the far-reaching constitutional reform had been agreed during Murad's reign, but Abdul Hamid had refused to sanction it until expediency forced him to change his mind. A national assembly was convoked, 'to be elected by universal suffrage without distinction of race or religion throughout the Ottoman Empire'.

The bewildered European diplomats now had nothing to do, for the changes they had felt necessary had already been announced. They were furious, suspecting that it was a trick, but there was little they could say or do. They hung around for a few days, held a few meetings, then packed their bags and returned to their capitals.

An exhilarated, uninformed electorate now went through the motions of electing parliamentary members of every race and religion. The first sitting of the Assembly was held in the opulent splendour of Dolmabache Palace bursting with light from the reflections of scores of crystal chandeliers on the mirrored walls and marble floors. The meeting was graced by Abdul Hamid, dressed in black; one gloved hand on his sword, he listened as his speech was read out to jostling members, some from the far corners of the Empire still dressed in sheepskins, the shrewder ones endeavouring to sit on his right because they had been told that this was the side of power. Solemnly Abdul Hamid swore to maintain the constitution, and with superb political acumen – as if to show his tolerance and wisdom – not only appointed Midhat Grand Vizier, but an Armenian as Vice-President of the Assembly, and two Jews as aides-de-camp.

In a matter of days the Sultan became the idol, both of the first reformers, the 'Young Turks', and of all the people who had put their faith in him.

They were rudely disillusioned. To the Sultan a gesture had been needed to stop the interference of Christian meddlers, but hardly had the

European statesmen departed before, without warning, Midhat was summoned to Dolmabache. As he made his way there, he noted an ominous sign: a cordon of soldiers encircling his house. And then, as he awaited the Sultan's pleasure, sitting in a Palace anteroom, he saw out of the window an even more sinister sign: the Sultan's yacht, moored at the landing-stage, was ready to sail, with smoke pouring from its funnels.

For an hour Midhat waited alone, the only sound the tinkling of an Offenbach tune on a distant piano, until finally the Sultan's Secretary with some embarrassment announced that the Sultan had dismissed him and the royal yacht was waiting to take him to exile, to any port in Europe Midhat cared to choose.

The Sultan had not acted only out of pique. In the brief spell of 'democracy' Midhat had unearthed incredible irregularities in the Treasury accounts, the Sultan having 'rearranged' them. Huge sums of state bonds and other Treasury moneys had disappeared. The Sultan had not dared to let the enquiries continue.

*

During these first months of the new Sultan's reign, war with Russia had always been in the offing; but it meant little to Abdul Hamid, for an extraordinary personal problem was occupying his mind.

Since his two immediate predecessors had each been deposed, fear and suspicion inevitably dominated the Sultan's mind and he decided to build himself a palace – if such a word may be used to describe the result – so impregnable that it would in effect be a prison locked from within.

The vast palaces at his disposal did not please him, nor was he inclined to build himself a towered, moated fortress. So he built himself a town.

With an irony doubtless lost on the mind of the ruler who finally brought about the death of the Ottoman Empire, most of it was constructed on two large graveyards. They lay beyond Pera on the northern side of the Golden Horn, a mile behind Dolmabache, where the ramshackle wooden houses thinned out and the road mounted unevenly as it wound towards an unpretentious kiosk called Yilditz – 'The Star Pavilion' – which his uncle Abdul Aziz had named after one of his favourite odalisques.

Here Abdul Hamid decided to live and, like Minos when he created the original labyrinth in his Cretan palace, the Sultan was determined that no one man should know every secret of the Yilditz he would build around the original villa; a township of hundreds of buildings scattered over many acres and which would house at least five thousand people.

A dozen architects worked, each one without knowing that the other eleven were employed. Bricklayers erecting a harem building in one corner of the grounds never met the men constructing an artificial lake. Those ordered to tear down an entire street to make more room had no inkling that a private zoo was being constructed a mile or so away.

Hundreds of builders worked on the hillside in shifts, never meeting, never knowing each other. One engineer advised on half of the electricity project, another on the second half. Men uprooting cypress trees in the Forest of Belgrade never met the men who transported them on hundreds of bullock carts to plant a forest in the palace grounds.

For a frightened man the site was perfect. The squalid streets of Pera lay to the landward side, cut off by high walls. In front of Yilditz, at the foot of the hill, lay the Bosporus. The sails of the Golden Horn merged into the cypresses of Seraglio Point across the water. To be certain that he could follow every movement of every ship, the Sultan erected pavilions, each with a powerful telescope, on every rise of land.

Each night for several months he rode up with one servant, almost furtively, to direct operations until the wilderness of old cemeteries had been transformed into a maze of buildings set in a park with a lake, fountains, tulip gardens, even a zoo, exotic birds fluttering in and out of the shrubbery – together with a hundred caged parrots because Abdul Hamid believed they invariably screeched at the sight of strangers. At the side of shaded gravel paths were coffee shops, each staffed by a trusted secret-service man in 'disguise', who helped to give the self-imprisoned Sultan an illusion of normality, especially as he always insisted on paying for his drink on his morning stroll.

The ugly yellow army-barracks lining one wall (and covering every strategic point on the landside) were the only large buildings; otherwise Yilditz resembled nothing so much as a badly planned development area. The rooms in which the Sultan lived – he changed houses regularly – were furnished in bizarre taste. Many walls were entirely covered with mirrors so that every stranger's gesture could be seen. Classic Turkish carpets and divans and priceless porcelain vases from China were cheek-by-jowl with cheap, plush upholstered French furniture, bric-à-brac ranging from cuckoo clocks to his latest toy – a British mousetrap on a table next to the Sultan's jewel-studded cigarette box. There were also four dozen grand pianos, strategically placed as decorative barriers by the doors so that visitors entering a room had to walk in single file. Most of the rooms, corridors, even entire buildings, were connected by secret underground passages threading their way among the bones of the past, and only Abdul Hamid knew every one.

As though to prepare for a siege, he filled many houses with furniture, clothes, guns, even children's toys, and cheap imported articles. Before long, one house contained a strange stack of machinery. It consisted of the essential parts of a cruiser purchased in Britain. The instant it arrived in the Bosporus, Abdul Hamid, afraid that it might be used against him, rendered it neutral. In every room, in every strategic corner of the vast estate, a loaded revolver lay at hand – in all, a thousand of them. And Abdul Hamid was a crack shot.

The Sultan's only concessions to modernity consisted of a small theatre in the grounds, an electric boat on his artificial lake, and a telegraph line linking him to his spies in every corner of the land. He also installed electricity in the palace, though electric light was still prohibited in Constantinople because Abdul Hamid had mistaken the word dynamo for dynamite. He also built a prison near the menagerie so that screams might go unheard.

This was the new home of Abdul Hamid, and it was from here, not Constantinople, that the country was governed. It was a government of secret police, its main functionaries being the Sultan's vast army of spies, many of whom reported daily to him by telegraph. To the gaunt, hook-nosed, unhappy young man, every action, every reflex was motivated by a fear of the silken bowstring. Soon one half of Constantinople was spying on the other. To be a spy was not only a possible way into the confidence of the Sultan, it was profitable; government salaries might be months in arrears, but the spies were paid on the dot.

Day by day the Sultan's obsessive fears became more and more macabre. The danger of poison was perhaps his greatest dread. The drinking-water for his sherbet – always from one particular spring – was placed before him in sealed bottles which he opened personally. His milk came from his own farm in Yilditz, and each cow was guarded day and night. All his cooking was done in kitchens with iron doors and barred windows. Though a frugal eater – pilaff, stuffed marrow, eggs and yoghourt were his favourite dishes – the Sultan insisted that the most extraordinary precautions were taken before he would touch a meal. Each dish had to be tasted by the Chief Chamberlain, Osman Bey, 'Guardian of the Sultan's Health and Life'. Then a portion was given to a cat or dog. At times portions were offered to government officials whom the Sultan suspected of disliking him. Only then was the meal served. Even when eating alone he insisted on ceremony. Two slaves in gold-embroidered uniforms first brought in the Imperial dinner service (covered by a carpet). The tasted, tested food followed on a large silver tray covered by a black cloth, hermetically sealed. Another slave bore the bread basket, also sealed.

Since the Sultan suffered from acute dyspepsia, the food often remained uneaten; instead he would occasionally take a pill prescribed by his doctor; but even this became an elaborate ritual bordering on farce. He sent a trusted eunuch to buy hundreds of pills, which were then shaken in a bag, into which the Sultan plunged a hand and picked one out at random. He felt this lessened the chances of poison.

An inveterate chain-smoker, Abdul Hamid refused to smoke high-grade tobacco because it could have been doctored but bought the cheapest brand in the open market, and the eunuch was not permitted to roll his cigarettes until the Sultan had personally opened the packet. (The eunuch took the first puff.) The Sultan also feared that his clothes might be poisoned. His foster-brother, Izzet, who was of the same build, 'warmed' them before he put them on.

Though not a voluptuary, the Sultan found that the harem was the only place where he could forget his terrors. For the harem, with its two hundred concubines, was his only real world, the heart of Yilditz, the only place where he could in some measure relax behind a wall of human beings whom he knew would protect him. But the women were more like mothers than mistresses, except for the 'maids of good fortune', who were presented to him at special festivals. Soon the Sultan began to rely on his concubines even in his governmental duties. Visitors from the world outside usually found a woman at the Sultan's side. None ever knew who was behind the thick veil, opening the bags of mail from spies and disinfecting the documents.

Though it was in the harem that he passed his happiest hours, often playing with his children, or strumming the piano (his favourite score was 'La Fille de Madame Angot') Abdul Hamid's dark, brooding mind also made him suspect even his women. Years previously he had, as a child, visited the French equivalent of Madame Tussaud's and now he had a life-sized waxen figure of himself placed in the shadow of the harem so that his odalisques would think he was watching them.

He had, in fact, one mistress at this time who was *not* in the harem – a rare circumstance for a sultan. For the first year or so of his reign Abdul Hamid's consolation outside the harem lay in the arms of 'a fair-haired girl with laughing eyes'. Flora Cordier was a Belgian who kept a glove shop on the Grand Rue in Pera, the 'West End' of Constantinople, on the northern shore of the Golden Horn. He met her two years before he became Sultan and fell madly in love with her, not only sensually but because she provided him with the latest gossip picked up from the young bloods who regularly visited her shop.

It was at first a warm and happy love affair, and it was not long before news of it reached Whitehall, so that at the time of Abdul Hamid's accession Disraeli wrote to Lord Salisbury, 'The new Sultan has only one wife, a *modiste* from Pera, a Belgian. He was in the habit of frequenting her shop, buying gloves, etc, and much admired her. One day he said, "Do you think you could marry me?" and she replied "Pourquoi non?", and it was done. It is she who has set him against Seraglio life and all that. In short a Roxelana. Will he be a Suleyman the Great?'

This was possibly the one time in Abdul Hamid's life when he was really happy, but it does not seem that the two did, in fact, marry. Flora never entered the harem, but was tucked away in a small house to await Hamid's occasional order to visit Yilditz in a closed carriage. Rather sadly, the isolation away from the Grand Rue meant that she lost her chief attraction for the Sultan – the cheerful, uninhibited gossip with which she had always regaled him. Presumably she became dull. Her shop was closed, and there were rumours she had been sent back to Belgium.

(There was a curious echo years later when Lady Layard, the British Ambassadress, visiting the harem, met a pretty slave girl who spoke

French. After all the years of gossip and mystery she was astounded when the Sultan explained to her that, ' She lived in the small house of a Belgian *modiste* of Pera who was very intelligent.' She was more surprised at the deference with which the eunuchs treated the girl, at the liberties she was allowed to take in teasing the Sultan. Was she Abdul Hamid's child by Flora Cordier? We shall never know, for the girl was indiscreet enough to keep a rendezvous with Prince Selim, Abdul Hamid's son of eighteen. When Hamid heard about the tryst he promptly banished his son and had the girl drowned in the traditional manner.)

From time to time the Sultan entertained. For the occasional lavish dinner, he used the Dolmabache Palace, but normally foreign diplomats ate relays of dishes in one of the Yilditz rooms, the food half-cold because of the long journey from the kitchens. The meal was often eaten in silence, ending with coffee, a ceremony which impressed Drew Gay of the *Daily Telegraph*, who became friendly with Abdul Hamid. When the Sultan signalled for coffee, wrote Gay, a servant 'picked up a tin very like one of those in which the celebrated Mr Colman retails his mustard', shook from it a little ground and very fragrant coffee into a silver saucepan, 'which would then be held over some burning charcoal in a brazier till the water boiled, when from the cupboard was drawn a little porcelain cup, without a handle, and a magnificently inlaid gold cup-holder, in shape exactly that of an English egg-cup'.

In fact, the oriental splendour of Abdul Hamid's forebears had vanished, and in its place was a tawdry travesty of the past. The swarm of parasites was there – the priests, dwarfs, deaf mutes, eunuchs, the Circassian slave girls, even 'the shimmer of hidden treasure, the shadow of imminent death'. But, like Shakespeare acted in modern dress, the mood had evaporated. The Grand Vizier, once magnificent in white satin lined with ermine, his egg-shaped turban glinting with jewels, now appeared in what. looked like an old German uniform and a fez. It seemed to turn him into a cringing old man. The black eunuchs, once terrifying in their oriental splendour, now looked horrible in their dingy black Stambouli coats. Obese, the layers of fat wrinkles drooping over unaccustomed collars, they reminded the British Ambassador of a corps of third-rate under-takers.

But then everything in Yilditz was now a parody of the pomp of the past. It was totally cut off from reality. The Sultan's only informants were his eunuchs, concubines and his vast army of spies – who furnished him with false information when it suited them. In Constantinople alone the police outnumbered the garrison. Soon Abdul Hamid was refusing even to meet his ministers except on rare occasions; and even then, when the Grand Vizier was given his orders, no discussion was allowed. More often government officials merely received messages – a polite term for orders – informing them of the Sultan's wishes. No wonder that he took little heed of the gathering storm clouds. And no wonder that his ministers did not dare to keep him informed. And so, when the European powers made a second attempt to solve 'the Eastern question' – in other words, the problem of Bulgarians and other Christians – the Sultan again indignantly rejected their overtures as interfering with the independence of the Ottoman Empire.

It was the moment for which the Czar had been waiting – and, for a different reason, the moment Queen Victoria had been dreading, for she regarded Russia as England's most formidable enemy. Ever since the Crimean War, Russia had been quietly advancing in central Asia, and even now Victoria was warning her government of Russian plans to invade India. It was one thing, however, for the Queen to complain about the 'Russian menace'; it was another to persuade her cabinet to take any action – even to issue a declaration of intent. In fact, she threatened to abdicate on the issue, writing to the Prime Minister, 'If England is to kiss Russia's feet, the Queen will not be a party to the humiliation of England and would lay down her crown.' And in a memorandum to the Cabinet she put the danger of a Russian victory over Turkey squarely: 'It is the question of Russian or British supremacy in the world.'

And yet it was unthinkable for Britain to go to war. Bulgaria was a comfortable distance from Whitehall, and though Gladstone could indulge in armchair indignation and cry passionately in his pamphlet, (which incidentally earned him £12,000) that, 'Five million Bulgarians, cowed and beaten down to the ground, hardly venturing to look upwards even to their Father in Heaven, have extended their hands to you', there could be no question of sending British boys, once again, to distant lands to fight.

In Russia, however, the feeling was very different. Above all, the Czar wanted Constantinople and had been preparing to seize it. He had extracted a Romanian promise to allow Russian troops through the Principality, and a promise of neutrality from Austria-Hungary. Now the Sultan's refusal to agree to the European protocol, following the excesses in Bulgaria, gave the Czar his opportunity.

On 24 April 1877, in words used over and again in history, the Czar announced that 'his patience was exhausted', and declared war on the Ottoman Empire. Any territorial ambitions were as usual masked by the pretence that this was to be a Holy War to save Christianity, a war between the Cross and the Crescent.

Using the impending war as an excuse, Abdul Hamid suspended Parliament. Almost immediately, two mighty Russian armies invaded Turkey. In Europe nearly 200,000 men under the command of the Grand Duke Nicholas crossed the Danube; in Asia 150,000 men from the Caucasus marched under the command of the Grand Duke Michael.

Constantinople was in chaos. The spies on whom the Sultan relied for information were helpless; indeed, the only way the Sultan could obtain the latest information was from Layard, the British Ambassador, who visited the Sultan regularly, remembering particularly his sunken eyes rimmed with black circles from lack of sleep, his face showing grey and strained under the rouge he applied daily, as he begged the Ambassador to ask Queen Victoria to help.

Yet, as Russia's European troops marched across the Danube, confident they would soon be at the gates of Constantinople, one stumbling-block halted them – a sleepy little town, lying in a valley twenty miles south of the river, the scene of one of the most heroic defensive struggles in the history of war.

The town was called Plevna.

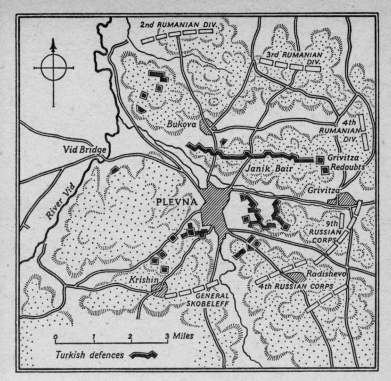

Battle plan of Plevna

Chapter ten
The siege of Plevna

The peaceful little Bulgarian town of seventeen thousand people, where the last great battle between Russia and Turkey was fought in the summer and winter of 1877, lay in a deep valley, the hillsides covered with vineyards and fields of Indian corn almost ripe for harvesting. On three sides ridges, defiles, ravines, rocky escarpments made Plevna almost impregnable. On the fourth it was protected by a large hill studded with orchards. Its strategic importance was that it was a road junction on the River Vid.

Facing Plevna from the north, a Russian army of 180,000 men, with eight hundred guns, waited to pounce. Already Russian troops had easily captured the Turkish stronghold of Nikopoli on the Danube, twenty miles to the north, while other Russian forces had taken the Shipka Pass, the mountain gateway through the Balkans. They had met with only dispirited Turkish resistance and there seemed no reason why Plevna should not fall just as easily, leaving the road to Sofia and Constantinople wide open.

For once Abdul Hamid reacted promptly to the threat. He telegraphed an urgent message to the Turkish Army at Widden on the Upper Danube which was under the command of Osman Pasha, ordering him to march to Plevna with all speed. 'The Ottoman Empire,' he cabled, 'lies between life and death.'

Osman Pasha, at forty already a veteran of the Crimean War, was a soldier's soldier. Short, taciturn, he had a commanding, dignified presence and a sense of iron discipline, and at dawn on 13 July his army of fifty thousand men set off for Plevna, 120 miles away. Each soldier in the ten-mile-long column carried a week's supply of biscuits so hard they could be broken only by a hammer before being soaked in water.

On reaching Plevna on 19 July, Osman Pasha toured the hills and scattered villages that encircled the valley and concluded that, apart from nature's ramparts, Plevna was totally undefended. Knowing that before long the Czar would launch the whole weight of his army against him, Osman's first task was to dig trenches and redoubts.

The bulk of the Russian Army was camped north and east of Plevna, so Osman felt certain the first attacks would come from that direction, where Plevna was dominated by a ridge called Janik Bair, four miles long and nearly four hundred feet above the valley. Digging in shifts, lit by camp fires after dark, Osman's troops worked for twenty-four hours a day on earthworks. Trenches and gun emplacements lined the actual saddle of the ridge for three and a-half miles, ending up near a village called Grivitza, east of Plevna. Behind it Osman Pasha built two great redoubts – known as the Grivitza redoubts – with walls twenty feet thick and twenty feet high, protected by moats and trenches angled to fire on Russians who might try to bypass them. Each redoubt held a thousand men in comparative comfort. Requisitioned furniture was hauled up the slopes, sleeping-chambers and storerooms were built into the walls. A magazine was dug deep under the earthen floor.

Before the end of July, Plevna had been transformed into a fortified town, and its defenders were standing to arms; each infantryman in the redoubts was issued with five hundred cartridges and an iron ration of biscuits and coffee; casks of drinking-water and plenty of food were stored in each redoubt. Carts waited to carry back any wounded, and horses were readied to drag the guns back into the town if a redoubt fell.

Now there was nothing to do but wait for the first assault. Plevna itself was as normal as could be expected, though no one could enter or leave. At first the terrified Bulgarian shopkeepers closed their shutters, but, after Osman had executed several Turkish soldiers for looting the shops, were encouraged to open again. There was a fair supply of food, and during these days of waiting, in which the Turks were successful in several skirmishes, the Grand Bazaar took on a new appearance as the Circassians sold plundered Russian uniforms, silver crosses, photographs, handfuls of roubles. These were the traditional Ottoman spoils of war, and Osman was powerless to interfere.

On the evening of 29 July, Archibald Forbes of the *Daily News** learned

---

* Forbes had become a legend in Fleet Street during the Franco-Prussian War when *The Times* chartered a train to carry exclusive news of the German entry from the Russian general staff that an assault against the Grivitza redoubts would take place the following day with thirty-five thousand men and 170 guns. The Russian order was, 'Succeed, cost what it may.'

At eleven o'clock the next morning, the assault began. In the redoubts the Turks stood firm, repelling three waves of grey-clad Russians, whose old-fashioned rifles were no match for the superior breech-loading American Peabody rifles, of which Abdul Hamid had bought half a million from Rhode Island.

Not until the Czar threw in ten thousand reserves did the Turks waver. From their entrenched positions they were firing at point-blank range into the faces of the Russians, but the sheer weight of thousands of fresh troops began to tell. The first Russians reached the parapet of a Turkish protective trench. Forbes could see the flash of steel in the sun as the Russians were 'in among the Turks like an avalanche', and the Turks retreated to the shelter of the gun batteries behind. The Russians had gained the first Turkish trench on the perimeter, and now, as a battery of their guns rattled into the newly-won position, it seemed to Forbes that nothing could save Plevna. A Russian officer turned to him and cried exultantly, 'We shall sup in Plevna tonight.'

And yet the Turks in the actual redoubts were throwing back every Russian attempt to advance, and at this moment Osman threw *his* reserves into the battle. Forbes heard a bugle in the distance – the Turkish command to charge – and the next moment the vineyards were swarming with men. This time it was the turn of the tired Russian front line to hesitate, then flee. In a matter of moments all had changed and now, as dusk was about to fall, Osman, sensing the spreading panic among the Russians, counter-attacked and recaptured the perimeter positions taken by the Russians. Long after dark the Circassians were still butchering the wounded, and the Turks had routed the enemy. In that one day of the first assault, 168 Russian officers and more than seven thousand men were killed.

'The entire campaign is altered,' wrote Forbes. 'Plevna must be taken. It is impossible for the Russian advance to continue with such a formidable

---

into Paris, and Forbes boarded the train disguised as a fireman and got his story into print first.

force of Turks left unaccounted for on their line of communication.'

In Whitehall, the British Government immediately decided to send a fleet of ironclads to anchor off Constantinople.

*

No one could have been more startled by Osman's unexpected victory than the Sultan in Constantinople and the Czar behind the lines. To Abdul Hamid, who immediately sent a jewelled sword to Osman and awarded him the title of *Ghazi*, or Victor, an empire which had seemed on the verge of collapse had been transformed in a single day's fighting into one capable of beating the infidel Russians. Furthermore, Osman Pasha had not only given him time to try to persuade Queen Victoria to help him, but also his unexpected victory had inspired reluctant admiration for the Turks and done much to erase the stigma of the Bulgarian atrocities.

In the Czar's headquarters behind the front lines, the reaction was totally different: distress bordering on panic. There were rumours that Osman Pasha was preparing to pursue the Russian Army. Thousands of troops fled into Romania where Prince Charles received a cable from the Grand Duke Nicholas, 'Come quickly to our aid. The Turks are annihilating us. The Christian cause is lost.' There was talk of retreating to the north bank of the Danube because the various Russian armies were spread out in a highly vulnerable arc 180 miles long. But the Czar was adamant. Such a retreat would mean leaving the Christian Bulgarians to the mercies of the Turks, and he could not – or dared not – face the loss of prestige.

*

Osman Pasha had no illusions. Though he had won a respite he was convinced the Russians would launch a new assault, certainly greater than the first, and he immediately set about erecting a ring of intricate new earthworks. On the northern front, he built five more redoubts connected by covered trenches to the first two on the Janik Bair ridge. In the south-east he built six, together with six more in the south. Considering the semi-primitive implements employed, they were remarkable achievements. One covered nearly 11,000 square yards. Most had walls 20 feet thick, 7 feet high on the outside edge, surrounded by fosses 15 feet wide and 10 feet deep. Traverse walls, deep rifle-trenches were constructed to repel attacks from the rear or sides. Many redoubts were sited to give complete command of the country for two miles, while others on the inner line of defence, nearer the bottom of the valley, were protected by steep, rocky natural slopes which could only be climbed by an enemy under intense fire. Each redoubt had a telegraph link to Osman's headquarters.

Each Turk in the self-supporting redoubts was issued with six hundred cartridges, with an extra thousand close at hand. Iron rations for eight days were issued, together with rice for pilaff, and maize for soup or bread. A few cattle were tethered behind each redoubt for extra food. Each gun was issued with a hundred shells; packhorses and ox wagons were prepared for the evacuation of the guns and shells, if that ever became necessary.

*

A thin drizzle and an impenetrable white fog masked the dawn of Tuesday, 11 September, the morning of the great assault. For four days the Russian artillery had pounded the Turkish positions – in all, raining thirty thousand shells on the redoubts and trenches, but though five hundred Turks were killed the damage wrought each day was easily repaired each night, and to the dismay of the Russians the shelling actually strengthened morale among the Turks. Dr Charles Ryan, an Australian in the Turkish medical corps, whose wounded patients had been apathetic all through August, now found them offering to help as the shells whistled over 'like railway trains'. Any Russian hope that a sustained artillery barrage would wreck morale showed a misjudgement of human nature as inaccurate as that among those who believed raids by a thousand bombers would shorten the Second World War.

September 11 had been chosen for the attack because it was the name-day of the Czar, and he decided to watch the battle from Grivitza, where a wooden platform with railings had been erected; from it he and his staff could look down on the muddy quagmires of each slope where Russian troops, in a twelve-mile semicircle, had spent the night lying in the merciless rain and mud. The Czar's platform was large enough to accommodate a marquee and a table covered with bowls of caviare, cold game and other choice foods and several cases of Russian vodka and French wines. It reminded Forbes of an English country point-to-point meeting.

The Russian attack was based on the tenets of military textbooks, which insisted that any attack must succeed provided one had enough cannon-fodder; the first waves of men would die, but finally, as the defenders tired, fresh troops, fighting over the bodies of the slain, must reach the objective and take it with the bayonet. It was all a question of men. There was, however, one flaw, as Rupert Furneaux pointed out in his excellent book, *The Siege of Plevna*: 'This theory may have operated successfully in the old days of the muzzle-loading musket and defenders drawn up in lines and squares, but magazine rifles and entrenched positions had rendered it as obsolete as the armoured knight at Agincourt. The Russian High Command knew nothing of what had been learned in the American Civil War where the combination of rapid fire and earthworks had proved its impregnability. Determined to belittle their adversary, the Russian generals ignored the already proven fact that the Turks were masters of applying field fortifications to battle tactics, and that the Turk by nature was superbly adapted to bulldog defence.'

Abruptly the fog lifted shortly before lunch, and at precisely 3 p.m. the Russians launched a three-pronged attack – in the north-east against the Grivitza redoubts, in the south-east against similar fortifications, and in the south against three new redoubts guarding the main roads. No correspondent could be in all three places at once, but J. A. MacGahan of the *Daily News*, whose reports from Batak had stirred the world, decided to move to the southern front, largely because the troops there were led by far the most colourful of the Russian commanders. General Skobeleff was a man of extraordinary panache, a handsome, fearless six-footer of thirty-five who spoke six languages perfectly and sang in each of them, usually ending an evening's roistering with 'Auld Lang Syne' rendered in an excellent Scots accent. He and MacGahan had become close friends, particularly after Skobeleff had explained why he always wore a white uniform and led his men astride a white charger. 'I dress in white,' he said, 'so that my men can see that I am always with them.'

Two more northerly assaults were soon bogged down in the fearful mud, though the Russian and Romanian troops captured one of the Grivitza redoubts by evening, at a price of nearly four thousand killed. Osman Pasha was not worried; he had sited the two Grivitza redoubts so that the loss of one without the other was not fatal, and he made no attempt to counter-attack until later, for he was soon fully occupied with Skobeleff in the south; the latter had brought his guns and twelve thousand men to within a thousand yards of the main Turkish southern redoubt. Built on a low hill, it was also the nearest redoubt to the town. In a hollow at the foot of the hill Skobeleff lined up half his force and under covering artillery-fire they marched up the hill with music blaring and flags flying. As they met the automatic Turkish fire, the Russian line wavered. Skobeleff threw in another three thousand men. A few Russians almost reached the redoubt, but once again the line wavered.

At this moment Skobeleff acted. In his white uniform, on his white horse, he led his last reserve troops up the hill. As he galloped past he shouted, 'Good-bye, MacGahan. Wish me luck, old friend.' Then Mac-Gahan heard him cry, 'Follow me. I'll show you how to thrash the Turks.' As MacGahan watched them charge the slope he could easily pick out Skobeleff's white tunic, and even saw his horse shot from under him as he reached the ditch. Skobeleff led the charge on foot, with the yelling mass of men following him across the ditch, over the parapet and into the redoubt itself. The firing ceased – or nearly ceased. It was now the moment of the bayonet. And almost immediately the Turks were bolting, stream-ing down the hill, and Skobeleff had gained for the Russians the most vital of all the defending redoubts, the one commanding the gateway into Plevna itself.

Skobeleff's losses had been fearful – three thousand men had died in the assault; but the Turkish rout was complete. Through his telescope Osman Pasha could see the Russian eagle fluttering from the captured ramparts, and Osman knew that if the Russians could take the neighbouring redoubt the following morning Plevna would surely fall. It was now nearly dark, and Osman telegraphed the northern redoubts to send in all the reinforce-ments they could spare. He would gamble on retaking the redoubt the following morning.

What Osman could not know, as he planned his counter-attack, was that Skobeleff was in such serious trouble that he could hardly hold the captured redoubt, let alone advance, without reinforcements. Yet all Skobeleff's requests to headquarters for more men were refused.

Skobeleff was, in fact, facing murderous fire from nearby Turkish positions. It was pouring on to his exhausted men, standing or lying in pools of blood. The redoubt was jammed with the dead and dying. The rain was pitiless. And yet, as Skobeleff told MacGahan later, he felt that with reinforcements he would be fighting in the streets of Plevna the following day.

Just before dark Skobeleff decided to gallop back to headquarters and 'try and convince those crazy textbook generals'. It was useless. 'We cannot send reinforcements because we have none,' he was told. The most he could manage to get before returning to the redoubt was some ammunition for his Krenck rifles. But some of his troops were equipped with Berdan rifles of a different calibre. The indefatigable Skobeleff arranged for a score of Russians to gallop to the redoubt with Berdan ammunition carried in horses' nosebags.

At dawn Osman counter-attacked. From his headquarters south of Plevna, he sent the first five thousand men to storm the redoubt, but they were repulsed, leaving five hundred dead on the edge of the parapet. In all, five Turkish assaults to recapture the redoubt were beaten off but then, unknown to Osman of course, a message reached Skobeleff from the Russian headquarters. 'If you cannot hold the captured positions,' it read, 'you are to fall back. The attack is not to be continued.' Skobeleff called it 'the worst instruction I ever received'. But he was a soldier and he had to obey, and started the unenviable task of getting as many men out of the redoubt as possible. By five o'clock that evening the redoubt was in Osman's hands again and, 'The banner of the Crescent waves again where for a moment of time the Russian eagle had looked down into the streets of Plevna.' As the Russians were routed in the south other Turks retook the Grivitza redoubt, and everywhere the Russians were retreating. The great assault had failed. In two days, the Russians and Romanians lost three hundred officers and fifteen thousand men. Shocked by the slaughter the Czar ordered the fighting to cease. Instead, Plevna would be starved into surrender.

*

Osman Pasha was above all a realist. He had twice defeated an army more than double the size of his own. Even more important, he had stalled the Russian war machine, forcing it to face a dreadful winter campaign. To Osman, his task was done. There was no point in staying in Plevna to be starved out – particularly as he had proved that his army was the finest fighting force in the Ottoman Empire. He planned to withdraw fifty-five miles southwards to the town of Orkanie, and there link up with the southern Ottoman forces. Between them they should be more than a match for any Russian offensive. Osman telegraphed his plans to the Sultan in Constantinople. He was astounded to receive an almost hysterical telegram from Abdul Hamid ordering him to remain in Plevna. The international prestige in Europe, the admiration for Osman, the resulting sympathy for Turkey, were of paramount importance for the political future, Abdul Hamid insisted. Plevna had become a symbol, and it must be held at all costs.

The Sultan, in fact, had a point. In England particularly the past behaviour of the Turks had been replaced, as Rupert Furneaux wrote, by 'a glorification of the courage and the valour of the bulldog Turk, and Osman . . . became the man of the hour. Innumerable dogs, not a few cats, the son of an English peer, and a new type of lavatory-pan were christened Osman.'

However dismayed Osman Pasha might have been, he could at least take comfort from one promise by his lord and master. A huge army was being assembled, cabled the Sultan, to march to the relief of Plevna. All that Osman had to do (and how easy it must have seemed in Constantinople) was to hold out until the new army arrived. Poor Osman had spent his life fighting, not in the courts of Yildiz, and apparently it never entered his head that a man so exalted as Abdul Hamid would make a promise he had no intention of redeeming.

Several immediate problems now faced the besieged garrison. A food supply from the south had to be organized. The redoubts had to be repaired, strengthened, improved; and – perhaps most urgent of all – the dead had to be buried, for the threat of disease was so great that guards in the redoubts had to be changed every twenty-four hours.

It took some weeks before Plevna was completely invested by the Russians, and to Osman Pasha this was a godsend. Not only was he able to bring up hundreds of wagonloads of food and thousands of cattle along the road from Constantinople which passed through Orkanie, but those who manned the convoys during September and October remained in Plevna to increase the defence force. At the start of the great assault Osman Pasha's forces totalled fifty thousand men of which he had lost four thousand. But by the time the Russians invested the town completely the garrison had swollen to sixty thousand, many reinforcements arriving in the last great convoy of 1,500 bullock carts which reached Plevna in early October.

While the Turks were busy preparing, the Russians seem to have taken life at an easier tempo. MacGahan was exasperated to see the huge force of men, apparently with no plans, and wrote, 'I think history offers no such example of a splendid army in such an utterly hopeless condition.' Of course, the Russians did not need to hurry – time was on their side – and Skobeleff took some well-earned leave in Bucharest. Despite the attractions of music, the theatre, good food and wine, and particularly the willing ladies who regarded him as the hero of the hour, Skobeleff could not forget the carnage of the great assault. 'I drink and drink but I still see that breastwork of dead bodies,' he told Forbes, who found Bucharest 'a ballroom wherein Mars, Venus and Bacchus were dancing the can-can in frantic orgies'.

By mid October heavy snow started to fall, and there was only one back door into Plevna – a redoubt controlling the road to Orkanie from where the supplies were coming. In the last few days of October it was attacked by a column of the Russian Imperial Guards; and after eight hours, in which the Turks held out against a force three times as strong as theirs, a white flag appeared on the ramparts. Nearly four thousand Turks lay dead, two thousand surrendered; and though four thousand of Russia's élite fighting corps died in the attack, the thirty-mile circle round Plevna had now been joined up.

The bitter Bulgarian winter dragged on. It was intensely cold, but Turkish spirits were sustained by hopes of the arrival of the army promised by the Sultan. As the thermometer dropped to ten below zero Turkish sentries near the front line were changed every hour. Each day the Russians shelled Plevna itself for a few hours. Every mosque still standing had long since become a hospital, the wounded on mattresses in every corner, trying in vain to warm themselves, for now there was no heating. Even the last of the vines had been uprooted and burned. The ration was soon down to half a pound of bread and a lump of meat a day, with buckets of soup for the wounded. In the black market a single cigarette cost the equivalent of ten new pence. An egg cost twice that amount. Despite the shortage of meat no one could kill the horses or bullocks for they might be needed for a breakout. Yet, while the troops in Plevna searched for cats and dogs, rats and mice to vary their diet, the Russians lived very differently. 'In this camp of grand dukes, princes and generals, every table is spread with gleaming silver and the whitest damask,' Furneaux wrote.

In the second week of November, five Turks taken prisoner by the Russians were seen to be crazily making their way, gesticulating and waving white flags, to the Turkish line. They had been sent by the Russians to show Osman Pasha the latest copies of *The Times* and the *Daily News*, both with details of major Turkish disasters in other warfronts – the rout of one Turkish army in Armenia, and the fall of Kars. Osman sent a polite message thanking the Grand Duke for giving him some reading, 'which will help to pass the long winter evenings'.

In case Osman should keep the grim news from his troops, the Russians started hoisting placards on long poles where the two front lines were close together. The Turks, confident that the Sultan had sent a large relieving army, took it as a joke and used the Russian placards for target practice. Morale was still high despite the terrible hardships and semi-starvation.

In fact, it was not until the end of November that Abdul Hamid even thought about the promised army. For, with the heroic defence of the garrison, he had achieved much of his purpose: he had gained the time he so badly needed, and the sympathy of Europe. At last, however, he decided he must do something about it. The effort was pathetic. An army consisting of a 'disorderly rabble', built by denuding other regiments from all parts of the Empire, was hastily sent to Orkanie. At the first sight of a Russian attack, it fled in panic. Only then did Osman Pasha realize that Plevna was doomed, and that his only alternative to surrender was to break out of the iron ring.

Preparations had to be made in the strictest secrecy, for Osman realized that his only hope lay in overwhelming surprise. All the redistribution of wagon trains, artillery and men was done by night, amid intense excitement; for now the thought of action, of fighting, galvanized the men. 'Sick men recovered miraculously and wounds that had refused to yield to treatment began to heal.' None minimized the danger that lay ahead, but Dr Ryan felt that most of the Turks – certainly those he spoke to – preferred to fight and die rather than remain in their prison.

It was unthinkable to leave the civilian Turks behind, for the Bulgarians would massacre them to the last man, woman and child. So he had to take them along. The severely wounded had to be left, but Osman took the only course possible: he assembled the Elders of the Bulgarian Church and made them swear on the Bible that the badly wounded would come to no harm.

As the moment of the breakout arrived, the wheels of the gun carriages were greased and wrapped in straw to deaden any sound. Each man was issued with three days' rations and a pair of sandals. Water, ammunition, forage were loaded, together with the last remnants of food. When the troops were slowly withdrawn from the redoubts, life-sized dummies were placed in the trenches to delude the Russians.

*

The breakout was, of course, doomed from the start. And yet Osman Pasha all but brought off another miracle. Security in Plevna had been so strict that the Russians were quite unaware of the plans until a Polish spy woke up Skobeleff at 4 a.m. on the day. The Russian troops had hardly assembled before masses of Turkish troops started streaming across the snowy plain west of the town. At their head rode Osman Pasha on a chestnut stallion. Behind them rumbled thousands of wagons. Without wavering, two thousand picked Turkish troops, with bands blazing and banners unfurled, charged the Russian trenches. By 8.30 a.m. they had annihilated one Russian regiment and broken the first links in the iron ring.

Without hesitation Osman charged into the attack on the inner Russian defence line, but here the opposition was stiffer as nearly fifty thousand Turks and Russians fought hand to hand. Yet the Turks were holding their own against heavy odds and might well have succeeded, but for a catastrophe. A stray bullet wounded Osman Pasha. Those around him saw him lurch, then fall from his horse. In fact he was only wounded in the leg, but in a matter of moments the rumour galloped through the Turkish ranks that he had been killed. It was more than the half-starved, half-sick men could bear, and in a panic they streamed away from the Russian defences. By the time they had been regrouped, it was too late, and the Russians had occupied the Turkish redoubts, cutting off any hope of reaching a temporary sanctuary there. By one o'clock, the last shot was fired in a siege that had lasted 143 days, and from a house near the bridge, where the wounded Osman had taken refuge, a white flag fluttered.

*

Osman Pasha was treated as a hero by the Russians. When the Grand Duke Nicholas finally came face to face with him, he shook his hand and cried, 'I compliment you on your defence of Plevna. It is one of the most splendid exploits in history.' The immaculately booted Russian officers echoed 'Bravo!' And when Osman Pasha first met the general in white uniform and realized it was Skobeleff, he took his hand and said to him, 'One day you will be commander-in-chief of the Russian Army.'

The Czar invited Osman Pasha to luncheon, and when Osman removed his sword the Czar returned it to him. As Osman prepared to leave for internment in Kharkov, a member of the Czar's staff offered him a sprig of myrtle – a traditional Russian sign that he was no longer their enemy.

A very different fate was reserved for the soldiers of the line. Despite repeated Russian promises that prisoners would be well treated, nearly forty-five thousand Turks were kept in the bitterly cold open air of Plevna for two weeks. They received virtually no food, drugs, medical aid; nor could they even drink the water of the River Vid, which was contaminated by hundreds of corpses. Three thousand men died before the rest set off in the snow to various internment camps. Of the forty-two thousand men who started, often barefoot, on the long march to prison, barely fifteen thousand reached Russia. A fate as terrible awaited the seriously wounded left behind by Osman. The Bulgarians, conveniently ignoring their promises, dragged them from the hospitals and massacred every man.

One last and gruesome echo of the heroic siege of Plevna appeared in, of all places, a Bristol newspaper. It consisted of one paragraph that escaped general notice in England. In an article dealing with fertilizers, it read simply: 'Thirty tons of human bones, comprising thirty thousand skeletons, have just been landed at Bristol from Plevna.'

Chapter eleven
The murder of a patriot

Now the road to Constantinople lay open. And to Abdul Hamid another dimension was added to his fear of assassination – the nightmare of total defeat, of Russian troops stalking the streets of the capital. In panic he sent for Henry Layard, the British Ambassador, and again begged him to ask Queen Victoria to help, finally breaking down and admitting that his real need was Britain's help in negotiating an armistice. When this came to nothing, Abdul Hamid sent a despairing personal cable to the Queen, imploring her to intercede.

As the Russians advanced, the Sultan retreated still further into his private, unreal world. He still maintained a travesty of an emperor's court. Pages and chamberlains, their uniforms glittering with decorations, ugly dwarfs, fawning eunuchs, guided men like Layard from room to room till the moment came to meet the Sultan. In the harem the Queen Mother adhered to a rigid etiquette, yet even there the ancient ceremonials had become a travesty. When from time to time Abdul Hamid was presented with a twelve-year-old slave girl who it was hoped would take his fancy, the chances were that she would instead be bundled off to school. When doctors were finally admitted to the harem, the lady patient was hidden behind a black curtain while the doctor, under the supervision of a eunuch, inspected her tongue through a hole.

Abdul Hamid's terror of death had increased. In many rooms he had built special cupboards with glass doors, though perhaps few realized that each cupboard was so placed that it faced the door. The cupboard doors were electrically controlled from the Sultan's couch, so that if anyone suspicious entered he could press a hidden button, causing the doors to fly open and pistols inside the cupboard to fire automatically. To his vast store of loaded revolvers he had even added two more which hung on either side of his bath.

In the gardens he killed at least two people, in a panic. When a gardener made a swift movement as he salaamed, the Sultan spun round and shot him through the head. When a favourite little slave girl (some historians say his daughter) gave him a playful push, the Sultan fired before he recognized her. As his terror bore increasing signs of madness, he chose the most incredible characters to guide him. His advisers included a slave he had bought in the market, a circus clown whose act he admired, the son of one of his cooks, a Punch and Judy performer and a bootblack.

He made few concessions to the public, apart from the weekly public prayers each Friday at the mosque. For this he was made up under the direction of the faithful Izzet, who not only wore his clothes, but superintended the bottles and jars needed for his toilet. Ready at last, he set off in a splendid procession to the mosque, a lonely, frightened man with a hooked nose and scraggy beard, dressed in a grey army cloak with red piping, crouching in his dark green carriage, with one of his younger sons on his knee as an insurance, for the Sultan knew no Turk would fire if there were any danger of killing a child. Behind him a procession of chamberlains, pages and troops, their gold-braided uniforms blazing with decorations, fat pashas, all on foot, sweated as they tried to keep up with the royal carriage.

When the Sultan approached the mosque a fanfare warned sightseers. Two officers in gold and crimson, their swords drawn, waited outside the door to escort the Sultan inside. But it was not until the weekly prayer was over that the scene was startlingly changed. With a frightened, almost furtive, air, the Sultan virtually ran out of the mosque and quickly entered another smaller, lighter carriage, grabbed the reins himself, and whipped the horses to a mad gallop up the hill to the safety of the secret other world of Yilditz.

*

By the middle of January 1878, the war was all but ended, for the fall of Plevna had released the bulk of the Czar's European troops. One army under General Gourko took Sofia in a matter of days. In bitter weather, with the temperature plummeting below zero, another army under the dashing General Skobeleff forced its way across the Balkan range (after Skobeleff had borrowed several thousand pounds from his father to buy fur coats for his men). Advancing along two sheep-tracks, Skobeleff led his troops through a wild countryside filled with dead and dying refugees. In the last week of January he took Adrianople – only sixty miles from Constantinople – and that was virtually the end. An armistice was signed on 31 January.

To the average Britisher, the swift onslaught of the Czar's troops posed the uneasy possibility of an altered balance of power in the Middle East; and to this was added another factor: the man in the street's hatred of the Turks had veered round completely after the heroic defence of Plevna by Osman Pasha. Possibly their feelings were compounded of a genuine admiration for the Turks at Plevna and a fear of the Russian bear. It took time, however, for the feelings of ordinary people to reach Downing Street. But the people had one champion on their side – the Queen. Victoria had been so deeply moved by the Sultan's pleas for help that she cabled the Czar directly, requesting him to stop the fighting. The Czar's reply was so high-handed that Victoria wrote to Disraeli, 'Oh! if the Queen were a man she would like to go and give those horrid Russians whose word one cannot trust such a beating.' To her daughter she wrote, 'Oh! that Englishmen were now what they were!' Gladstone was now jeered in the streets for his old-fashioned anti-Turkish bigotry.

Finally the Queen shattered the complacency of the British Cabinet, which suddenly woke up to realize that the tents of the victorious Russians were almost within sight of Constantinople. Russian arrogance had to be checked. Parliament voted £6 million 'for war purposes'. Reservists were called to the colours. Troops from India were rushed to Malta. Using the pretext of protecting 'the Christians in Constantinople during a time of crisis', a British fleet equipped with the world's first torpedoes sailed up the Dardanelles to the very shores of the city. Their guns, of course, were trained on the Russians, who replied that they too had lives and property to protect and moved their army to the village of San Stefano, facing the Sea of Marmora, six miles from Constantinople.

The Treaty of San Stefano was signed between Russia and Turkey in March 1878, but the terms were so brutally onerous to the Turks that at the instigation of Britain it was subsequently revised at the Congress of Berlin in June 1878, with Prince Bismarck serving as the 'honest broker'. All the European leaders were present at the most important gathering of its kind since the Congress of Vienna in 1815. There were banquets, receptions, operas – and secret agreements. Lord Beaconsfield, now seventy-four, led the British team, and was delighted to discover how many people were reading Disraeli's novels.

The Balkan states were deeply unhappy with the results. The Bulgarians were furious because Britain insisted that it would be safer to carve the country into three smaller states. The Romanians had to surrender Bessarabia, the Serbs acquired little new territory. Bosnia and Herzegovina were horrified when placed under Austrian administration, Britain feeling that an Austrian occupation was the simplest way to prevent a dangerous chain of small states in the Balkan Peninsula. Yet this move led directly to Sarajevo and the First World War. The Turks, in fact, lost little in the way of territory, and Abdul Hamid's empire was still greater than Germany, France and Austria put together. The Russians suffered a major blow – the Balkans had slipped through their fingers – though they had recovered Bessarabia and extended their Asian empire. But, above all, Russia was denied access to the Mediterranean, which she had hoped to reach through the Bulgarian back door. 'And that,' as Disraeli wrote to Queen Victoria, 'was the real object of the late war.' The Russian General, Prince Gortchakov, said bitterly, 'We have sacrificed a hundred thousand picked soldiers and a hundred million of money for nothing.'

But what really infuriated the Russians was that Britain, amidst the confusion, managed to pick up the island of Cyprus. 'Trust the Englishwoman,' one wrote to the Czar, 'to land a fish from the troubled waters.'

*

Despite its size the Ottoman Empire was, in fact, now down and out, and the Young Turks plotting in exile – with Midhat Pasha lecturing in Geneva or Paris – became an added source of terror to the Sultan. There had already been one unsuccessful attempt on his life, and when the Czar Alexander II was assassinated by Nihilists the Sultan's terror was so abject that for days he would only eat food cooked by the Queen Mother, and would never go to his bed until it had been thoroughly searched. More and more he became convinced that Turkish revolutionaries were plotting his death and, since foreign newspapers regularly reported the activities of Midhat, the exiled Pasha soon became, in the semi-deranged mind of the Sultan, the one man above all others he feared.

He decided that Midhat must die, and a plan to this end was born when a sycophantic courtier who hated Midhat suggested that the late Sultan Abdul Aziz had not died from self-inflicted wounds caused by his scissors but had been murdered by assassins hired by Midhat. Abdul Hamid seized on the story. But where was the proof? There were living witnesses, he was told, and Pertevalé, the ex-Queen Mother, now living in 'retirement' at the long-abandoned Grand Seraglio, would have a very different story to tell now to the one she had babbled incoherently in her first moments of grief.

On a bleak, windy March day, the Sultan, warmed by his sable-lined coat, set off for the old Grand Seraglio to find out for himself if the story were true. It must have been a moment of great pathos and poignancy when the harem heard of his visit, for this was, in effect, an old ladies' home. Behind the Gate of Felicity lived the remnants of the harems of three reigns – women, now old and toothless, who had been loved either by the great Mahmud, by Mejid or Aziz. For years they had seen no man but the eunuchs. Now, however, as the rain pelted down on the leafless trees in the deserted gardens, the ladies of yesterday reached for their powder and paint and their finest jewels.

All in vain. The Sultan made his way immediately to the apartments of Pertevalé, looking neither to right nor left. The ex-Queen Mother had been forewarned of the purpose of his visit, and because at the time of Aziz's 'suicide' she had indirectly shared in the guilt for his death by handing him the fatal scissors she was now only too grateful to retract her first story. No persuasion was necessary for her to believe, or pretend to believe, that Midhat had hired a palace gardener and wrestler to stab her son to death. She even 'remembered' a tiny mark made by a stiletto which she had forgotten to mention three years previously.

Pertevalé was sworn to secrecy, for one last hurdle had to be overcome. Midhat must be lured back to Constantinople from the comfort of Switzerland. The Sultan cabled him personally that 'all was forgiven', that his banishment was ended, that his country needed him. Would he return to help Turkey, still reeling from the body blows it had received? Abdul Hamid banked on the fact that above all Midhat was a patriot. In fact, within a matter of weeks Midhat walked straight into the trap, and was arrested and charged with regicide.

The farcical state trial of Midhat Pasha and the two alleged assassins took place in a large oval green tent at Yildiz, the court packed day after day as scores of witnesses were called. Not that many were needed after the first day when the gardener and wrestler both admitted they had been bribed by Midhat to murder Abdul Aziz. But this trial had to convince not only the Turks, but Europe. So day by day damning evidence was piled up against the great reformer. Then came the defence. Midhat spiritedly denied all charges – until he was curtly informed that he would not be allowed to cross-examine the prosecution witnesses. From that moment the verdict was a foregone conclusion. The 'conspirators' were immediately sentenced to death.

There can be little doubt that the trial was rigged. The gardener and wrestler were never executed, but lived comfortably for the rest of their lives on pensions granted by the Sultan. Nor was Midhat executed – not immediately. Bowing to outraged world opinion, Abdul Hamid commuted the sentence to one of banishment to Taif in Arabia, a country under the Sultan's firm jurisdiction. Yet, even so, the Sultan still dreaded Midhat more than any man alive, and after biding his time for two years he had the great Turkish reformer strangled. Even that was not enough. Abdul Hamid needed proof, and was not satisfied until the victim's embalmed head was sent to Yildiz. (According to one version, the head arrived from Taif in a packing-case addressed, 'Japanese Ivories – To be personally delivered to His Majesty the Sultan.')

Whatever the method, the Sultan had, as Sir Henry Elliot summed up, 'secured an iniquitous conviction . . . but it was at the cost of an indelible blot upon his reign'.

*

Abdul Hamid had lost a war against Russia; he had traitorously trapped the leading Turkish reformer of the day; but now the Sultan was responsible for an even more staggering defeat: he managed to lose the huge vassal state of Egypt to Britain without a Turkish rifle being fired. And this despite the fact that Britain begged the Sultan for cooperation.

Egypt was only nominally a Turkish province, and the Khedive of Egypt had assumed the airs of an independent sovereign. But by 1879 Egypt's debts were so staggering that the Khedive put himself, financially speaking, into the hands of France and Britain. It was then that Britain bought its shares in the Suez Canal for a niggardly £100,000. When in 1882 Egypt flamed into revolt against 'foreign financial domination', Suez had to be guarded, and since the country was a Turkish province Britain wanted, indeed insisted, on Anglo-Turkish cooperation. In vain the British Ambassador tried to convince the Sultan that it was in his own interest not to lose his hold, however tenuous it might be, on Egypt, where the rebel leader, Arabi, was inciting the sheiks to launch a Holy War.

Abdul Hamid dithered. He condemned the Egyptians, still nominally his vassals, but he would not, or dared not, ally himself openly with the British against the Arabs. He took consolation from the advice of his Court Astrologer, Abdul Huba, who wielded enormous power over the superstitious Sultan and had told Abdul Hamid that Britain would never go to war alone in Egypt. The crisis came on 15 September 1882 when the British Ambassador made a last attempt to persuade the Sultan to act. He was kept waiting at Yilditz for five hours. All hints that he was pressed for time were met with bland smiles from the eunuchs, and innumerable cups of coffee. Finally, 'A tall thin figure in flowing silk appeared, moving silently in the direction of the Sultan's apartments.' It was Abdul Huba. Half an hour later, the Sultan sent a message that the stars precluded him from reaching a decision.

Though less spectacular than some of Abdul Hamid's many follies, this was perhaps the greatest single mistake he made, for now Britain moved into Egypt alone and quickly stamped out the rebellion. The occupation was described as 'provisional'; but for the Ottoman Empire the loss was permanent.

Within a few years, the chain of events that had cost him Egypt was followed by the first link in another chain – one that would eventually drag Turkey into the German side in the First World War.

Relations between Turkey and Germany had changed considerably since the seventies when Bismarck snorted, 'I never even trouble to open the mailbag from Constantinople.' There was a personal reason behind the change. Abdul Hamid had for long been quietly transferring Treasury bonds into the neutral safety of German banks. Understandably he came to admire the Germans, who in their turn wanted railway concessions, not only for the Hejaz railway along which Abdul Hamid planned to carry the pious making the pilgrimage to Mecca, but in commerce, banking and, subversively, politics. It was the famous policy which the Austrians had pursued in vain – *Drang Nach Osten*, the 'Trend towards the East', and which now became purely German.

So the Kaiser, Wilhelm II, paid a state visit to Constantinople, arriving on 2 November 1889, to the boom of a 101-gun salute. Abdul Hamid was only forty-seven, but he looked much older. His beard was grey, his body emaciated; but he was determined to give the Kaiser a taste of oriental splendour. The State dinner for 120 guests was served on the solid gold, gem-studded plates which Abdul Aziz had ordered from Paris. Even the goblets were encrusted with jewels. Chefs imported from Paris prepared a sumptuous meal, though the Sultan, afraid of poison and dyspepsia, ate only rice and eggs cooked in his iron-barred kitchen.

During the five-day visit the Kaiser was shown the treasures of the Seraglio, and he had only to admire an item for it to be presented to him; and when the Empress congratulated the Sultan on his beautiful gardens Abdul Hamid himself picked a bouquet for her, whispered to an aide, and finally presented the flowers to the Empress, nature being adorned with a huge diamond nestling in the flowers.

(The German state visit was touched by one item of unintended humour. When the Empress visited the harem, she was met at the Gate of Felicity by the Kislar Aga, and it was explained to her that the Chief Black Eunuch was a highly important personage; at which the Empress, trying to make conversation – and knowing nothing of eunuchs – brightly asked the Kislar Aga through the interpreter whether his father had also been a eunuch.)

The Kaiser had hardly left Constantinople when quite by chance the beautiful Empress Elizabeth of Austria was assassinated by an Italian anarchist. What perturbed the crazed mind of Abdul Hamid was not the murder itself but the fact that the murderer – crying 'Long Live Anarchy' – admitted at his trial that his only grievance against the Empress was that she wore a crown.* From that day onwards, the Sultan always wore a shirt of mail under his drab frock coat when he went to Friday prayers. Yilditz became more of a fortress. Every door was lined with steel,

---

* The assassin had intended to kill King Umberto of Italy as a protest, but he could not raise the extra fifty lire needed for the journey to Rome, so assassinated Elizabeth instead.

and an army of workmen started increasing the number of secret passages. Though the 'Young Turks' as a party consisted of exiles plotting in Paris, the Sultan's spies continued to provide him with disturbing evidence that their doctrines were finding increasing favour inside Turkey. Intelligent young Turks were uneasily ashamed at what was happening, at the way in which power had corrupted, at the manner in which the limbs of the Empire were being dismembered. And they had useful allies particularly among underpaid schoolmasters with 'revolutionary' tendencies. It was all very well for the wealthy, who had been able since 1888 to travel on the grandiloquently named Orient Express all the way from Paris to Constantinople, or who could communicate by telegraph in seconds to a distant town or city; but, for the poor in the interior, the roads, which still followed the tracks of the Greek Empire, were still tracks, often impassable. A bridge washed away by flood was rarely repaired. For the peasants this meant incredible difficulties in transport so that at times the people of one valley would starve while their neighbours a few miles away lived in plenty. (In all the Middle East the only good road had been constructed by the French between Beirut and Damascus.)

The intellectuals inside Turkey could not yet achieve the status of a 'party' – the spy system was too powerful, and the torture chamber at Yilditz resounded nightly with the screams of those at the forced confessional. But news from the exiles, numbering many thousands, did trickle through, and Abdul Hamid was discovering that it was infiltrating not only the schoolteachers ('that hotbed of revolt' as he described them) but also the younger army officers, some of whom the Sultan had foolishly (from his point of view) sent to Germany for training. They despised the Sultan. They wanted a leader in the tradition of the sultans of old, who would ride at the head of his troops when they marched into battle.

Perhaps it was this terror of plots that finally caused Abdul Hamid to organize and direct a ruthless plan of extermination against the Armenians that far surpassed the Turkish butchery of the Bulgarians.

Of all races which the Ottoman Empire subjected to intolerance, the two million Armenians suffered most. Their history had been long and hard. Some historians say their forebears were one of the Ten Lost Tribes, which would account for their resemblance to the Jews; and, like the Jews, they had dispersed across the face of the earth, mingling but never fusing after their country, round Mount Ararat, where Noah's Ark traditionally landed, was ravaged by the Mongols in the tenth century.

Because of their aptitude for commerce and finance they stood out in nineteenth-century Turkey, both as industrious peasant workers in the six north-eastern provinces where most lived, and as men of commerce in the cities. Lamartine called them the Swiss of the East: 'Regular in their habits, they resemble them also in calculation and love of gain. Commerce is their god and they would engage in it under any master.'

The half-mad Sultan banned the word 'Armenian' in all newspapers, even school text-books, which in many cases had to be reprinted. When he suddenly discovered that a man who for years had regulated the hundreds of clocks in Yildiz was an Armenian, he reached for a revolver, and would have shot him had he not run for his life.

Many honest Moslems felt thoroughly ashamed of the manner in which Armenians were treated. The British Consul, Sir Alfred Billiotti, received one letter from a Moslem who wrote that:

It is impossible to give an idea of the state of things. Tyrannized over, robbed, and driven from their lands by Government officials and agas, Moslems as well as Christians shed tears of blood. The aspect of the country is desolate. No care is taken to preserve or restock the forests. The villages are only collections of mud huts in plains devoid of trees, water, gardens, or vegetables. The inhabitants are coarsely fed and coarsely clad. Neither roads nor bridges are in a serviceable state. There hardly remains a single public building whose interior or exterior is not partially in ruins. The nomad population is constantly entering the settled districts.

Perhaps the Turks liked the Armenians because they were at heart oriental, nearer the Turks in ideas and habits than the Greeks or Albanians, so that they felt, like Moltke, that, 'An Armenian is but a baptized Turk.'

Now Armenians outside Turkey – many of them influential in the United States, Britain and Russia – started demanding better living conditions for their brothers in the Ottoman Empire. They did not ask for autonomy. Most Turkish Armenians were content to remain members of the Empire whose north-east corner was the home of their race. They asked only for administrative reforms, security, respect for their women and property.

Unfortunately, the relatives abroad were at times too zealous; and they were often the tools of Russians anxious to provoke trouble, so that though nothing could excuse the massacres which followed they were certainly due in some cases to deliberate provocation by the Armenians or their 'friends'.

In 1894, following serious outbreaks, the Sultan decided to teach them a lesson. As he said after a quiet dinner to Professor Vambery, 'I will soon settle those Armenians. I will give them a box on the ears which will make them smart and relinquish their revolutionary ambitions.'

He sent agents to every area inhabited by Armenians. They were armed with express instructions to tell the Moslems in those areas that they could take by force any goods belonging to the Armenians and kill them if they resisted. It was the beginning of a cold, calculated campaign in which at least a hundred thousand men, women and children were slaughtered.

Massacre had always been regarded in the Ottoman Empire as a legitimate arm of warfare, but perhaps the single most horrifying factor – apart from the murders themselves – of the atrocities that followed was the manner in which the butchery started, not as a result of savage, inflamed passions, but with the cold precision of the professional obeying a signal, usually a trumpet sounded with the impersonal indifference of a factory hooter. As sundown approached, another trumpet proclaimed that the day's activities were over, and like workers at the end of a shift the Ottoman troops returned to their camps to await the following morning's call to arms.

The massacres were to put the last nail in Abdul Hamid's coffin. Their significance in the history of the Empire lay in the fact that Abdul Hamid was the mastermind behind every outrage; no detail was too small to escape his attention. From every area his agents sent daily reports. He knew every single fact, and never once was he stirred by the slightest twinge of compassion for peasants whose only crime had been a half-hearted uprising against the exactions of the Moslems. Significantly, many of his subjects joined the outside world in their condemnation of the Sultan's creed of extermination. During the three years of the intermittent massacres thousands of pious Moslems, sickened by the debauchery, sheltered their Armenian neighbours.

At times like this, the dead became statistics and unreal; but, despite the most rigorous censorship, stories of savage torture, prison murders, burnings began to come out in unexpected ways. In many cases Moslems smuggled letters out for Armenians whom they had known for years. At other times chance played its part. Details of the massacre at Trebizond, in which every Christian in the city was killed, came from the captain of an Austrian Lloyd's steamer who saw Armenians caught and drowned by Moslem boatmen as they tried to swim to freedom. A member of the British Embassy, Gerald Fitzmaurice, gave the world the first details of how three thousand men, women and children were deliberately roasted alive inside the cathedral at Urfa. The Armenian families had gone to the cathedral, large enough for a congregation of several thousand, in the mistaken belief that no Moslem would molest them in a house of God. For the moment, their faith seemed justified. They were surrounded by a double ring of troops. At the midday prayer on the Saturday a priest waved a green flag, emblem of the Moslem faith, as a signal for a general attack in the city. Every house in the Armenian quarter of Trebizond was plundered, and then began a ghastly ritual slaughter. In the words of Fitzmaurice, 'A certain sheik ordered his followers to bring as many stalwart young Armenians as he could find. To the number of about a hundred they were thrown on their backs and held down by their hands and feet, while the sheik, with a combination of fanaticism and cruelty, proceeded, while reciting verses of the Koran, to cut their throats after the Mecca rite of sacrificing sheep.'

Shortly before sunset a bugle sounded and the butchery ceased. The next morning, Sunday 29 December, the trumpet called the troops out. This time their target was the cathedral, whose flock had obviously expected the worst, for Fitzmaurice found a record written on one of the cathedral pillars by an Armenian priest, stating that on the Saturday night he had administered a last communion to 1,800 people.

The Turks started firing through the windows. Then the iron door was smashed in, and troops killed everyone on the ground floor, the women and children having fled to a large gallery running round three sides of the cathedral.

Because many had spent the night in the church it was strewn with straw mattresses. Thirty tins of petrol were poured over them, and set alight. Everyone who had not been killed was burned alive. At precisely

3.30 p.m. a trumpet sounded and the Moslem troops withdrew.

An attack on a smaller scale was to have repercussions in another part of the world. Two Armenian professors working for the American missionary college at Marsovan were accused of printing seditious leaflets. They were brought to trial at Angora in chains and condemned to death. And for the first time in Ottoman history Abdul Hamid had to face not only the violent reaction of Europe, but the wrath and outraged horror of the American nation.

The American Minister in Constantinople at the time was Judge Terrell, 'a rough-hewn Texan' whom the Sultan disliked intensely because he chewed tobacco and spat whenever he felt like it. Yet Abdul Hamid felt he had to see him and 'explain'. He invited the entire Terrell family to dinner at Yilditz and listened patiently to an hour's lecture on the art of government. Terrell told His Majesty that he was 'a plain man, unused to courts, but confident that truth was a commodity that rarely reached the ears of Sultans'.

Terrell recounted details of the dinner to young Arthur Nicolson (father of the late Sir Harold Nicolson) of the British Embassy, confiding that he thought he had hit the mark because of 'the way the Sultan hung his head and sighed'; indeed Terrell was now convinced that Abdul Hamid 'was the best man that ever breathed and only his agents were vile'. Nicolson's tart reaction was much crisper. 'The U.S. Minister has been nobbled by the Sultan,' he noted.

Even so, American indignation was so bitter that the Sultan also felt it wise to receive one of the world's greatest princes of the Press – Gordon Bennett of the *New York Herald* – who persuaded him to allow a *Herald* reporter to visit the Armenian provinces. The Sultan agreed, provided an independent 'commissioner' accompanied him, and the man chosen was the Reverend George Hepworth, a Presbyterian who dabbled in journalism, and who, in a model example of impartiality, wrote that, 'It would be but a moderate estimate to say that fifty thousand were killed.' The figure, he added, took no note of those who died from cold or exposure.

Within a year, Armenian 'revolutionaries', who had nothing to lose, fought back – in Constantinople of all places, and in a daring bank raid bearing a startling resemblance to those of the present day.

In broad daylight in the last week of August 1896, twenty desperate men armed with bombs seized the premises of the Ottoman Bank. Their objective was not money but rather to draw the attention of Britain and America to the plight of the Armenians.

For three hours the men rained bombs on the police outside until the foreign embassies, all of whom used the bank, negotiated a surrender after promising a safe conduct. The British director of the Bank, Sir Edgar Vincent, played the leading role in this 'cynical but essentially practical policy'. At the first alarm he had crawled to safety across the roof of the building and it was he who persuaded the embassies to use their influence with the Sultan. The twenty desperadoes were escorted to Sir Edgar's yacht while seven thousand Armenians in Constantinople were butchered in revenge.

And yet, the 'bank robbers' did achieve their aim. Trebizond and Urfa might still be only distant names to many people, but once the massacres started in the streets of Constantinople itself, diplomats, the rich, even tourists were suddenly confronted with the same horrors. Arthur Nicolson found that, 'Venice in its darkest days was light and freedom compared to the Stamboul of today.'

The reaction was swift. Diplomats reported urgently to London. Within days an open telegram signed by every European power warned Abdul Hamid to stop the massacres immediately. If the situation continued, said the telegram, 'it would imperil both the Sultan's throne and his dynasty'.

In fact, only one final push was needed to overthrow the last of the Ottoman despots. It came from within.

Chapter twelve
The brave and the damned

The Armenian massacres had not been isolated episodes, but an attempt at genocide, sustained on and off with varying savagery for three years. The effect on people was a sense of shame that mounted each time evidence of a new atrocity was unfolded. Abdul Hamid had earned himself the title of 'Abdul the Damned'.

Scores of disillusioned Turks were fleeing the country to join the Young Turks abroad. Even the Sultan's brother-in-law, Mahmud Damat, fled to Paris with his two sons and put himself at the service of the exiles. So did one of their bravest early members, Niazi Bey, a young lieutenant who was also disgusted by corruption in the Army and Civil Service. Unwisely he voiced his criticisms, and the Sultan's spies were soon tapping the information back to Yilditz by telegraph. Fortunately for Niazi, many spies were also becoming disaffected, and he was warned in time to flee to Paris.

Niazi, a man of action, decided to return to Turkey in disguise. Dressed as a Turkish hawker, he was smuggled first to Smyrna. He travelled all over, sometimes as a hawker, at others as a begging dervish or a teacher. He boldly spread the doctrine of revolution, particularly among army units. Everywhere he found a growing hatred of Abdul Hamid, so that it was not difficult to organize the first revolutionary cells inside the country.

Meanwhile the Sultan was becoming even more of a recluse. He now often refused to attend the Friday prayers but sent Izzet, whose likeness was so uncanny that he could 'warm his clothes', even for state occasions. Those who did see the Sultan around the turn of the century found his long, melancholy face the colour of ashes. His clothes hung on his body, his fez seemed too large for his head as he shuffled from one room to another. His suspicious nature was now matched by an uncontrollable temper and he would never allow a man to put his hands in his pockets in his presence. When Sadyk Pasha, one of his innumerable ex-viziers dipped into his pocket to hand the Sultan a document, he nearly lost his life and was dismissed in disgrace. The Sultan's fear of poison was still so dominant that he would never open letters himself, because of possible contamination. Yet he seemed unaware of the precise nature of the unrest bubbling under the surface, probably because the Young Turks were now beginning to have their own spies in all government departments and among the five thousand people living in Yilditz. The only interest the Sultan seemed to take in any reforms concerned the harem where his sultanas were now dressing in tea-gowns from Paris and whalebone corsets, never before seen in Turkey. Comfortable slippers were replaced with tight patent-leather shoes. Artificial flowers were all the rage, standing on the gimcrack furniture which arrived from every capital in Europe. The face of Constantinople was changing as the twentieth century was born. Horse trams clattered along some streets. Though the streets were badly lit and no one went out at night without a guard, the new hotels blazed with light because the Sultan wanted the tourists' money. He firmly refused, however, to allow telephones to be installed because his ministers, aghast at the prospect of the Sultan on the end of a line twenty-four hours a day, persuaded him that his enemies would be able to listen-in to his conversations.

Abdul Hamid had now become a living legend, particularly when the new century coincided with his Silver Jubilee. Twice he barely escaped assassination: in 1904 a young officer tried to stab him outside his private theatre at Yilditz, and a year later a carriage loaded with dynamite exploded outside the Mosque as the Sultan attended Friday prayers.

Hundreds of innocent people were tortured as the Sultan tried in vain to discover how the dynamite had got past his trusted guards. The truth was that the bomb attack was only one sign of increasing sabotage instigated by the revolutionary cells inside the Empire, all unswervingly loyal to the exiled Young Turks, who by now had changed their name to the more portentous Committee of Union and Progress.

By 1906 the Committee felt strong enough to form their central base in Salonika, then the capital of Macedonia, for long a hotbed of hatred for the Sultan, doubtless because Macedonia, more than any other Turkish province, was composed of many different races – Turks, Greeks,

Serbs, Bulgars, Albanians, Bosnians and the largest group of Jews in the Empire. In short, Macedonia was the ideal spot from which to launch a revolution. Niazi Bey planned the operation in conjunction with a brilliant young officer called Enver Bey, a graduate of the Turkish Military Staff College. Conveniently Niazi had been forgiven by the Sultan and reinstated in the Army with the rank of major, an admirable cover for revolutionary tactics, which he now employed more circumspectly than before.

From time to time there were outbreaks of violence, though there did not seem to be much coordination among the revolutionaries in various parts of the country, but Abdul Hamid accepted them as part of an established pattern; probably his spies had for so long been feeding him with reports of disaffection in the Army that when they at last urged him to take action, 'The spies found themselves in the position of the boy who cried "wolf" too often.'

He did, however, send a commission to Salonika in May 1908 to investigate – a step which precipitated events, for on 11 June the officer in charge was shot as he left for the capital to hand in his report. The Sultan immediately sent a replacement, and suddenly the Committee realized that, as they were the focus of Abdul Hamid's attention, they must act before the Sultan. Six days later an Inspector of Police was shot, and a number of army officers were arrested.

Niazi and Enver struck on 2 July 1908. Niazi broke open the Mess safe and stole his battalion funds, then made off for the mountains behind Lake Ochrida with a small band of loyal followers. At the same time Enver deserted from Rezna with 150 men. For the first time in five centuries the standard of revolt had been raised by the Moslems themselves.

Abdul Hamid does not seem to have sensed how perilous his position had become. In his eyes, Macedonia had always been a centre of disaffection, and presumably he thought that a battalion of troops would soon settle the problem. Niazi was branded as a traitor and outlaw, but the Sultan did decide to woo Enver back to the fold. He was recalled to Constantinople with the promise of preferment. Enver did not even answer the Sultan's personal invitation, at which Abdul Hamid immediately despatched eight hundred troops to Monastir in Northern Macedonia. The troops refused to fire on their comrades. Instead they assassinated two of their senior officers; one was openly shot in the street. The news spread like a bush fire, and from every corner of Macedonia Turkish garrisons rushed to join the colours of Enver Bey. The entire Third Army Corps revolted, including a fiery, revolutionary officer called Mustafa Kemal. The Second Army Corps followed suit.

Events now moved with astonishing swiftness. On 23 July, the Young Turks in a formal ultimatum from Monastir informed the Sultan that unless the constitution drawn up by Midhat Pasha was restored within twenty-four hours the Second and Third Army Corps would march on Constantinople.

To the Sultan this would mean an abject admission of defeat for a policy of oppression from which he had never wavered since he had exiled Midhat. Yet to refuse could mean civil war. For the first time in years he asked his Council of Ministers to discuss the matter. Almost all were in favour of conceding to the Young Turks, but now, with every minister aware of the vindictive temper of the Sultan, a problem arose. They had made their decision but no one could be found with the courage to tell the Sultan personally. All knew that if he were in a rage he might easily draw a pistol.

At last, a messenger was found – none other than Abdul Huba, the court astrologer, who had lost Egypt for the Empire, but one of the few men the superstitious Sultan respected. Abdul Huba was a man with a keen, intelligent mind, afraid of no one, and the councillors tactfully suggested that their decisions might be more welcome to the Sultan if his astrologer announced them as being inspired by a message from the heavenly bodies. To encourage the astrologer to emphasize how close was the threat of civil war, he was given access to the stream of warning telegrams arriving hourly from all corners of the Empire.

That night, alone at Yilditz with one of the few men he trusted, the Sultan was told by his court astrologer that the stars favoured an accommodation with the Young Turks. Abdul Hamid did not hesitate to follow his trusted counsellor: that evening he sent telegrams to Macedonia, and on the next morning, 24 July, a staggered and unbelieving Constantinople woke to find a message from the Sultan in the morning newspapers proclaiming the restoration of Midhat's constitution.

There was a day of frenzied rejoicing in Constantinople. As Joan Haslip wrote in *The Sultan: the Life of Abdul Hamid*: 'Eye-witnesses in Constantinople described the amazing scenes which took place in the square of Aya Sofia and Galata Bridge, when Greeks and Bulgars, Kurds and Armenians embraced one another as brothers and Young Turk officers harangued the crowds, telling them that Jews, Christians and Moslems were no longer divided, but all working together for the glory of the Ottoman nation. Caught on the swelling tide of enthusiasm, softas and mollahs were seen wearing the red-and-white cockade of liberty. Even the shopkeepers, leaving their shops wide open, and the guild of butchers in their white overalls joined in with the crowds which surged round the Sublime Porte, cheering for the Sultan and the Constitution.'

For four days the rejoicing hardly ceased, culminating when a crowd of nearly seventy thousand burst into the courtyard of Yilditz to hail the Sultan who had provided for them a new dawn. Few, if any, had ever seen him, but now nothing would stop the crowd's wave of emotion but the appearance of the Sultan on a balcony, and they had their first glimpse of the master of Yilditz looking a trifle pathetic as he blinked at them in the sunlight.

It was as though the Empire had wakened from a fearful nightmare, and the optimism was instant and infectious. In the town of Drama, a Turk was thrown into jail for insulting a Christian. At Serres, the head of the Bulgarian Committee embraced the Greek Archbishop. Turks reverently attended a memorial service in an Armenian cemetery for victims of the Armenian massacres. And in the wild excitement it was all too easy for the mass of people to hail Abdul Hamid as their liberator, to believe that it was the palace cliques who had deliberately kept the Sultan in ignorance of the truth.

It was this that prevented the Young Turks from immediately deposing Abdul Hamid. 'The Committee of Union and Progress did not feel strong enough to force the issue in 1908,' wrote Dr Ernest Ramsaur in *The Young Turks*. 'The Sultan had stolen their thunder to some extent by giving in to the demands for the restoration of the constitution and had even been fairly successful in making it appear that the idea was his own,' but 'the exalted position which he occupied still blinded the Turkish people to his real character.' Enver in fact had to be content with demoting the Sultan to the role of constitutional monarch, robbed of most of his power.

Abdul Hamid's popularity was not so evident in Macedonia where the dashing Enver Bey, resplendent in a new uniform, drove in a triumphant procession through the streets of Salonika, escorted by an artillery regiment, with a band blaring out the 'Marseillaise'.

With the Sultan now only a constitutional monarch, the Committee set about reducing the vast overheads of his entourage. His theatre was closed, two hundred musicians were dismissed, his three hundred aides-de-camp reduced to thirty and his stud farm taken over by the State. The Young Turks ordered the Sultan, who had dismissed his Cabinet, to issue a royal decree abolishing espionage. And in the general election which followed, men of all races and religions voted for the new parliament which was inaugurated on 17 December.

It must have been a memorable scene. Snow whitened the beautiful city on a crisp, cold day, with the sun glinting on the minarets. A procession formed up in the great square of Aya Sofia with the scarlet flags of the Star and Crescent vivid against a bright blue sky. All the panoply of the past glittered in the first real show of pomp since the frock-coat became the national costume. Zouaves in their green turbans, Albanians in their white skirts, mitred priests in flowing robes, paid homage to the Sultan as he led the procession to the Parliament House, filled with newly elected members, including three men destined to lead the new Turkey in its first stumbling steps towards democracy: the dashing, perfumed Enver, whose photographs were sold by the thousands in the streets; the swarthy Talaat who looked not unlike a gipsy, and was said to be the brains of the party; and Djemel Bey, once the willing page-boy of a pasha who preferred pages to paramours, but whose gallantry in the Salonika uprising was already legendary. Three ill-assorted men who, alas, in the end, were found sadly wanting.

*

Nursing a nation from despotism to democracy was not easy, particularly as foreign powers quickly moved into the arena. Prince Ferdinand of Coburg proclaimed himself Czar of an independent Bulgaria, formed by the fusion of Bulgaria and Eastern Rumelia; Austria-Hungary annexed Bosnia and Herzegovina, which she had been 'administering' for the Sultan since 1878. Crete announced a union with Greece. As all these limbs were unceremoniously lopped off the Empire, the Committee made only formal protests, presumably regarding them as the price they must pay for foreign recognition and help. But the effect on the average Turk of this wholesale dismemberment of his cherished empire was to rouse him to open indignation; and it did not take long for this growl of protest to pass through the gates of Yilditz and reach the ears of Abdul Hamid.

It is difficult not to believe that Abdul Hamid was behind the disorder that followed; that it was his money which bribed the Albanian troops to break out against the Committee; that he was bribing thousands of spies, now out of jobs which had cost the government £1·2 million a year. Certainly many people began to believe that their only hope for the future lay in restoring the Sultan's powers. They were encouraged by a small section of fanatical priests and inadvertently helped by hundreds of criminals who had been granted an amnesty and now started to terrorize the city and countryside.

On 13 April 1909, troops in Constantinople revolted and a counter-revolution was proclaimed. It did not appear to have any leader, for Abdul Hamid kept carefully in the background. All members of the Committee of Union and Progress were forced to flee, and if Abdul Hamid had had the courage to come out into the open he might have kept his throne.

He did not – and lost all. Within a fortnight, troops from Salonika, loyal to Enver, were marching on Constantinople. On 23 April, a cold, bright spring morning, as Abdul Hamid was dressing for the Friday prayers, he heard the sound of gunfire. Enver had reached the Golden Horn and was advancing towards the Taxim barracks in the centre of the city. Here the garrison had prepared for a siege, but after a four-hour battle Enver, with great dash and bravery, personally led his troops in storming the barricades under heavy shellfire. By sundown he controlled most of the city and his men were encamped less than a mile from Yilditz.

The Sultan, incredibly, had no real knowledge of what was happening, even when the guns stopped firing, since none of his eunuchs or chamberlains dared to tell him. All he did know was that his personal garrison at Yilditz had not been brought to battle. In fact, he was completely cut off; his royal yacht had been taken over by the Salonikans, who also ringed the vast park. Abdul Hamid spent much of that night on a divan listening

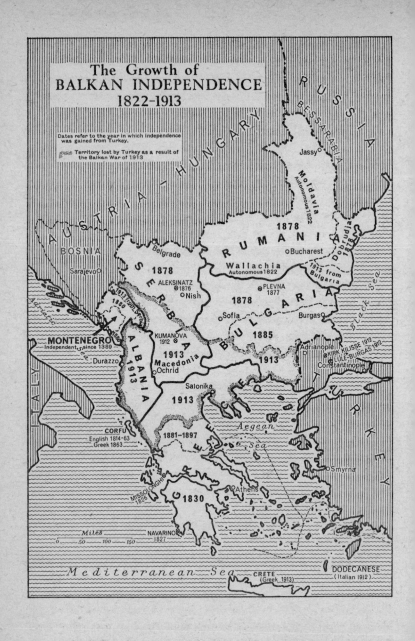

The Growth of
BALKAN INDEPENDENCE
1822-1913

Dates refer to the year in which independence
was gained from Turkey.

Territory lost by Turkey as a result of
the Balkan War of 1913

RUSSIA

AUSTRIA - HUNGARY

BESSARABIA

Jassy

BOSNIA

Sarajevo

Belgrade

Moldavia
Autonomous 1822

1878
RUMANIA

Bucharest

Wallachia
Autonomous 1822

Dobrudja
1878

1913 from
Bulgaria

1878
SERBIA

ALEKSINATZ
1876
Nish

PLEVNA
1877

1878
BULGARIA

Sofia

Burgas

Black Sea

MONTENEGRO
Independent since 1389

1913 from Serbia
1880

KUMANOVA
1912

1913
Macedonia
Ochrid

1885

1913

Adrianople
KIRK KILISSE 1912
LULE-BURGAS 1912
Constantinople

Durazzo

ALBANIA
1913

Salonika

1913

ITALY

Adriatic Sea

TURKEY

CORFU
English 1814-63
Greek 1863

1881-1897

Aegean
Sea

Smyrna

MISSOLONGHI
1826

1830

Athens

Miles
0   50   100   150

NAVARINO
1827

Mediterranean Sea

CRETE
(Greek 1913)

DODECANESE
(Italian 1912)

to a page reading aloud from an English book. It was *The Adventures of Sherlock Holmes*.

Even as Saturday dawned, the farcical life of Yildiz continued. When gunfire woke the Sultan he dashed out in his dressing-gown to ask a eunuch what was happening and was told, 'Your Majesty's loyal soldiers are crushing the rebels.' In fact Enver had opened the assault on Yildiz itself.

As it became clear to everybody else that the Sultan's garrison would soon be overwhelmed, the parasites who had lived on the Sultan's bounty began to flee in their hundreds. By evening a bare handful of servants were left. The cooking fires had gone out. The electricity no longer worked. And in all the kiosks of the vast, dark park no one could even find a candle. For the first time in thirty-three years Abdul Hamid ate a cold supper that had not been prepared in his personal kitchen. It was the servants' leftovers, all the few eunuchs who remained could find in the deserted pantries.

One problem faced the Committee. What to do with the Sultan? The counter-revolution had clearly shown that they must tread warily. Any thought of assassination was out of the question. The revolutionaries must be seen to treat the head of the Empire with constitutional decorum; so they fell back on the age-old Ottoman formula of asking the Sheik-Ul-Islam. To him they put this question:

What should be done with a Commander of the Faithful who has suppressed books and important dispositions of the Shenel Law; who forbids the reading of, and burns, such books; who wastes public money for improper purposes; who, without legal authority, kills, imprisons, and tortures his subjects and commits tyrannical acts; who, after he has bound himself by oath to amend, violates such oath and persists in sowing discord so as to disturb the public peace, thus occasioning bloodshed?

From various provinces the news comes that the population has deposed him; and it is known that to maintain him is manifestly dangerous and his deposition is advantageous.

Under these conditions, is it permissible for the actual governing body to decide as seems best upon his abdication or deposition?

In his white-and-gold robes, his head under a huge yellow turban, the Sheik answered, 'Yes.' It was enough for the National Assembly to make its decision, and on the morning of 27 April a committee of four parliamentarians – an Albanian, a Greek, a Jew and an Armenian – went to announce that decision to the Sultan.

One of them, General Essad, remembered the atmosphere of apprehension, almost fear, that seemed to engulf them as they sat in the Tchitli Kiosk, a long one-storeyed building with a secret door to the harem. They were guarded by thirty terrified eunuchs as they waited to meet the man who for so long had dominated every life in Turkey. 'His presence seemed to fill the room.' On one table stood his bottle of medicine. Peeping out from behind a stove were his galoshes. In one corner was a crumpled heap of old reports from spies. A tin of cheap cigarettes stood on a table next to the greasy stub of a candle. On the floor between the inevitable piano and a large Japanese screen lay a pile of cigarette ends. The deputation could see each other's faces whichever way they looked, reflected in the mirrors placed strategically on each wall.

Without warning the door opened and in walked the Sultan dressed in a military greatcoat hanging over his skeletal thinness. To the General, the only one who had met him before, Abdul Hamid seemed even smaller than he remembered as he waited with quiet dignity for the customary ceremonial greetings. Then he asked, 'What do you want?'

Essad replied, 'The nation has deposed you, and we are charged with the security of you and your family.' And because this straightforward soldier still could not quite absolve himself from loyalty to the Sultan, he added quietly, 'You have nothing to fear, sir.'

For a long time there was no sound in the room except the ticking of eleven clocks. Then, still maintaining his dignity, the Sultan, using the words of his uncle in similar circumstances, said simply, 'It is Kismet. I am not guilty. Will my life be spared?'

It was. His brother, Reshid, promptly rechristened Mahomet V, ascended the throne. To the Young Turks who wanted no fuss from the Sultanate, he had at least one qualification which no doubt pleased them greatly: his confession that, 'I have not read a newspaper for twenty years.'

Abdul Hamid was deported to Salonika, with three wives, his two small sons, four concubines, four eunuchs and fourteen servants. At midnight the carriages arrived to take them away. White-faced and barely able to stand, he said his farewells to the sobbing women of the harem.

The troops presented arms. The eunuchs kissed the hem of his coat for the last time. Then, with a cavalry escort, he set off to board the royal train, which had been presented to him twenty years previously but which he had never seen.

Doubtless to his surprise, Abdul Hamid was installed in a comfortable villa, and his 'guards' – two personable young officers – told him they had express orders to grant any reasonable request he made. They did. When he complained that the eggs and milk were not fresh, fifty pedigree fowls and two cows from his farm at Yilditz were sent out to him. So were a number of younger concubines.

There was good reason to pander to him. Abdul Hamid had been milking the Treasury for decades, but where was the money? Some was quickly discovered in the Yilditz cellars – eleven sacks of gold coins, and boxes crammed with precious gems. Something else was discovered – a small notebook which Abdul Hamid had left behind in the confusion. It contained details of his foreign holdings, money stacked away when he expropriated some Mesopotamian oilfields, large funds secretly deposited in the Deutsche Bank and with certain American oil companies.

Apart from the Sultan himself, only Izzet knew the secrets of the note-book and Izzet had escaped during the revolution. So the pleasantly mannered guards in Salonika had the task of persuading, by subtle suggestion, that exile might not be permanent if the sixty-year-old Sultan agreed to return the money to the Government.*

As the lions in the zoo roared with hunger, the Committee started clearing out Yilditz, which resembled nothing so much as an immense junk shop. 'No large city store, and still less the household of any other monarch, could produce an array of contents to compare with that of Yilditz,' wrote Alma Wittlin in *Abdul Hamid, Shadow of God*. 'There was an immense cupboard containing nothing but shirts – thousands of them. Nor could these be hurriedly piled up and removed. Each individual shirt had to be searched for the costly objects which were found concealed in some of the garments – strings of pearls whose value ran into tens of thousands of pounds, small bags of precious stones. One drawer contained

* Eventually a great deal of the money was returned before Abdul Hamid died peacefully in 1915, but he never gave away all his financial secrets, knowing that they were his guarantee against assassination.

two hundred medals mixed up with rubies and railway shares, and probably stowed away in this fashion by Abdul Hamid himself. Whole bookcases were filled with five-pound notes.'

The parasites who infested Yilditz also had to be ejected. Those who had not escaped – servants, spies, astrologers – left in a dismal, rain-soaked procession half a mile long. Most were well treated, though known 'criminals' were hanged in public on Galata Bridge by gipsy executioners who received a fee of ten shillings per head. Among them was the grotesque, bloated Kislar Aga, known for his cruelty, and Mehmed Pasha, the head executioner, whose favourite method was to drown suspects by slow degrees.

The Committee had to face another problem: what to do with the harem? Out of the thousands who had fled, there still remained some nine hundred women of the harem – odalisques and their servants – together with hundreds who had served in the suites of the sons and daughters of the Sultan. They could hardly be turned out into the streets, for most had spent their adult lives under a fairly beneficent umbrella of protection. Mostly slaves, mostly unversed in the ways of the world, 'freedom' to them must have been an unpleasant prospect.

Accordingly, with a touch of modern panache, the Young Turks advertised in the newspapers, requesting anyone whose daughter or sisters had been kidnapped for the harem to come to Constantinople at the Government's expense and claim their relatives. They circularized the Circassian villages, for generations a centre of the slave trade. The response was remarkable, culminating in a long procession of women and eunuchs, passing for the first time in history *out* of the harem and into the streets of Constantinople. It was followed by a bizarre scene. At the head of a long room sat a Commissioner of the Young Turks. Down one side sat the ladies of the harem, down the other an assortment of roughly dressed tribesmen, mostly armed. At a word of polite command, the concubines, protesting and praying, unveiled in public for the first time in their lives, to recognize or be recognized by long-lost fathers and brothers. Scores were reunited and, after tearful farewells with their fellow odalisques, set off for the rigours of a life in the mountain homes of their families – with regret or relief no one will ever know.

Many relatives were never traced. Some girls disappeared. The rest

5 Abdul Mejid in his youth

6 *below* Dolmabache, Abdul Mejid's
alace on the Bosphorus

17 Circassian slaves – the most beautiful in the harem –
were at one time raised on slave farms

18 *top* 'The Turkey at bay' – a British cartoon at the time of Plevna
19 *above* Plevna : a few of the dead

20 The Mosque of Sultan Ahmed – still one of the most magnificent sights in Istanbul

21 Enver Pasha

22 Victory at Smyrna

23 Kamal Ataturk with his wife Latife

made their way to the old Grand Seraglio Palace, where they joined the ranks of discarded concubines from past imperial harems. It was comfortable, at least, and secluded from the problems of the outside world. This was the end of the harem life, the last link with the excesses and debauchery of an era that had closed.

The new dawn had broken. And the excesses and debauchery would be of a different kind.

Part 3
The alternative despots

Chapter thirteen
The unholy trinity

As the Young Turks stumbled blindly on to the totally unfamiliar stage of democracy, three men ruled the destinies of the Empire. They were Talaat, Djemel and Enver, each destined to transform a dawn of high promise into a fatal nightmare before dying by violence in distant lands.

The power behind the Committee of Union and Progress for most of the disastrous years between 1908 and 1918 was Talaat Bey. Every inch the boss of the party machine, he was a man of such enormous, almost grotesque, stature that when Henry Morgenthau, the American Ambassador, first met him he was staggered by his 'huge, sweeping back and rocky biceps' and 'wrists twice the size of an ordinary man's'.

Talaat liked to remember that he was a man of the people. A one-time telegraph operator who became Minister of the Interior (an admirable post for running a party machine) he lived simply, almost humbly, as Morgenthau discovered when he paid an unexpected visit to his home. Talaat might have been the most powerful man in the Turkish Empire, but his house was at the end of a narrow street little more than a slum, where the Ambassador waited in a room scantily and cheaply furnished with a few gaudy prints on the walls and worn rugs on the floor. Presently Talaat came lumbering into the room to meet the unexpected guest, dressed in carpet slippers, a fez and thick grey woollen pyjamas.

Though utterly ruthless, Talaat was able to disguise his instincts with a veneer of cheerful bonhomie, like a shambling bear who looks friendly but has to be watched. Nothing, however, could disguise Djemel Bey, the Military Governor of Constantinople and Minister of Marine, a hard-drinking, insatiable gambler who spent all his spare time at the card tables of the Cercle d'Orient. Djemel's black, piercing eyes took in everything. His shock of black hair, his black beard heightened the impression of savage energy, so that when he dined with Harold Nicolson at the British

Embassy the young British secretary was most impressed by 'his white teeth flashing tigerish against his black beard'. Djemel was perfectly cast in a role which demanded assassination and judicial murder as part of his daily routine.

Enver Bey was different. He was only twenty-seven when he stormed the barricades to depose Abdul Hamid and was above all others the man who captured the imagination of the people, a soldier renowned for audacity in battle, with dark good looks, clean-cut features, unmarred by a single wrinkle so that he seemed almost effeminate. His small hands with tapering fingers played the violin moderately well and heightened the effect. So did his immaculate uniform, in which he cut a dashing, almost foppish figure, particularly as he sported an upturned Kaiser Wilhelm moustache, after visiting Berlin where he had acquired a fore-taste of the good life. When Enver became War Minister, he installed himself in a study with three pictures on the wall – Napoleon, Frederick the Great, and himself in the middle. It did not take his acolytes long to nickname him 'Napoleonlik' – Little Napoleon – and it was hard to believe that his youth had been wretchedly poor, that his mother had followed the lowest occupation in the Empire – that of laying out the dead. But then Enver had the most complex character of the three. Though vain, he could hide it with an air of shyness. Though dynamic he never seemed to be hurried, but always calm. He moved well. He had a sort of diffident charm so that, as Alan Moorehead, in *Gallipoli*, felt, 'It was no wonder that he was made so much of by the hostesses of the time; here was the young *beau sabreur* in real life, an unassuming young hero. All this was a most effective cover for the innate cruelty, the shallowness . . . the megalo-mania that lay beneath.'

Enver's first years as the popular 'hero of the revolution' were tumul-tuous. A man of unflagging energy, he seemed to have an uncanny instinct for being in the right spot at the right moment, particularly when every-thing the Young Turks planned seemed to go wrong, as their dreams – no doubt sincere at the outset – crumbled.*

When, in the autumn of 1911, the Italians launched an unprovoked

* Though the Committee of Union and Progress sometimes preferred to allow 'old Turks' to hold nominal positions of power, it was the Young Turks who, except for one brief interval, were always the real masters.

attack on Tripoli – the Ottoman province in north Africa – Enver was the first to dash from his mission in Berlin to fight at Benghazi. From there he speeded to fight the Balkan wars in which many old enemies of Turkey, hitherto kept apart by friction, joined together in the common cause so that the Young Turks faced Bulgarians, Serbians, Greeks, Montenegrans. They overran Macedonia, invested Adrianople, while one army reached the Chatalja lines defending Constantinople. When, in January 1913, Europe proposed an armistice which would have lost Adrianople to the Empire, Enver appeared again, more dramatically than ever. To a bewildered Turkey all seemed lost, and even party members listlessly allowed Nazim Pasha, then War Minister, to negotiate the armistice.

Not so Enver. As the peacemakers wrangled, Enver quietly bribed the officer in charge of the conference security to take a day's leave. His armed conspirators formed small groups which sat drinking coffee in nearby cafés with hidden flags ready to be unfurled at a given signal – the appearance of Enver himself.

The Government had no inkling of possible trouble until without warning Enver burst into the Foreign Ministry. At this signal scores of coffee drinkers, brandishing revolvers and carrying red flags emblazoned with messages from the Koran, appeared at every corner, rushing up the steps behind Enver crying, 'Down with the government!' and, 'We will hold Adrianople.' Outside the gates, 'about a hundred more sympathizers cheered and handed round copies of a manifesto.'

Still the peacemakers did not realize that something was amiss. At the main entrance, Enver demanded to be allowed into the council chamber. In reply the ADC at the door foolishly fired a shot at the demonstrators. It was his death sentence, for Enver coldly drew his revolver and killed him.

By now the noise of the uproar and cheering must have reached the ears of the conference, though whether or not they heard the actual shooting is doubtful, for at this moment Nazim, hands in pockets, a cigarette dangling from his lips, walked to the door and said almost cheerfully, 'Come, boys, what's all the noise about? Don't you know it's interfering with our deliberations?'

They were the last words the War Minister spoke. Enver or one of his colleagues shot him dead. Enver then rushed into the conference chamber and at the point of the pistol forced the Grand Vizier, who was over eighty, to resign. When the Grand Vizier hesitated, Enver stuck a pistol in his ribs and told him, 'We didn't hesitate to kill the War Minister to save Adrianople. Why should we worry about killing you?' The old man's protests stopped, and Enver was able to seize the opportunity to purge the Army. He did so with his usual flair for the spectacular, dismissing 1,200 officers in a single day.

Though Enver was in effect directing the Ministry of War, it was action for which he really craved. Almost immediately he returned to the front, routed the enemy and at the head of his troops saved Adrianople for the Empire.

When he returned to Constantinople, every street was strewn with roses, every roof-top precariously crammed with hundreds of thousands of people awaiting the hero, who celebrated one victory with another of a different kind. He married the Sultan's daughter, took the title of pasha, installed himself in an ostentatious palace with a retinue of servants and a personal bodyguard, causing one of his comrades to mutter, 'God damn Enver Pasha for murdering our Enver.'

*

One man was missing, at least from the public eye. Mustafa Kemal was a military officer in the shadows, often under Enver's orders. The two men hated each other, though Kemal had taken part in the original march on the capital, had served in Tripoli and in the Balkan Wars. But Kemal was not just a morose and moody man; he happened to be a military genius, who could not stomach the fact that he had to serve under this popinjay who, however brave at the ramparts, was hopelessly inept as a military strategist.

*

The tragedy of the Young Turks in those early years was that their original hopes and aspirations became lost in the march of events that engulfed them. Nationalistic aspirations among the subject peoples ended forever their dreams of an empire consisting of free and equal members. Talaat himself was soon forced to admit that, 'There can be no question of equality until we have succeeded in our task of Ottomanizing the Empire': a speech which caused the British Ambassador to comment wryly, 'To them "Ottoman" evidently means "Turk" and their present policy of "Ottomanization" is one of pounding the non-Turkish elements in a Turkish mortar.'

At first the results consisted only of a bewildering series of nonsensical edicts. Overnight French signs which for decades had been placed next to the Turkish instructions in public places were removed, so that the growing European population was faced with totally incomprehensible street names, public notices, directions on streetcars. And yet, while one department zealously obliterated this trace of 'infidel foreigners', writers like Abdullah Cerdet, using the new freedom of the Press, were demanding that 'Civilization means European civilization, and it must be imported with both its roses and its thorns.' At times it *was* imported, with ludicrous results, as Ismail Hami, another writer, discovered, for, 'by simultaneously introducing Russian uniforms, Belgian rifles, Turkish headgear, Hungarian saddles, English swords, and French drill, we have created an army that is a grotesque parody of Europe.'

Mark Sykes, the British writer, returning to Constantinople in 1913, did not like the change at all. 'Four times, at almost equal intervals, have I been to Constantinople since the Constitution was proclaimed,' he wrote. 'What a strange mood the city is in today – after five years of progress, of folly, of squalid intrigue, of violent negation, of senseless destruction, of ignominy, of instability, of wars and devastating fires. Outwardly, the change is trivial. The streets are cleaner, the roads smoother, the dogs have gone and cholera has come to stay.' But, he discovered, 'In Turkey, where, until the Constitution, no man had wanted for bread from his fellows, the first act of the mock Parliament was to invent a Poor Law.'

By 1913, after five years of mounting difficulties, of wars and internal troubles, little if anything remained of the original concepts of the Committee of Union and Progress. The Government – a ramshackle affair in Turkey at the best of times – had run to seed, and Enver and Talaat were now wholly preoccupied in a struggle in which their own political survival could only be maintained by a ruthless party machine as sinister in its way as that of Abdul Hamid.

During these years, and indeed until the Sultanate was later abolished, the Sultan played no part in the affairs of State. A powerful man might have been able to exert some influence, but Mahomet V had spent thirty-five years under the watchful eye of his brother, Abdul Hamid. He had been allowed no friends, no newspapers or books, even his servants had been spies, so that he had devoted his life to the harem. Though he lived ostentatiously after ascending the throne, he had in effect changed one guard for another, for he was the virtual prisoner of the Young Turks, a pathetic old man described in *The Near East from Within*:

The very appearance of Mahomet V suggests nonentity. Small and bent, with sunken eyes and deeply lined face, an obesity savouring of disease, and a yellow, oily complexion, it certainly is not prepossessing. There is little or no intelligence in his countenance, and he never lost a haunted, frightened look, as if dreading to find an assassin lurking in some dark corner ready to strike and kill him.

Mahomet had not been a party to the conspiracy to oust his brother but the fear of death was so deeply lodged that he never lost it and, in the words of Eversley, 'A portrait of this degenerate would better explain than words, if it were not too cruel, the depth to which the once proud race of Othman had fallen. It was probable, however, that the cunning men who engineered the revolution thought it would better serve their purpose to have a cipher as a figure-head of the Empire than a man with a will of his own.'

And there was one more irremediable note. Years of German peaceful penetration was now bearing military fruit. Germany had already financed the Baghdad railway project; she had invested heavily in municipal transportation, electricity, mining, agriculture. Krupp and Mauser had branches in Constantinople. The offices of the three largest German banks were more ostentatious than any of their European competitors. As the First World War approached, Enver was completely captivated by the German war machine – and more than ever captivated by assiduous flattery from the Kaiser himself. Thousands of Germans packed the city's bars and clubs each night and picnicked on Sundays on the Sweet Waters of the Bosporus. They were not tourists, but technicians training and re-organizing the Turkish Army as the long hot summer of 1914 approached.

Not all the members of the Committee of Union and Progress welcomed their presence. Talaat certainly had grave doubts. So did some of the elder statesmen who felt that if war came Britain, France and Russia would be more than a match for Germany. They counselled caution; or, to put the matter more crudely, they wanted to play a waiting game, so that if war came they would be able to auction their services to the highest bidder.

But Enver, who spoke fluent German, was now Minister of War, so could act in secret, though he took care to hedge his bets with diplomats. 'The Turks and Germans,' he told the American Ambassador, 'care nothing for each other. We are with them because it is our interest to be with them; they are with us because that is their interest. Germany will back Turkey just so long as that helps Germany; Turkey will back Germany just so long as that helps Turkey.'

Enver's enthusiasm for Germany was one thing, but one wonders whether it might have been reduced had allied diplomacy in Constantinople been good enough to parry the thrusts of Baron von Wangenhein, the German Ambassador, a close friend of the Kaiser and a frequent visitor at his villa at Corfu.

Von Wangenhein was a huge hulk of a man with a cold, imperious manner and 'strong, arrogant eyes', to look at, a caricature of a Prussian aristocrat. Knowing that Germany was planning a war, he had an advantage in his dealings with Enver over the British, French and Russian representatives, to whom a European war was unthinkable. Furthermore, the Allied ambassadors tended to look down on the new government which had so crudely usurped the sultans, causing Morgenthau to note, 'It was apparent that the three ambassadors of the Entente did not regard the Talaat and Enver regime as permanent, or as particularly worth their while to cultivate.'

This age-old symptom of diplomatic snobbery to newcomers was possibly due to a malign influence in the British Embassy, which employed in a key position a man who loathed the Young Turks and whose influence on the Entente ambassadors was unbounded. His name was Fitzmaurice, and just before the war T. E. Lawrence met him in Constantinople. His impression of the man was hardly complimentary. 'I blame much of our ineffectiveness upon Fitzmaurice, the Dragoman, an eagle-mind and a personality of iron vigour,' he wrote to his biographer, Liddell Hart. 'Fitzmaurice had lived half a lifetime in Turkey and was the Embassy's official go-between . . . He knew everything and was feared from end to end of Turkey. Unfortunately he was a rabid R.C. and hated Freemasons and Jews with a religious hatred. The Young Turk movement was fifty per cent crypto-Jew and ninety-five per cent Freemason. So he regarded it as the devil and threw the whole influence of England over to the unfashionable Sultan and his effete palace clique. Fitzmaurice was really rabid . . . and his prejudices completely blinded his judgement. His prestige, however, was enormous and our ambassadors and the F.O. staff went down before him like nine-pins. Thanks to him, we rebuffed every friendly advance the Young Turks made.'

Given this kind of advice, it is easy to understand why, even after the Archduke Ferdinand was assassinated at Sarajevo, the British Ambassador felt it quite safe to depart for England on leave.

Thus the Ambassador was absent from Constantinople when in the last days of peace von Wangenhein persuaded Enver to sign a secret pact. He did not ask Turkey to go to war, but proposed a more subtle plan directed against Russia: that the Bosporus should, at the right moment, be closed to international shipping, a precaution by a neutral country to which no belligerents could really take exception. Germany would certainly not, because by bottling up a strip of water two or three miles wide and barely twenty miles long a fatal wedge would be driven between Russia and Europe. Without a shot being fired, von Wangenhein had arranged to sever the major route along which Russian men and machines would be ferried to the Allied war theatres in the West. It was a tactical triumph of the first order.

Enver agreed, but he had to place the details squarely before the Committee of Union and Progress. However, he forestalled any arguments from his colleagues by ostentatiously placing his loaded revolver on the conference table, then asking them to continue. The agreement was signed two days before the First World War started. And yet, despite this secret pact, Turkey might still have remained neutral had it not been for one fatal incident.

In his brilliant *Gallipoli*, Alan Moorehead wrote that the secret pact 'still did not commit Turkey to war, and there was still no real feeling of belligerence anywhere in the country. But now, in the changed atmosphere of these last few hours of European peace, there occurred one of those incidents which, though not vitally important in themselves, yet somehow contrive to express and exacerbate a situation and finally push peoples and governments to the point where, suddenly and emotionally, they make up their minds to commit all their fortunes, regardless of what the consequences are going to be. This was the incident of the two warships Britain was building for Turkey.'

The warships had been ordered by Turkey many months previously. The money had been raised largely by public subscription. Collection boxes appeared outside every mosque, on the Galata Bridge, at every village store. More money was raised by village fêtes, charity bazaars, jumble sales. Agents had walked from house to house collecting pitifully small contributions, and Turkish women had even sold their hair to help. These two vessels, already christened the *Sultan Osman* and the *Reshadiye*, belonged to the people of Turkey, and Turkish sailors were already in England to sail them to the Bosporus. By August 1914, the *Sultan Osman* was ready to sail, the *Reshadiye* would be ready in a matter of weeks.

Then came the bombshell. The day before war was declared, Winston Churchill, the First Lord of the Admiralty, announced that 'in the interests of national security' the two vessels had been requisitioned by the British Navy. Morally and legally he acted within his rights, and in fact he may have known that Enver in his secret agreement had promised von Wangenhein that he would direct the *Sultan Osman* to a German port in the event of war.* But to the national pride of the Turks it was a terrible blow. Their fury and indignation gave von Wangenhein a golden opportunity. As crowds of angry Turks stormed through Constantinople, smashing the windows of British firms, the German Ambassador paid a call on Enver. Sitting in the study, facing the three photographs, von Wangenhein made the Turkish War Minister a stunning offer. In the name of the Kaiser he was authorized to replace the two warships which the British had 'stolen' with two German warships, the *Goeben* and the *Breslau*, both conveniently in the Mediterranean.

For the Young Turks, who had inevitably been blamed by the public for the catastrophe, it was a godsend, and Enver readily agreed. Talaat, however, had his doubts. What, he asked, would happen to Turkish neutrality? But Enver as usual won the day, and all that now remained was

* German official papers, Wangenhein to Foreign Office, 2 August 1914, no. 404.

for the two German warships to reach the safety of the Golden Horn.

It was a close-run thing, for British battleships had been shadowing the *Goeben* during the week before war was declared, and on 4 August, with the ultimatum to Germany running out at midnight, they could have sunk her had not Churchill expressly forbidden any action until midnight. Even as late as five o'clock, when it was obvious that war was inevitable, the First Sea Lord, Prince Louis of Battenberg, turned to Churchill in the Admiralty and said there was still time to sink her before sunset. But nothing could be done, and once it was dark the vessel got away. On 6 August, both ships were reported coaling at Messina and then they vanished.

It is not difficult to imagine the intense excitement, mingled with official apprehension, as Constantinople waited for news and possible repercussions; for Britain and Germany were now at war, and, as Talaat kept reminding Enver, if the German warships passed through the Straits, Britain would certainly regard it as a hostile act. And Talaat, like millions of Turks, was heartily sick of the wars that had impoverished the Empire since the Young Turks took power. 'We want nothing more than to be left out of war, and have a period of peace in which we can build for the future,' he told Enver.

For once Talaat shook Enver's nerve, and the Minister of War wavered, then decided to cover himself by double-crossing von Wangenhein. Sending for the Russian Military Attaché he blandly proposed a Russian–Turkish alliance which would automatically cancel his secret agreement with the Germans.

Poor Enver assumed that the Germans would never know, though it showed naivety. Indeed, it is possible that Talaat, who was highly alarmed at the prospect of receiving the German ships, might have warned von Wangenhein, for he was in the habit of reading all diplomatic cables before they entered or left the country and may have deliberately leaked the news.* Von Wangenhein, however, had kept a trump card up his sleeve. Too practised a diplomat to confront Enver with a charge of treachery, he

---

* Talaat astounded the American Ambassador by mentioning the contents of a cable which Morgenthau said he had never seen. 'Oh, but you will,' said Talaat cheerfully, 'I always get all your cables first, you know. After I have finished reading them I send them round to you.'

made a proposition which would immediately solve the vexed neutrality problem. Why not arrange for the two German warships to be 'sold' to neutral Turkey, in the same way as Britain had offered to build and sell their two warships? The question of payment, he added, could be left to the future.

The next day the *Goeben* and the *Breslau* arrived at the entrance to the Dardanelles and von Wangenhein's aide asked Enver to permit them to enter. When Enver said he must consult his colleagues, he was told curtly that he must decide instantly or the warships would leave. After the briefest pause, Enver said, 'Let them come in.' The two warships steamed towards the Golden Horn; the proposed alliance with Russia was forgotten.

Within days the German sailors, farcically donning the fez to show they were members of the Turkish Navy, were roistering in the nightclubs of Pera, and German cars sporting the Kaiser's sacred eagle were tearing up and down the steep twisting streets of the capital, while to the perplexed Turks a new pun was born – 'Deutschland über Allah.'

It was the turning-point in the fortunes of the Young Turks, aptly summed up after Djavid Bey, the Minister of Finance, told a distinguished Belgian journalist sympathetically, 'I have terrible news for you. The Germans have captured Brussels.' Icily cold, the Belgian pointed to the *Goeben* and *Breslau*, anchored in the Bosporus and replied, 'I have even more terrible news for you. The Germans have captured Turkey.'

Then came the final episode. Towards the end of October, the *Goeben* and the *Breslau* steamed up the Black Sea and, without warning, opened fire on Odessa and Sevastopol, sinking all the shipping they could find. Though they were Turkish ships – in theory anyway – Djemel, the Minister of Marine, knew nothing of the event until a messenger interrupted his game of cards at the Cercle d'Orient.

The British, French and Russian ambassadors could stand no more. On 30 October they asked for their passports. The following day Turkey was in the war.

*

During these stirring days Mustafa Kemal had been Turkish Military Attaché in Sofia, banished by Enver after he had written to him, bitterly criticizing the presence of German troops in Turkey. 'Only the Turks themselves can find their salvation,' he wrote. 'It is madness to allow the Germans to control the Army, the basis of our power to live.'

Kemal accepted the post as a form of banishment, so this perplexed, deeply frustrated man decided to take advantage of his post as a diplomat. He had always been a compulsive womanizer, but now, to his chagrin, he found himself snubbed. He took dancing lessons, and this helped him to enter Sofia's social life – until he heard that the father of a girl he escorted regularly had told a friend that he would kill any Turk rather than let him marry his daughter. Kemal's reaction was to rush to the other end of the female spectrum. 'Society women' were beneath contempt, and he turned instead to the more obliging ladies of the brothels. For months he hardly ever returned to his own bed before dawn. He had no work of consequence to occupy him. He hated his job. It was far more pleasant to spend the night in the beds of ladies with whom he could indulge in all the frustrations that had been bottled up inside him for years. As a result he contracted venereal disease.

Dissolute, lonely, now despising all women, he begged for permission to return to active service. Every request was refused, even after Turkey entered the war, for an anti-German officer was the last man Enver wanted around. By February 1915, he had decided to leave Sofia anyway, to find his way back to Turkey and enlist as a private soldier. He had packed his bags when a routine order came posting him to Rodosto on the Gallipoli peninsula. 'It was an event which, passing quite unnoticed at the time, was to change the whole course of the campaign that lay ahead.'

It changed, too, the course of Mustafa Kemal's life, for by his courage and brilliant military strategy he became the hero of the greatest Turkish victory of the war. Had it not been for Mustafa Kemal, there is little doubt that Churchill's plan to wrest control of the entrance to the Bosporus would have been realized. Though victory was at times almost within the grasp of the thousands of Allied troops landed on the shores of the peninsula, the attack failed, not only because of Mustafa Kemal's tenacity, but because he, like Osman Pasha, was able to extract out of weary Turkish troops 'all the tenacity they have always displayed in every form of defensive warfare'. By the end of 1915, the British, after suffering 112,000 casualties, evacuated the peninsula, and though Kemal's losses had been even greater he had thwarted Churchill's dream of shortening the war by two years. He returned to Constantinople, to newspaper banners shrieking, 'The Saviour of the Dardanelles'. But he returned also to an implacable Enver who promptly posted him to Diarbekir in the Caucasus, no doubt because it was as far away from Constantinople as possible.

*

Gallipoli may have stirred the Turkish newspapers to flights of lyrical prose, but while the soldiers of the Ottoman Empire were fighting so resolutely in the west the newspapers forbore to mention a war of a very different kind being mercilessly waged during the same months of 1915 in the east. It was a one-sided war, personally instigated, personally directed by Enver with such savagery that it placed him in the same category as the sultans from whose tyranny he had 'freed' Turkey, for Enver decided on the enterprise with only one thought in mind: to exterminate the Armenians. Abdul Hamid had tried, but even he could not match the genius for genocide now displayed by the virtual dictator of the Ottoman Empire.

The Armenians living in the north-east of Asia Minor bordering Russia had been an island of Christianity in a Moslem world for 1,500 years. Saracens, Tartars, Mongols, Kurds and finally Turks had crossed and recrossed the 'Belgium of the East' which formed a link between Asia and Europe. Early in 1915 there had been savage fighting between Turkey and Russia in the region, and using the excuse that some Armenians had helped the Russians, Enver seized the opportunity to eliminate any possibility of an 'Armenian problem' after the war by the simple process of exterminating the population. Even for a so-called 'enlightened' government it seemed that Ottoman habits were hard to forget.

He made a start in the province of Van by replacing the moderately inclined Moslem governor by his hypocritical, unstable brother-in-law, Djevet Bey, who on 15 April set about exterminating all Armenians he could find. In the village of Arkantz five hundred Armenian males were rounded up and shot. Djevet then repeated the procedure in eighty nearby villages. Hundreds of women were raped, thousands of men tortured in attempts to make them confess they had weapons, and soon Djevet was known throughout the province as 'The Blacksmith' – because his favourite torture was to nail horseshoes to men's feet. Other tortures were just as fiendish, for the Chief of Police in Constantinople, Bedri Bey, frankly admitted to the American Ambassador that he had 'delved into the records of the Spanish Inquisition and adopted all the suggestions found there'. According to Dr Usher, the American medical missionary at the hospital at Van, fifty-five thousand bodies had to be burned when the killing ceased.

This, however, was only the beginning, for what Enver had in mind was systematic massacre or deportation of Armenians to Aleppo, across the Syrian Desert. He was not motivated by the religious fanaticism which prompted the horrors of the Spanish Inquisition, but by a psychopathic hatred not unlike Hitler's attitude later to the Jews. 'The whole ghastly process was carried out in complete coordination between the military and civil authorities under Enver and Talaat,' said one official report. 'It was a deliberate and calculated scheme of policy concocted in Constantinople.'

According to the British Bryce Report, placed before Parliament in October 1916, one-third of the two million Armenians in Turkey perished, one-third escaped to Russian territory and one-third remained unmolested in the large cities, mainly Constantinople and Smyrna, where their business acumen was useful.

'The procedure usually adopted,' according to the official report, 'was to summon all the male Armenians in the district. They were then marched away in batches, roped man to man, to some distant destination, they were told, but in fact merely to the first lonely place where bands of Kurdish or other cut-throats were in readiness to exterminate them.' The women and children were then told to prepare for deportation in convoys. At the start of the long journey to Aleppo they were provided with soldiers 'for their protection'. After a few days, however, they were stripped of every rag, every penny and cast adrift.

One authenticated case-history of a caravan, on file in the American State Department, tells more of the misery inflicted on hundreds of thousands of innocent people than any battery of figures.

On the first of June a convoy of 3,000 Armenians, mostly women, girls, and children, left Harpoot. All the way to Ras-ul-Ain, the first station on the Bagdad line, the existence of these wretched travellers was one prolonged horror. The gendarmes went ahead, informing the half-savage tribes of the mountains that several thousand Armenian women and girls were approaching. The Arabs and Kurds began to carry off the girls, the mountaineers fell upon them repeatedly, killing and violating the women, and the gendarmes themselves joined in the orgy. One by one the few men that accompanied the convoy were killed. The women had succeeded in secreting money from their persecutors, keeping it in their mouths and hair; with this they would buy horses, only to have them repeatedly stolen by the Kurdish tribesmen. Finally the gendarmes, having robbed and beaten and killed and violated their charges for thirteen days, abandoned them altogether. Two days afterwards the Kurds went through the party and rounded up all the males who still remained alive. They found about 150, and these they butchered to the last man. But that same day another convoy from Sivas joined this one from Harpoot, increasing the numbers of the whole caravan to 18,000 people. Another Kurdish Bey now took command, and summoned all his followers from the mountains. Day after day and night after night the prettiest girls were carried away. Whenever they reached a Turkish village all the local vagabonds were permitted to prey upon the Armenian girls. When the diminishing band reached the Euphrates they had all been so repeatedly robbed that they had practically nothing left except a few ragged clothes, and even these the Kurds now took, the consequence being that the whole convoy marched for five days completely naked under the scorching desert sun. For another five days they did not have a morsel of bread or a drop of water.

Hundreds fell dead on the way, their tongues were turned to charcoal, and when, at the end of five days, they reached a fountain, the whole convoy naturally rushed toward it. But here the policemen barred their way and forbade them to take a single drop of water. Their purpose was to sell it at from one to three liras a cup, and sometimes they actually withheld the water after getting the money.

After seventy days of forced march through the desert, the remnants of the combined convoy reached Aleppo. Out of the eighteen thousand who had set off, only 150 naked women and children remained.

With America still neutral, which meant that American consuls worked in various parts of the Ottoman Empire, the Young Turks were powerless to prevent the news reaching the outside world. Even in Britain, engaged in a life-and-death struggle for survival, the horrors of the Armenian massacres replaced the war on the front pages of the newspapers. In America the reaction was one of frustrated fury. When the American Ambassador sought an interview with Enver in Constantinople he received a shock.

Thinking it might be more diplomatic to save Enver's face by not accusing him personally, Morgenthau opened the conversation by saying, 'Of course, I know that the Cabinet would never order such terrible things as have taken place. You and Talaat and the rest of the Committee can hardly be held responsible. Undoubtedly your subordinates have gone much further than you have ever intended. I realize that it is not always easy to control your underlings.'

To the Ambassador's amazement, Enver took great offence, and answered curtly, 'You are greatly mistaken. I have no desire to shift the blame on our underlings and I am entirely willing to accept the responsibility myself for everything that has taken place. The Cabinet itself has ordered the deportations.'

Talaat was equally forthcoming. To friends he boasted, 'I have accomplished more towards solving the Armenian problem in three months than Abdul Hamid accomplished in three years.' And to a reporter from the *Berliner Tageblatt* he propounded an incredible philosophy. 'We have been reproached for making no distinction between innocent Armenians and the guilty,' he said, 'but that was utterly impossible in view of the fact that those who are innocent today might be guilty tomorrow.'

But it was to Morgenthau that Talaat made 'what was perhaps the most astonishing request I had ever heard'. For many years American life-insurance companies had done considerable business among the thrifty Armenians, and this intrigued the Turks.

'I wish,' Talaat asked the American Ambassador, 'that you would get the American life-insurance companies to send us a complete list of their Armenian policy-holders. They are practically all dead now, and have left no heirs to collect the money. The Government is the beneficiary now. Will you do so?'

*

With the Turkish Army victorious in Gallipoli and Armenia, and with Allied reverses on the Western Front, the Young Turks should have been content to be allies of Germany. In fact, just the reverse happened, for it was in the Middle East that the first cracks occurred, and it was the Turks who suffered. Early in 1916 Enver planned a new attack against the Russians in the Caucasus using two hundred battalions released from

Gallipoli, but the Russians, fighting in intense cold, captured the great Turkish stronghold of Ezerum, thrust deep into enemy territory to take Trebizond, while another Russian army drove the Turks out of western Persia. Though Russia never reached her intended goal of Baghdad, she drained hundreds of thousands of Turkish troops from the Middle East where Enver now faced a far more serious blow – nothing less than a proclamation by the Sherif of Mecca, Islam's holiest city, to overthrow the Turkish yoke and fight for Arab independence. From the Arab world the response was enthusiastic – and it was backed by firepower. Almost all the Turkish garrisons in the Hejaz were annihilated, and by December 1916 Britain formally recognized the Sherif as King of the Hejaz. It was a mortal blow to the spiritual authority of the Sultan, for now he was no longer custodian of the sacred shrines of Mecca and Medina. To the intensely devout Turks it was a disaster from which they never really recovered.

The new King of the Hejaz lost no time. He appointed his son, the Emir Feisal, as commander of the Arab forces and, together with T. E. Lawrence, thrust into Palestine and Syria. By March 1917 ecstatic crowds were hailing the British 'liberators' as they marched into Baghdad. Soon Jerusalem surrendered, then Damascus and Aleppo.

Distrust between Germany and Turkey was mounting; after all, the Germans had milked Turkey of seven divisions and many Germans had died in the Middle East. Bismarck, who once grunted that, 'The whole of the Balkans is not worth the bones of a single Pomeranian grenadier,' must have turned in his grave. At times Turkish and German officers literally fought each other, so that the British had to keep all Turkish and German prisoners-of-war in separate compounds.

For Enver and Talaat the end was near. After four years of war, in which Turkey lost 427,000 killed alone, disagreement among the Young Turks was growing more and more acrimonious. Finally Enver was publicly denounced for selling economic concessions to Germany, and accused of having made a fortune out of profiteering in foodstuffs, at a time when disease and famine were rife over all Turkey.

The game was up, and the pashas of the once-glorious Committee of Union and Progress prepared to flee. Enver, Talaat and Djemel met secretly on the night of 2 November 1918 in the house of Enver's aide-de-camp, and were spirited out of Constantinople on a German torpedo-boat.*

It was the end of the Young Turks, and the moment for a new and dynamic character to step on the scene, the man destined to preside over the death of the Ottoman Empire and the birth of the Turkish nation.

* In 1922 Enver was killed in Russia while leading a cavalry charge on Red Army troops. Talaat and Djemel were both assassinated in Berlin in the twenties by Armenians.

Chapter fourteen
The rebel

Mustafa Kemal was thirty-eight when in May 1919 his moment of destiny arrived. All his life so far, as a student, a plotter, a soldier, showed him to be, in the words of one biographer, 'a man born out of due season, an anachronism, a throwback to the Tartars of the Steppes, a fierce elemental force of a man'. In a different age he might have been a Genghis Khan, conquering, pillaging empires, 'and filling in the intervals of peace between campaigns with orgies of wine and women'. This was the heir to a prostrate empire, a man with vision enough to see that, though the Empire might be dead, a country could rise from its ashes.

Mustafa Kemal's father, a customs official turned timber merchant, died in 1888 leaving a son of seven with only one ambition: to be a soldier, a career not favoured by his widowed mother. When he was twelve (and behind her back), he passed the entrance examination for the Salonika Military School, and within six years was attending the War College at Constantinople, graduating in 1903 with the rank of staff captain. He also acquired a burning hatred of Abdul Hamid (which earned him a spell in prison) and an equally burning zeal for the Young Turks. Yet even though he had taken part in the stirring events leading to the downfall of Abdul Hamid, he never entered the inner circle of the Young Turks because he despised the Germans on whom Enver was becoming more dependent, and had no hesitation in voicing his contempt for Enver's policies.

Now, however, all had changed. Constantinople was suddenly thronged with victorious British and French troops who were hailed by many Turks almost as deliverers. Soldiers with well-lined pockets crammed the dance halls of Pera while the officers dined to tzigane music in the Tokatlian Hotel. There were requisitioned motor-boats to take men – and girls – to the pretty white villages lapped by the Bosporus. There were picnics on the beaches of the Black Sea. 'Life was gay and wicked and delightful,' for the occupation forces – and the black-eyed Greek and Armenian girls who preferred them to the Germans.

The euphoria was further heightened by the vague administration of the Allied officials. Constantinople was not formally 'occupied'; the troops were merely there to keep order while the politicians drafted the peace treaties. None of the troops expected to stay more than a few months. The French and British were soon getting on each other's nerves, perhaps because senior officers had no clearly defined duties.

The armistice was barely a month old when Mustafa Kemal reached Constantinople, after months of fighting the Arabs. He found the enemy everywhere – British warships in the Bosporus, French troops in the capital, Italians guarding the railways. The Ottoman Empire had been smashed, all the leaders of the Young Turks were abroad in hiding, the Government was led by an old pro-British diplomat from the reign of Abdul Hamid called Tewfik Pasha.

Mustafa Kemal should have been in a unique position, for with Enver gone he had no rival as the only successful general in Turkey. He was also known to have consistently opposed joining the Germans in the war. Yet political power eluded him, largely because of his own lack of tact. He passionately advocated 'Turkey for the Turks' in political speeches, demanding generous peace terms. He publicly attacked Tewfik's government and the occupation forces; he tried to stem the timid acceptance of total defeat; he tried to form a new political party as the months rolled by – until Turkey was shocked by a blow which to them was even graver than defeat.

In February 1919, Venizelos, the Greek Prime Minister, made a formal claim to the Peace Conference in Paris for the possession of the city of Smyrna on the Aegean coast of Anatolia. It was the price which Britain and France had already agreed on as a reward for Greek entry into the war. So many Greeks lived on the Aegean coast that Venizelos's demands seemed reasonably fair, but there was also a more cogent argument in favour of them. Lloyd George regarded Venizelos as 'the greatest statesman Greece had thrown up since the days of Pericles', and it seemed to him highly expedient for the Greeks to replace the Turks as protectors of the British route to India. To President Wilson, a Greek occupation of Smyrna would be preferable to Italian threats to make the Mediterranean an Italian lake. According to the American author, Edward Hale Bierstadt, 'At the suggestion of President Wilson Greece was authorized to occupy Smyrna in order to forestall any Italian move in that direction.'

Three months later, on 15 May, twenty thousand Greek troops landed at Smyrna, backed by British, American and French warships, and, as Churchill put it, 'set up their standards of invasion and conquest in Asia Minor'. Delirious crowds of Greeks – for centuries a subject race of the Ottoman Empire – welcomed *their* 'liberators', who immediately sought revenge by massacring as many Turks as they could find in the city and province.

At first the Turks could not believe the Greeks were in Smyrna. It was one thing to suffer the occupation even of Constantinople by alien troops of the victorious Western powers, but for a former subject people to be presented with one of the greatest cities in Anatolia was an altogether different kind of humiliation. A crowd of fifty thousand gathered in protest before the Mosque of Sultan Ahmed in Constantinople. Under the machine-guns of allied troops, they carried black flags while black curtains shrouded the national flag of Turkey. Mustafa Kemal was there and (as he later wrote) was obsessed with only one thought – somehow to reach Anatolia and organize resistance to the Greeks, and the docile Turkish government which had given Smyrna away.

To Mustafa Kemal, distrusted by both Turks and British, it must have seemed an impossible dream. He was already known to the Allied occupation authorities as an intractable hot-head with dangerous left-wing sympathies. And, though respected for his military prowess, he was at this time hardly a figure to inspire confidence. Furious and impotent, he had let himself run to seed. Down-at-heel, short of money, he was living at the modest Pera Palace Hotel overlooking the Golden Horn. His face was lined and grey from a recurrence of his disease.

Yet, unknown to Mustafa Kemal, the British, even before the Greeks stepped ashore at Smyrna, had suggested that the Sultan should send a high-ranking officer to deal with increasing violence in the area. The request was not exactly a threat, but it masked an alternative distasteful to the Sultan. If the Turks could not keep their Anatolian house in order, the Allies would have to send in troops.

Mustafa Kemal was the last man anyone would have imagined would be nominated to handle the gathering storm in Anatolia. And yet that is exactly what happened, for he *was* the last man – the only man – available. At their wits' end, the Sultan and Damad Ferid, the Grand Vizier, turned to him. The British were horrified; they already had evidence that he was concerned with plots to prepare centres of resistance, and his name was on a list for possible deportation to Malta. The Grand Vizier, however, finally persuaded the British that the troubles in Anatolia were due to rebel factions loyal to the memory of Enver and anxious to restore the Committee of Union and Progress.

'Though Mustafa Kemal was nominally a member of the Committee,' he told the British, 'in reality he is known as its most determined opponent. He has a great reputation in the country. He can be trusted. He is clearly the man to go.'

So Mustafa Kemal was appointed Governor-General of the Eastern Provinces. Before leaving he arranged a secret code by which he would be able to communicate with sympathizers in the War Office, and chose two 'disciples' to accompany him: Colonel Refet, who would command the Third Army Corps; and Colonel Mehmet Arif, a staff officer who bore an uncanny resemblance to Mustafa Kemal, with whom he had fought in Gallipoli. They had similar tastes, particularly where wine and women were concerned. Arif was the only man to whom Mustafa Kemal ever showed any public affection. In public he would put his arm round Arif's shoulders, or call him by 'endearing names'. Many of Mustafa Kemal's enemies swore the two men were lovers.

Mustafa Kemal planned to board a tramp steamer which would sail up the Bosporus for the Black Sea coast, but just before he was due to sail the British High Commissioner belatedly realized the dangers of the mission and at midnight Wyndham Deedes, his military attaché, hurriedly woke the Grand Vizier with a warning that Mustafa Kemal's avowed aim was to raise insurgent groups in Salonika. 'He would have to be stopped at all costs.'

There was nothing the Grand Vizier could do. 'It is too late, Your Excellency,' he said. 'The bird has flown.'

Mustafa escaped from Constantinople by barely an hour, thanks to the blundering jealousies of the Allies. Urgent orders were certainly sent to intercept him, but the British, French and Italians all played varying parts in the control of passenger vessels, and each distrusted the others. While they were bickering, Mustafa Kemal slipped through the net.

He landed at Samsun on the Black Sea coast on 19 May 1919 – four days after the Greeks had occupied Smyrna. His orders were to disband the Turkish forces in the area. Instead he immediately started to organize a resistance movement and raise an army.

*

When Mustafa Kemal arrived at Samsun it was with the complete conviction that he could form a government and muster an army powerful enough to oust not only the supine Turkish Government but also the victorious occupation armies of Britain, France and Italy. It was a stupendous challenge.

Within a week of landing at Samsun, Mustafa Kemal moved inland to the town of Amassia astride the main road linking East and West Turkey. Here he called a series of secret meetings of army and civilian leaders. Nothing could be done, he knew, without the backing of the Army; but already tens of thousands of armed guerrillas in the mountains behind Smyrna were fighting the Greeks, and it was not difficult for Mustafa Kemal to persuade the Army – or the remnants of the skeletal divisions – to back him. Then he spent weeks touring towns and villages, preaching resistance to the Allied occupation troops and the Turkish Government, always taking care not to involve the sacred person of the Sultan, who, he cried, was in effect a helpless prisoner of the British. 'You, the Turkish people, must save yourselves,' he said, 'before the Allied troops destroy us.' Mustafa Kemal was an electrifying orator and his words made sense, for he was the Sultan's accredited representative, and one can imagine the reaction among simple, devout peasant communities when he cried, 'Your Sultan has sent me to help you.' In the name of the Sultan he even despatched 'orders' to military leaders to refuse to hand over arms to the Allies. To the civil authorities in towns and villages he issued instructions to stop local taxes being sent to Constantinople.

By 22 June – little more than a month after his arrival – he sent a circular cable in cypher to all trustworthy military and civil leaders in Anatolia. Its first three sentences perfectly expressed his political platform.

1 The integrity of the country, the independence of the nation are in danger.

2 The central government is unable to discharge the duties for which it is responsible. As a result the nation is regarded as non-existent.

3 Only the will and resolution of the nation can save the independence of the nation.

Mustafa Kemal then suggested a secret congress at Sivas, 'which is the safest place in Anatolia for that purpose', where, free from interference, delegates could assert the Turkish nation's rights before the world. The Constantinople Government quickly heard of the planned meeting, and soon after Mustafa Kemal had sent out his telegrams the Ministry of the Interior countered with a circular which read:

Although Mustafa Kemal Pasha is a great soldier, his political sagacity is not of the same standard . . . He has added to his political mistakes the administrative error of sending telegrams on behalf of certain illegal bodies whose only function is to extort money from the people. To bring him back to Constantinople is the duty of the Ministry of War. The Ministry of the Interior, however, orders you to recognize that this man has been dismissed, to enter into no official dealings with him whatsoever and to see that no request of his relative to governmental affairs is complied with . . .

Early in July, after an exchange of telegrams ending with an abrupt refusal by Mustafa Kemal to return to Constantinople, he was dismissed from his post. Mustafa Kemal immediately resigned his commission and started wearing civilian clothes. 'I shall stay in Anatolia until the nation has won its independence,' he cabled the Sultan.

That cable marked the point of no return for Mustafa Kemal. As Churchill wrote later, 'Loaded with follies, stained with crimes, rotted with misgovernment, shattered by battle, worn down by long disastrous wars, his Empire falling to pieces around him, the Turk was still alive. In his breast was beating the heart of a race that had challenged the world. In Constantinople, under the guns of the allied fleets, there functioned a puppet government of Turkey. But among the stern hills and valleys of "the Turkish Homelands" in Anatolia, there dwelt that company of poor men . . . who would not see it settled so.'

*

Every aspirant for political power needs a little luck, and as the delegates to the Sivas conference made their way in secret by night across the mountain passes the Constantinople government ordered the police to intercept Mustafa Kemal. Less than five miles from the place where the trap was laid, a horseman galloped towards him with a warning. Mustafa Kemal detoured and arrived at Sivas, where the strength of armed units loyal to him made an attack impossible.

During the conference he had an even bigger stroke of good fortune. Many delegates were afraid to give Mustafa Kemal all the powers he demanded, but on the third day of endless discussions a message from Constantinople to the Governor of Malatia, a Kurdish province south of Sivas, was intercepted. It ordered the Governor to raise a levy of Kurdish tribesmen, march on Sivas and arrest the delegates.

To the delegates Mustafa Kemal sneered, 'How dare they send a bunch of tribesmen to arrest true Turks.' After that he dominated the conference, not only with his ideas but with his oratory. Sivas was the moment in which the Nationalist movement changed from local to a national level. A provisional government was formed with Mustafa Kemal as chairman. Among his first tasks was to prove by captured documents that the Kurdish raid had been personally ordered by Ferid, the Grand Vizier who had originally sent him to Anatolia. He also found proof of British participation in the form of Major E. W. C. Noel, a political officer of unorthodox activities who was with the Kurds and who (incredibly) sent a cable in clear to Constantinople implicating the British.

Mustafa Kemal sent an ultimatum to Constantinople that Ferid must be dismissed, and when he received no reply he decided on more drastic action. Ordering the military to take over the post and telegraphs, he cut Constantinople off from the rest of Turkey, diverted all mail – and that meant the revenue – to his National Congress, which had just moved to Angora (later to become Ankara). It was a small town chosen for its central position in Turkey, its strong natural defences and doubtless because it was one of the few towns in the area linked to Constantinople by a railway.

Within a few days, the Sultan capitulated. Ferid was sacked, and new elections were held in which the Nationalists won a large majority. 'Now,' as Mustafa Kemal told a friend, 'the first phase is at an end' – and it was an astonishing victory, measured by any standards, for in four months he had brought about the downfall of the government which had dismissed him and the Grand Vizier who was the tool of the Allies.

Mustafa Kemal himself was elected deputy for the town of Ezerum, but as the newly elected deputies cheerfully set off from remote and drab Angora to sample the fleshpots of Constantinople Mustafa Kemal refused to go. He was convinced that any parliament sitting cheek by jowl with Allied occupation forces in Constantinople must fail.

It did. Within a week of Parliament convening (in January 1920), the Allies managed to persuade the Sultan to dismiss the Minister of War and Chief of Staff, following several large thefts of arms from Allied dumps, in which it was known that they were implicated. It made no difference. Their dismissals were followed by another major raid on a French depot at Akbas, in which the Nationalists made off with eight thousand rifles, forty machine-guns and twenty thousand boxes of ammunition.

To the exasperated Allies only one course seemed possible for, as Lord Curzon told the House of Lords, 'The Allies cannot any longer acquiesce in a state of affairs in which they are flouted at Constantinople while persecution and massacre occur elsewhere.' Powerless to check the fighting in the interior with their insufficient troops, the Allies could at least show who were the masters of Constantinople. Up to now they had behaved with circumspection as a military 'presence', but before dawn on 16 March 1920 British warships anchored almost at the Galata Bridge and British armoured cars rattled through the cobbled streets into the Turkish quarter of Constantinople, seizing the War Office, the Admiralty and the radio station. The capital was formally placed under military occupation. The Grand Vizier was arrested and bundled off to Malta, together with every Nationalist deputy who had not made good his escape. Parliament was dissolved; back in Angora, Mustafa Kemal said, 'Today, by the forcible occupation of Constantinople, an end has been made of the seven hundred years' life and sovereignty of the Ottoman Empire.'

Mustafa Kemal immediately arrested every British officer he could find in Anatolia.* Those deputies who escaped made their way to Angora, where on 23 April 1920 the Grand National Assembly of Turkey held its

* They were exchanged in 1921 for the Nationalists deported to Malta.

first session. Mustafa Kemal was elected President and issued to the world his statement of faith: 'Sovereignty belongs unconditionally to the nation. The Grand National Assembly is the true and sole representative of the nation. Legislative authority and executive power are manifested and concentrated in the Grand National Assembly.'

Yet these brave words ignored an important fact. He was 'the head of a provisional government without money, power, or any of the machinery of government'. Allied planes were soon dropping leaflets urging 'the rebels' to capitulate. Mustafa Kemal was court-martialled and sentenced to death *in absentia*. The Sultan, though forbidden a regular army by the allies, was allowed to form 'the Caliph's Army', which was despatched to Anatolia, together with a large number of priests who summoned their religious brethren in every town and village and warned them of the dangers of tinkering with the cause of a man who despised God and their Sultan. Backed by religious fervour, many were soon up in arms against the Kemalists all over Anatolia, and before long Mustafa Kemal's men were wholly occupied in fighting for survival, even at times on the outskirts of Angora itself. The country was on the verge of civil war.

One wonders what the outcome would have been had the attacks on the 'rebels' been sustained. It is hard to believe that Mustafa Kemal could have held out indefinitely, for many of the army chiefs who had swept him to power were becoming disgruntled. So were the peasants, who now only wanted to be left in peace to reap their harvests.

Angora itself was hardly a headquarters to inspire confidence, for it was little more than a village built on twin hills 'rising like nipples from the bosom of the Anatolian plateau'. Baked in summer, snow-clad in winter, the town had never recovered from a disastrous fire during the war, and every mud street was scarred with blackened, shattered buildings. A Turkish war-correspondent, Alaeddine Haidar, who arrived and innocently enquired for a room was told he would be lucky to find a numbered stair on which to sleep. (In fact he ended up in a cupboard.)

This was the headquarters of new Turkey, and here Mustafa Kemal was surviving on a day-to-day basis. He and the faithful Arif slept in turns, in their clothes, their horses saddled in the courtyard below ready for instant flight. Mustafa Kemal and his forces, many growling with disaffection, could hardly have lasted much longer, had not the victors of the First

World War, meeting in a distant land, made two incredible errors, of the kind which so often seem incomprehensible to less exalted citizens.

*

In Paris, in the spring of 1920, Lloyd George, President Wilson and Clemenceau were preparing to dispose of the estate of The Sick Man of Europe in what was to be called The Treaty of Sèvres (signed later, but never ratified). When details of the treaty became known by the end of May, Turkey announced a national day of mourning, for its terms were intolerably harsh – far more onerous than those imposed on Germany. The immediate reaction inside Turkey was electric: if there were no organized resistance, Turkey was doomed. And, since the Sultan seemed to agree with everything the great powers demanded, only one man could save the Turkish nation. Had the Allies in Paris been determined to back Mustafa Kemal, they could not have hit on a neater method. The civil war started to change shape. Though it was still chiefly a war of daring irregular bands, thousands joined Mustafa Kemal's colours and some of them actually reached Constantinople and for two days opened fire on the building where the British High Commissioner had his headquarters.

The first error of 'the peacemakers' had been bad enough; but now it was followed by another, as they faced the problem of deciding with whom to negotiate – a guerrilla leader with power but no legal status, or a legal puppet-sultan with no power? Obviously the internal disasters in Turkey had to be stopped before 'a just, honourable and lasting peace treaty' was signed. But how?

Attending the conference was a mild-mannered, placid man with glasses, all of which 'gave him an air of child-like simplicity'. He was Venizelos, still Prime Minister of a Greece that now included Smyrna, and whose ambition for twenty years had been to extend the Greek Empire along the Mediterranean coast of Anatolia. Lloyd George knew perfectly well that Venizelos had a huge concentration of well-equipped troops in Smyrna. He had bought vast stocks of surplus war-stores from Britain and France at cut-rate prices. Indeed, Greece now probably had the best-equipped army in the Middle East, sitting idle, while the Allies were each engaged with their own particular post-war problems. Italy was in the throes of a Communist revolution; France was tied up in Syria; Britain was faced with civil war in Ireland and rebellion in India. The United

States could not become involved because of the illness of President Wilson, who within a few months would vanish from the conference table, 'a broken and baffled prophet', in the words of Lloyd George, 'unable to put up any further fight for his faith'.

So when Venizelos quietly offered the services of his Greek army to the victorious but hard-pressed Allies, his suggestion was hastily and gratefully accepted. By early June Britain's Mediterranean fleet gathered at the Golden Horn. On 22 June 1920, two Greek armies marched inland from Smyrna.

The hatred between Greek and Turk stretched back to the age of Byzantium. Now, in one moment of folly, the Allied statesmen themselves provided the final factor needed to reunite Turkey, to bring brothers divided by civil strife together to fight the common foe.

*

At first, unity was not enough. The Turks might have been able to fire a few impertinent shots at the High Commissioner's office, but the bands of bedraggled irregulars, often in rags, sometimes without shoes, armed with a variety of ancient flintlocks and muskets, were no match for the well-drilled, superbly armed Greeks, who, with British military advisers, swept everything before them.

The Greek war fell roughly into three major campaigns – one each in 1920, 1921, 1922 – and in the first, the motley Nationalist forces, hurriedly sent from the east to the western front, were completely routed, while a second Greek army advanced into Thrace – European Turkey – clearing the last Nationalist soldier from the province almost as far as Constantinople.

Lloyd George was delighted, though he did not seem geographically acquainted with the scene of battle, for at an Allied conference in Spa he boasted, 'They [the Turks] are beaten and fleeing with their forces towards Mecca.'

'Angora,' Curzon corrected him acidly.

'Lord Curzon is good enough to correct me on a triviality,' replied Lloyd George. 'Nevertheless . . .'

As the Greek summer campaign of 1920 ended, the situation was not without irony. In Constantinople the Allies waited, powerless. Though the Sultan had brought Damad Ferid back to head a government which

Churchill described as a new 'Ministry of Marionettes', and though he still thundered against 'the rebels', he was equally powerless; his only protection from Mustafa Kemal was a fence of hateful Greek bayonets.

The defeats had been an ignominious blow to Mustafa Kemal's pride, for in Turkey victory or defeat was always identified personally with a leader. And if the Nationalists had fared as badly in 1921, he might have been submerged forever by deputies thirsty for his blood. But this was the year when the tide turned for Mustafa Kemal.

As he prepared for the expected Greek onslaught, he was also busy politically. Soviet Russia was sending him money and arms. So was Italy, while France was in secret contact with Angora with promises of help. The Turks were united, except for the Sultan's clique, while Greece was now split following the fall from power of Venizelos.

Untiringly and unsparingly, Mustafa Kemal set about transforming his guerrillas into some sort of cohesive army, employing at times the most primitive methods. 'Every dwelling without exception has to supply a kit consisting of a parcel of underwear, a pair of socks and a pair of shoes,' he decreed. The noise of creaking oxcarts covered the land when Kemal (as Churchill remembered) 'called upon the wives and daughters of his soldiers to do the work of camels and oxen which he lacked.' Mustafa Kemal demanded total mobilization of women while the men trained. As they neared the fighting zone, women, often with babies tightly bound on their backs, not only drove the carts, but carried the heavy shells, one on each shoulder, to the guns.

Mustafa Kemal had moved to a large stone house at the village of Chankaya, which lay on a bare ridge four miles outside Angora. We have a picture of him in those days: 'He often growled and complained at those around him, and often unjustly. He rarely, and then only grudgingly, showed his gratitude to his subordinates. He was a man to avoid, for his mood decided his outlook; he was more often ill-natured than pleasant, and, if displeased, would be harsh and merciless. He also changed very rapidly in looks. One day he would seem young and full of life, and the next, ten years older, lined and tired.'

This was until the arrival of a young and attractive relative. Fikriye was dark and slender, 'a delicate, fragile girl, quiet and refined, with a white oval face and deep brown eyes'. She was Mustafa Kemal's cousin and

The War between
GREECE & TURKEY
1922

Miles
0   200

Greek Minority areas 1918
Awarded to Greece at Treaty
  of Sevres 1919
British controlled zone
  of the straits 1920-22.

Turkish advances, 1922.

Transfer of populations
after 1922 :—

Greeks......1,377,000
Turks......410,000
Bulgarians......250,000

Final western frontier
of Turkey

BULGARIA

YUGOSLAVIA

BULGARIANS
250000

GREEKS
50,000

GREEKS
310,000

GREEKS
625,000

TURKS
360000

Salonika

Athens

GREECE

CRETE

GREEKS
FROM CAUCASUS
50,000

GREEKS
FROM
RUSSIA
12,000

GREEKS FROM
TREBIZOND
280,000

Black Sea

Constantinople

Mudania

Chanak

Ankara
(Angora)

ANATOLIA

T U R K E Y

Smyrna

TURKS
25000

GREEKS
75000

RHODES

DODECANESE
(Italian)

GREEKS FROM
SOUTH TURKEY
50,000

they had known each other all their lives, though it was not until the year before Mustafa Kemal went to Salonika that she became more intimate with him. Fikriye had been married and divorced, she liked to laugh and gossip and make love, and to a man like Mustafa Kemal with a sporadic sexual appetite she served a delightful purpose, for she asked nothing in return. Now he installed her as his mistress in Chankaya. She was not only gay but had a natural intelligence. She never interfered with his work, she left him and his cronies alone during bouts of drinking, yet, since she was his cousin, she could, and did, act as his hostess whenever he wished. 'To Kemal Fikriye gave that sense of familiarity and ease which marriage afforded.' It was an admirable arrangement for a man who, when asked once what quality he admired most in a woman, replied laconically, 'Availability.'

Far to the east of this 'Sultan' in Angora the Sultan in Constantinople – now over sixty – was similarly engaged, for he too faced problems since he had been (as Lloyd George put it) 'vaticanized'. He too needed feminine companionship, and he found it in the arms of a gardener's seventeen-year-old daughter called Navsad whom he installed in a villa at Yilditz, doubtless more comfortable than Fikriye's, but employed for much the same purpose. Though the Sultan's privy purse was empty, the friendly British gave him a substantial allowance.

*

In July the Greeks attacked in force, and once again swept everything before them until they advanced on the vital railway junction of Eski Shehir, the key to western Anatolia. The advance had not been made without heavy Greek losses. Ernest Hemingway, then a war correspondent for the *Toronto Star*, cabled that it was the first time he had seen 'dead men wearing white ballet skirts and upturned shoes with pompoms on them'.

The losses, however, could not disguise the threat that faced Mustafa Kemal: that the Greeks planned not only to capture the junction but to encircle the main Turkish army. It was now that Mustafa Kemal showed his genius as a military strategist. Any counter-attack would probably fail. Yet, if he evacuated the area, he would be sacrificing the Turkish civilian population to Greek brutality. Without hesitation he evacuated not only the immediate territory, but ordered a general retreat of over two hundred miles to the Sakkaria river which twisted through mountainous country. This, he reasoned, would give the army time to reform and cover Angora, and embarrass the Greeks by lengthening their lines of communication.

On 24 August 1921, Turks and Greeks met on the Sakkaria river, with Mustafa Kemal in personal command. For three weeks of bloodshed on a sixty-mile front neither side gave way in a terrain of valleys, gorges, hill-tops that at times isolated entire units, leaving them to fight personal wars of their own. It was a battle at close quarters, with Mustafa Kemal in the trenches with his men. One Turkish division lost seventy-five per cent of its men. Seven divisional generals on both sides were killed, mostly at the point of the bayonet. Finally, the one factor which Mustafa Kemal had foreseen gave victory to the Turks. The Greek supply lines broke down. In the burning August sun, drinking-water started to give out, the food ration was reduced to a handful of maize a day. At the end of the third week the Greek line showed its first signs of cracking and then abruptly the noise of battle was stilled. The Greeks retreated for two hundred miles, with Mustafa Kemal in hot pursuit.

It took nearly a year before the Turks were ready to attack again, but the significance of Sakkaria was not lost on neighbouring nations, and Mustafa Kemal soon found himself immersed in politics while his generals further improved the Army in preparation for the final *coup*. Within five weeks Nationalist Turkey had signed an agreement with France, thus tacitly recognizing that Mustafa Kemal was the true leader of the country. Equally important, large supplies of French arms were promised. He made another agreement with Soviet Russia, another with Italy which also promised him arms.

The British Government frowned on these semi-secret arrangements by their allies, and their displeasure was followed by a sinister British Secret Service move in which a spy was sent to Angora with, apparently, the promise of £100,000 if he succeeded in assassinating Mustafa Kemal. The spy was an Indian, Mustafa Seghir, who arrived ostensibly as a deputy for the 'Indian Committee of the Caliphate', and when it was learned in Angora that he was there to dispense a £1 million fund raised to help Nationalists he was wined and dined. But he was a clumsy fellow, for when the £1 million did not arrive Mustafa Kemal's men intercepted letters in invisible ink to the British Secret Service.

He was arrested and confessed that he received a regular salary from the British, had spied in Switzerland during the war, in Persia, and even handed the judges a list of Turks in Istanbul who were wanted by the British. When the judge asked why he had been selected for such a perilous and difficult commission, he replied, 'Because shortly before this I had successfully carried out a mission which was at least quite as dangerous as this – the murder of the Emir of Afghanistan.'

The unlikely espionage agent – who had remained perfectly calm and courteous throughout the trial – was sentenced to death by hanging, and received the sentence with no show of emotion. Indeed, the Turkish newspapers reported a macabre twist to his last moments on earth. As he mounted the scaffold, he sat down. A bewildered hangman tried to explain through an interpreter that it was customary to stand. 'Please excuse me,' said Seghir politely, 'this is the first time I have been in a situation like this.'

*

The year following Sakkaria must have included other bizarre scenes, for though Mustafa Kemal was now dealing with the heads of major European countries on equal terms, the business of State was conducted in Angora in conditions resembling nothing so much as a Western film. A small, dreary Assembly Hall had been built on the outskirts of the city, isolated and looking 'more like a small railway station than anything else'. Delegates sat on school benches, recalling to one American 'the early meetings of the North American farmers after the Declaration of Independence'. The effect was heightened as the delegates arriving from long distances tethered their horses to a rail outside the building.

Meanwhile shipments of arms from Russia, France and Italy arrived, and by the summer of 1922 Mustafa Kemal was ready to strike the mortal blow against a Greek army sorely weakened by internal dissension. At 4 a.m. on 26 August he issued a battle call: 'Soldiers, forward! Your goal is the Mediterranean.'

The Greeks were taken completely by surprise. By dusk on the first day he had cut through their main army which was soon in headlong retreat.

By the end of the month its tattered remnants were rushing for the ships that awaited them at the coast. As the rout continued, Smyrna, almost to the last moment, remained convinced that a conference in London would find a solution before the Turks reached their city. After all, British and American warships were anchored in the gulf, reassuring shapes that spelled a hope for 'fair play'. It seemed impossible, in those last days of false optimism, that anything could happen. The dinner-dances still continued on the terrace of the Hotel Naim, and an Italian opera company still performed *Rigoletto* at the Sporting Club.

Then, suddenly, the Bourse was closed. The first wounded trickled back into the city, begging for crusts of bread as they told tales of appalling butchery. 'They looked neither to the right nor to the left but straight ahead, like men walking in their sleep,' George Horton, the American Consul, remembered.

By the first week of September, ten days after the attack started, the Turkish Army had covered 190 miles and the first troops were marching through the streets of Smyrna.

Mustafa Kemal was not with them. Deliberately he had remained behind the front line at his headquarters, a tent perched on the roof of a stable. Though sure of success, he was unwilling to bask in its glory until the stage was set. For to the Turks the recapture of Smyrna was more than a military victory. It was symbolic.

On 9 September, when the fighting had died down, Mustafa Kemal made his triumphant entry into Smyrna, driving the last few miles at the head of a convoy of cars decked with boughs of laurel, through crowds of cheering, weeping, praying, hysterical Turks.

It was, perhaps, Mustafa Kemal's greatest moment of triumph; but it was blotted by an insane act.

Chapter fifteen
The fire of Smyrna

Smyrna was unlike any other city in the Ottoman Empire. Blessed by a benign climate, backed by a rich, fertile hinterland where even the poorest peasant at least had more than enough fruit, bread and cheese, it was the heart of an area drenched by the perfumes of almond trees, mimosa and oleander. Turk, Jew, Greek, Armenian, European made up the population of a seaport whose export trade surpassed that of Constantinople, and though they all lived in their own separate quarters they mingled in the main streets in a dazzling variety of native costumes making one European feel that he lived 'in an eternal masquerade'. Cosmopolitan and wealthy, many people lived by the harbour, shaped as perfectly as the crescent on the Turkish flag, and lined with two-storey houses far more imposing than the villas of Constantinople. The warehouses were jammed with figs, apricots, raisins, pomegranates, for this was harvest time, and cargo boats from all over the world waited to load up.

The people of Smyrna were famous for their gambling and dancing and beautiful women. Most of them spoke three or four languages. They had clubs, restaurants, houseboats, tea dances, golf and racecourses.

Yet the city still remained a curious mixture of yesterday and tomorrow. At one end of the town – agreeably named Paradiso – was the American colony, its trim gardens, large American schools and the dollar-backed YMCA and YWCA making it, as one schoolmaster's wife wrote home, 'a veritable little corner of America set down in Smyrna'. Yet the placid routine of Paradiso was interrupted almost daily by caravans from the east, plodding along routes unchanged since Biblical times.

It was a city with an anguished past. From its earliest days the cradle of Greek legends, it inspired its native philosopher, Homer, to write his *Odyssey*. The Romans, after they had taken it, described it as 'the finest city in Asia'. Time after time it was destroyed – by earthquake, by the

Persians, by Tamerlane at the start of the fifteenth century. And finally in 1424 the Greeks and Armenians, whose fathers and mothers had lived there for 1,500 years, became the unwilling slaves of the Ottoman Empire.

*

On the morning of Saturday, 9 September 1922, the vast harbour was so choked with vessels that, 'It was almost possible for a man to walk across, jumping from ship to ship.' Humble freighters, lofty passenger-ships, anchored next to Levantine caïques so fragile they bobbed as each wave slapped them, and behind them stood the maritime might of four naval powers: two British battleships, protected by three cruisers and six destroyers; three American destroyers; three French cruisers and two destroyers; an Italian cruiser and destroyer – in all, twenty-one warships.

They were there for one purpose only – to protect their nationals. Strict neutrality was to be observed, for with the peace treaties still being drafted in Paris the Allies had firmly resolved that on no account must they interfere with Turkey's domestic problems.

On 10 September, Mustafa Kemal entered the city. His uniform bore no badges of rank, and he immediately made for the Greek government building on the quay, where a Greek flag had been spread over the steps like a carpet. Mustafa Kemal refused to walk on it, protesting, 'That is a symbol of a country's independence.'

Already there was sporadic street-fighting and individual excesses by both sides; looting was widespread, and the tension caused by thousands of Greek refugees pouring in from the devastated countryside was mounting. There was little food, no lodging. Holding precious bundles containing all they had salvaged, and obsessed by fears of an Ottoman massacre, men, women and children were sleeping in the streets, 'hungry and hopeless and often sick'. But there was still no sign of the violence to come, and that evening Mustafa Kemal strolled unrecognized into a hotel popular with foreigners where a waiter told him there was no table free – until a Turk suddenly recognized him and jumped to his feet, offering him his chair. As Mustafa Kemal toasted victory – his first sip of alcohol since the campaign started – he turned to a group of Greeks at the next table and asked, 'Did King Constantine ever come here to drink a glass of raki?' Apprehensively they shook their heads. 'Then why did he bother to take Smyrna?' he asked.

That was Sunday, the day that Mustafa Kemal issued an official proclamation ordering the death penalty for 'any Turkish soldier who molested non-combatants'. It was one of history's hollowest promises. That very day, the Turkish commander, Nurredin, a man with a reputation for sadism, sent for the Greek Patriarch, Monsignor Chrysostomos. As the Patriarch entered the room, Nurredin spat at him, pointed to a dossier and told him that he had been sentenced to death by a tribunal in Angora. 'There is nothing left but for the people to give their judgement,' he shouted. 'Now get out of my sight.'

The old man was walking down the steps when the Turkish general appeared on the balcony above and yelled to the mob, 'Treat him as he deserves.'

A patrol of twenty French marines had accompanied the Patriarch to the general's headquarters, but as a gesture, and under the strictest orders not to interfere. Now they watched horrified and helpless as the crowd tore the old man to pieces, gouging out his eyes, cutting off his ears, nose and hands. One of the French patrol later gave evidence that, 'The men were beside themselves and were trembling with indignation and wished to interfere, but, acting in conformity with orders received, the officer forbade them to move, at the point of the revolver.'

The murder of the Patriarch was soon accepted as a licence to murder and loot. Mrs Anna Birge, the wife of an American missionary, who escaped at the last moment, watched, terrified, as Turkish troops stormed into their home and stripped it. Then, in her words, the Turks 'started the most terrible looting, raping and killing. Whole companies broke into the stores and swept them clean of their goods. The American teachers in our American Girls' School watched the soldiers kill civilians in the street in front of the school, enter homes and kill families and throw them out into the street. When the sun set that evening dead bodies were lying all over the streets.'

Within a few hours, twenty women who had taken refuge in a British house were taken out and violated. An American's grave was opened, the body exhumed and torn to pieces. Every Greek and Armenian made, as though by instinct, for the quayside as the Turks systematically started flushing them out, raping the girls, murdering the men, until 'every Armenian and Greek in Smyrna had become a refugee'. Thousands lined

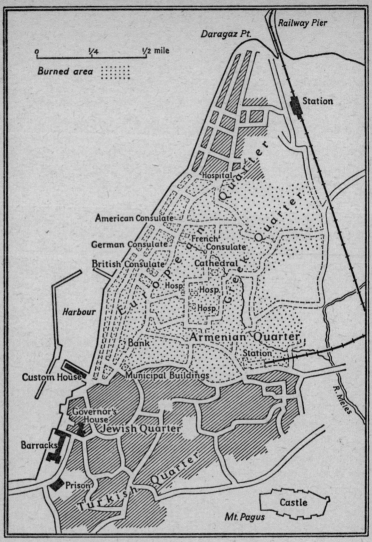

Smyrna: the extent of the fire

the edge of the harbour. Hundreds jumped into the water and swam – but not to safety; for under the policy of strict neutrality the warships could not take them aboard.

It was not until Wednesday, 13 September, that the great fire started – or rather several fires which broke out simultaneously. Among the first to see the flames was Miss Minnie Mills, Director of the American Girls' College, who remembers, 'Soon after lunch fire broke out very near the school, and spread rapidly. I saw with my own eyes a Turkish officer enter a house with small tins of petroleum or benzine and in a few minutes the house was in flames. Our teachers and girls saw Turks in regular soldiers' uniforms, and in several cases in officers' uniforms, using long sticks with rags at the end which were dipped in a can of liquid, and carried into houses which were soon burning. While the fire started just across the street from our school, throughout the quarter [the Armenian quarter] every third or fifth house was set on fire. The wind, though not very strong, was away from the Turkish quarter and blowing toward the Christian quarters, and it looks as if they waited for a favourable wind.'

The Director of the Near East Relief Organization, Mr Jacquith, saw Turks throwing oil on the waterfront buildings. A Major Davis of the Red Cross watched them sprinkling streets and houses along the line of fire with petrol. Mrs Birge saw Turks entering houses, carrying tins. Within a few moments the buildings erupted in flames.

Among those thrown into prison was a Smyrnean merchant called Socrates Onassis who was on a Turkish blacklist for being involved with the Greeks during the occupation. Socrates' brother, Alexander, was publicly hanged, his sister perished when trapped with five hundred in a church which the Turks set on fire. Socrates, however, was saved, thanks to the energetic efforts of his sixteen-year-old son, Aristotle, who, it is said, gained influence with a Turkish general and the American Vice-Consul by producing large supplies of whisky, then in short supply, which he exchanged for a safe-conduct pass enabling him to reach his father's fortune and buy his freedom.

By late afternoon on the first day more than a thousand flimsy lath-and-plaster houses had been burned to ashes, and the blaze, fanned by a mounting wind, was moving towards the waterfront, as though chasing tens of thousands of refugees trying to reach the sea. Over everything hung the odour of burning flesh. At midnight the whole line of houses along the front caught fire simultaneously. As the crowds surged towards the water's edge, Captain Bertram Thesiger, of the battleship *King George V* remembers hearing 'the most awful scream one could ever imagine'. It was a scream which Ernest Hemingway, who was still reporting for the *Toronto Star*, would later describe. 'We were in the harbour and they were all on the pier and at midnight they started screaming,' he wrote.

Ward Price, of the *Daily Mail*, who had managed to reach Smyrna on the *Iron Duke*, wrote, 'The surface of the sea shone like burned copper. Twenty distinct volcanoes of raging flame were throwing up ragged, writhing tongues to a height of a hundred feet. The towers of the Greek churches, the domes of the mosques, the flat roofs of the houses, were silhouetted against a curtain of flame.'

The thousands of Greeks and Armenians on the waterfront were now so tightly crushed that when a man died he was still supported in a standing position. To those still alive there was an incongruous note – the occasional bar of music wafted across the water. Determined that the routine of the British Navy should not be disturbed, the band of the British flagship played selections of light dinner music on deck.

Despite injunctions to remain neutral, the Allied navies the following morning reversed their orders, and all available boats were sent ashore to pick up women and children. The *Iron Duke* alone took on two thousand refugees; but, though the naval vessels did what they could, the number saved was pitifully small, as the fire continued to spread across the entire city, with the exception of the Turkish quarter which stood on the slopes of Mount Pagus, higher than the rest of the city – 'a labyrinth of narrow, crooked, vine-covered streets dotted with ancient fountains that exuded a flavour of the Arabian Nights'.

It was untouched.

*

There was one other oasis of peace in this dark moment of Smyrna's long and tortured history. It centred round Mustafa Kemal, who had fallen in love.

Shortly after setting up headquarters in Smyrna, a young woman asked to see him and, brushing past an orderly, walked straight into Mustafa Kemal's office. Furious at being interrupted, he was about to shout at her, then stopped, for, 'This was no peasant woman, but a lady of evident breeding, unveiled and wearing sober but elegant clothes.'

Her name was Latife, and she was the 24-year-old daughter of a rich shipowner. She was short, round-faced, but with large, intelligent eyes and a beautifully modulated voice. Her parents were on holiday in Biarritz but she had, she said, insisted on returning to greet 'the hero of modern Turkey'. She wore a locket round her neck in which she carried his photograph. She asked if he minded.

'Why should I mind? I'm flattered,' Mustafa Kemal replied.

Latife now made a proposal. Her parents' house on the outskirts of Smyrna was cool, large, comfortable – and empty. It lay up the hillside at Bornova, renowned for its beautiful gardens. It had a staff and servants. Why not use the empty villa as his headquarters? She spoke several languages, she added, and would be delighted to help in any way she could.

Mustafa Kemal accepted without hesitation, and found the house, surrounded by gardens and vineyards, much to his liking and, 'Above all there was the girl. Already he desired her. Within a day or two he was in love with her.'

On the first night of the great fire, they held a party at Bornova for guests, including several journalists with long memories. Latife received them with dignity and charm at the top of the veranda stairs suffocated with wistaria, roses and jasmine. She was, one remembered, 'a delicate little lady in black'. Mustafa Kemal wore a casual white-belted Caucasian-type shirt. After dinner he and Latife stood on the veranda with their guests. Below them, like a raging furnace, lay burning Smyrna, the flames outlining the grey battleships at anchor.

'It is a sign,' Mustafa Kemal pointed to the fire, 'a sign that Turkey is purged of the traitors, the Christians, and of the foreigners, and that Turkey is for the Turks.'

Not until the last guest had left, however, did Mustafa Kemal come to the real point of the evening. A man who still regarded his women as chattels – particularly those who so obviously adored him – he had been irritated by her reserve. She would allow him to kiss her, but that was all, and Mustafa Kemal could not understand why she would not go to bed with him. As she later told friends, she told him that she loved him and would be happy to marry him. But she was, she said, an emancipated modern woman and on no account would she ever become his mistress.

Mustafa Kemal raged and stormed. 'What is marriage?' she remembers him asking. 'A few empty words said by a dirty, bearded priest. Do they make so much difference?'

Apparently they did. For when Mustafa Kemal left Smyrna at the end of September – in a rage with her – Latife was still a virgin.

*

By the Friday the desolation was fearful, and the *Daily Telegraph*'s correspondent cabled to London:

Three-fifths of Smyrna are in ashes. More than 300,000 persons are homeless this morning as the fire burns itself out, after destroying the entire Armenian, Greek and foreign quarters.

The loss of life is impossible to compute. Every Allied ship in the harbour volunteered its services in clearing the refugees, many of whom were badly wounded. The streets are littered with dead. Thus, despite Kemal Pasha's assurances, Turkey has 'regulated past accounts'.

Now the tragedy took a new turn. On 16 September Mustafa Kemal issued a proclamation: All Greek and Armenian men between fifteen and fifty were to be deported in labour gangs into the interior by 30 September. All other refugees – and that meant Christians of all sexes and ages – had to be evacuated by the same date, or they would be rounded up too. It was a fate which Dr Esther Lovejoy, the only American doctor in Smyrna at the time, described as 'nothing less than a sentence of death. It is in fact worse than death, because it is preceded by slavery on the part of men and a fate even worse on the part of girls and women.'

By 26 September, four days before the ultimatum expired, nineteen merchantmen arrived to evacuate the inhabitants. Dr Lovejoy was down on the quay helping, and remembers 'the mass of miserable people pushed on down toward the quay and the long railroad pier in order to get aboard the rescuing ships'. Many women carried their sick and their babies on their backs. Dead animals and bodies floated in the water before them. As the crowd surged down the line they were blocked by five fences near the end of the quay. Everyone had to go through the five gates guarded by Turkish soldiers looking for men – which, as the doctor noted, 'afforded an opportunity to search and rob the women'.

Many old women and expectant mothers were pushed into the water to drown. Dr Lovejoy's special task was to watch out for pregnant women, 'and as I stood there one poor woman in the agony of her labour was thrust through this gate just as her baby came into the world. I give you the details of this one terrible case because it is the worst thing I have ever heard of or seen in my life. But there were hundreds of cases occurring at that time.'

If a Turk saw a prosperous-looking woman 'he would seize her, pull her aside, examine her – going over her body and lifting up her skirt, and looking into her stockings to see whether she had any money they could take. I am now telling what I saw with my own eyes, and I would take oath to what I say.'

In those last fearful days – and knowing that those who were not evacuated would be consigned to a living death in the interior – Smyrna became a city of astonishing contrasts. 'The Grand Rue de Pera offered some unusual sights,' wrote Marjorie Housepian later. 'One man, jogging along with five coffins strapped to his back, explained to an astonished reporter that he was searching for the likely location of a massacre; another man was seen staggering towards the docks carrying a red-hot kitchen stove.' Turkish belly dancers were in tears because the Greek jazz bands which supported their act had vanished; but Turkish barbers were delighted because they were buying up modern dentists' chairs for next-to-nothing from Greeks anxious to raise the last possible penny before escaping.

By 1 October the Allied vessels had performed a feat little short of a miracle; 180,000 women and children had been taken on board, and when Mustafa Kemal was persuaded to extend the time limit until 6 October another sixty thousand escaped to freedom.

It is impossible, even today, to say with certainty how many died in Smyrna. George Horton, the American Consul, was probably nearest the truth in his estimate that at least 100,000 perished.

*

One question remains: Did the Turks start the fire, or was it the result of a Greek and Armenian 'scorched-earth policy', as Mustafa Kemal insisted time and again?

According to Edward Hale Bierstadt, the blame lay undeniably with the Turks. Bierstadt, as Executive Secretary of the United States Emergency Committee, forced a Refugee Bill through Congress after the fire and then wrote a book, *The Great Betrayal*, in which he so shocked the American State Department that Allen Dulles, in charge of the Near East desk in Washington, sent for him personally to refute the 'lies' it contained. Dulles was unable to find one exaggeration of fact, even in the following passage:

What do the facts show for themselves? The fire broke out almost simultaneously at four points along the southern extremity of the Armenian quarter. The direction of the prevailing wind, the *imbat*, which blows as regularly as clockwork from noon or two o'clock until sunset, is usually from south-west to north-east. Knowing this, the Greeks and Armenians would know likewise that to start the fire when and where it was started would be to destroy their own quarters and leave the Turkish and Jewish quarters, the poorest part of the city, intact. Why should the Greeks and Armenians burn their own homes, to which they still hoped to return? The Turks had a reason. They wished to hide forever all trace of sack, massacre, and rapine that had been going on for four days. And more, they had determined that Christianity should be obliterated from the Christian capital of Asia Minor, that it should be wiped out utterly with fire and sword. So it was done. There is not and there never has been one shadow of doubt as to who burned Smyrna, or why they burned it. Every scrap of evidence points to Turkish responsibility.

Yet despite the overwhelming evidence of eye-witnesses, there was a studied reluctance on the part of government officials to implicate the Turks and a frenzied attempt to minimize the 'gross exaggerations' of the Press. To Edward Bierstadt, this was because of huge commercial interests in Turkey, and certainly at the time Standard Oil, American Tobacco and the Chester Concessions had large commitments in the area; but there was another factor. Ever since the war, nations had taken sides between Greece and Turkey. This doubtless coloured the on-the-spot reports, particularly of Admiral Mark L. Bristol, the 'genial, self-assured' American High Commissioner at Constantinople, who was also in command of American naval forces in the area. Even before Mustafa Kemal entered Smyrna, Bristol had written to a naval colleague, 'To me it is a calamity to let the Greeks have anything in this part of the world. The Greek is about the worst race in the Near East.' Consequently it was not surprising that he cabled the American Secretary of the Navy, 'That the Christians could have set fire to their own homes before leaving them is highly probable especially in view of the fact that when they evacuated the interior they set fire to their own villages before they left them.'

The State Department, which was pleading for 'restraint of expression', was no doubt delighted when Bristol cabled them (on 22 September) urging them to publish an official account to counterbalance the 'exaggerated and alarming reports'. Thoughtfully the Admiral provided them with the raw material, cabling his views:

American officers who have been eye-witnesses of all events occurring at Smyrna, from time of the occupation of that city by Nationalists up to present, report killings which occurred at that city were ones for the most part by individuals or small bands of rowdies or soldiers, and that nothing in the nature of a massacre had occurred. During the fire some people were drowned by attempting to swim to vessels in harbour or by falling off the quay wall, but this number was small. When mass of people were gathered on quay to escape fire, they were guarded by Turkish troops but were at no time prevented by such troops from leaving the quay if they so desired. It is impossible to estimate the number of deaths due to killings, fire and execution, but the total probably does not exceed two thousand.

A very different conclusion was reached by a British judge who studied the evidence during a lawsuit in December 1924. Most of the fire insurance in Smyrna had been in the hands of the British and did not cover 'hostile and warlike operations'. So the Guardian Assurance Company refused to pay $600,000 to the American Tobacco Company, which promptly sued them. Eye-witnesses who had been in Smyrna formed a procession to testify that the Turks had started the fire – a major from the Royal Marines, Sir Harry Lamb, the British Consul-General, a lady who had been raped, members of the Smyrna Fire Brigade. Without hesitation, Mr Justice Rowlatt found in favour of the insurance company, settling the blame fairly and squarely on the Turks.

Chapter sixteen
The dictator

Sakkaria had been a victory of profound consequence perhaps not yet appreciated in Europe; Smyrna was a flashing demonstration of revenge. Ahead, however, lay a mountain far more difficult to scale: the tortuous path to total power. Though Mustafa Kemal was hailed with delirious excitement as the leader of Turkey, though he was all-powerful in Angora, three obstacles blocked his path: the Greek Army had escaped across the sea and was regrouping in Thrace beyond Constantinople; the Allied occupation forces stood between Kemal and them; and finally the old and doddery Sultan was still hanging on pathetically to the remnants of power in Constantinople.

The only way to reach the Greeks lay across the Dardanelles; but Chanak on the Asiatic coast, where Mustafa Kemal and Arif had fought against the British seven years previously, was held by Allied troops. A strip of land on either side of the Bosporus had been established as a neutral zone, and to infringe it meant challenging the Western powers. Mustafa Kemal, however, decided to make it an international issue by moving Turkish troops into the area. He admitted later that he always hoped the matter would be settled by diplomacy, but even though he knew that the British had air and naval power he felt himself strong enough to threaten them, the more so as he was asking only for the right to drive the Greeks out of Turkish territory.

The British did not see it in this light. At the first sign of a Turkish threat Lloyd George received guarantees from the French and Italian troops that they would fight if necessary, and as Mustafa Kemal's threats became more bellicose, Churchill, who was Colonial Secretary, issued a defiant anti-Turkish communiqué. It was a curious document for one who for three years had supported the Turks in violent opposition to Lloyd George; it seems that the prospect of a Turkish army on the rampage in

Europe, in control of the Dardanelles, was too much for Churchill. Unfortunately, he omitted to tell Curzon at the Foreign Office what he had done, and thus the Allies remained in ignorance. It was an extraordinary omission on his part. Curzon, who was furious, described the communiqué as a 'flamboyant manifesto'. The *Daily Mail* cried 'Stop This New War'. The Dominions, who had given qualified promises of support, were soon growling about 'colonial rule from Whitehall'.

Worst of all, it gave the French and the Italians the excuse to extricate themselves from a position which they found distasteful, and so now only the British flag flew at Chanak, under the command of Lieutenant-General Sir Charles Harington.

In the end, barely twenty yards separated Britain and Turkey from war, and neither would give in. Harington was ordered to stand fast in the neutral zone. Mustafa Kemal sent him a cable saying he no longer recognized the neutral zone – and, to prove his words, sent his first patrols of an army totalling nearly 100,000 men to within a few yards of the British barbed wire. He did, however, order them to advance with their guns pointed downwards. The British troops were told not to open fire unless fired upon. To Captain J. C. Petherick, in command of the British patrol, it was obvious that the mock skirmish consisted of 'tactics in reverse'. Each side revealed, rather than concealed, the size of its forces, the extent of its defences.

The two patrols fraternized, 'with the exchange of pots and pans and camp equipment', while Mustafa Kemal and Harington exchanged a flurry of polite telegrams.

The man who really averted war was Harington – and this despite the politicians in London, who now drew up an ultimatum for the British general to deliver to the Turkish commander. In essence its message was brief: retreat or war. But Harington had been told that the French were in contact with Mustafa Kemal, trying to find a formula for peace, and so with great courage he turned a blind eye to the telegraph office and ignored his instructions. At the same time Mustafa Kemal (from his point of view) was behaving with equal patience. As he told Clare Sheridan, a British war correspondent, 'I am acting with such patience in order to give them every chance of retiring with dignity from the attitude they have adopted.'

The delay saved the two sides from war. As British reserves poured in from Malta and Egypt, and the Fleet steamed into the Dardanelles, the French emissary promised Mustafa Kemal that the Allies would instruct the Greeks to evacuate Thrace. Britain had to agree – and Mustafa Kemal had beaten the Greek armies without firing a shot.

The vexed question of the neutral zone was left to a conference held at Mudania, a shabby town of cobbled streets, alive with mosquitoes, on the southern shore of the Sea of Marmora. The only suitable place for the conference was the former Russian consulate, a tiny-roomed, miserable house with dirty white walls hurriedly covered with carpets. The discussions opened in teeming rain, and though Harington was empowered to agree in principle to the evacuation of all British troops in Turkey by stages, he and the Turkish delegate fought for hours over trifling points until Harington almost despaired. Then, as he remembered later, 'The scene is before me now – that awful room – only an oil lamp . . . I paced up one side of the room . . . Ismet [the Turkish delegate] paced up the other, saying he would not agree. Then quite suddenly he said, "J'accepte!" I was never so surprised in my life.'

Fearful that the Turks might change their minds, Harington insisted that the treaty be signed immediately. The agreement took fifteen hours to type in five languages with the limited facilities of Mudania's secretarial corps, but a Turkish military band played tunes to keep the delegates awake.

Now only one step lay between Mustafa Kemal and absolute power.

*

One of Mustafa Kemal's most remarkable traits was his ability to realize just how far he could go when suggesting reforms that might be unpalatable; of confining himself to the art of the possible and yet, while doing so, guiding events in the direction of his ultimate aim to which every apparent compromise inevitably led.

These were his tactics now. He wanted to dismiss the old Sultan from office, yet he realized that to tamper with the religious feelings of the people could be suicidal. With great skill he secretly engineered a campaign of vilification *against* the political actions of the Sultan, branding him and his cabinet as 'pliant tools of the foreigner and politically traitors to Turkey'.

When anger swept the country Mustafa Kemal rushed to the *defence* of the Sultan – as a religious power. Politics and religion might never mix, he agreed, but the Sultan was also the Caliph, so why not abolish the Sultanate which had always been political and retain the Caliphate which had always been religious? It meant that the dynasty of Othman could continue, respected as the religious head of the country, but politics would be left to the politicians.

When the Assembly met in Angora to vote, Mustafa Kemal could sense that many deputies were still against a reform which struck at the foundation of Turkey's historical greatness. He collected trusted friends around him. Some were armed. Mustafa Kemal demanded an immediate vote by show of hands. Cries for a vote by name were shouted down.

'I am sure the House will be unanimous in accepting,' said Mustafa Kemal as his followers ostentatiously fidgeted with their guns. 'A show of hands will be enough.' Mustafa Kemal put the motion. A few hands went up.

'Carried unanimously!' cried the President. Enraged deputies leapt on their benches in protest. In the mêlée, members spat at each other, scuffled and several were injured. With an eye on Mustafa Kemal, the President shouted above the din, 'By the unanimous vote of the Grand National Assembly of Turkey the Sultanate is abolished.' In a few minutes of angry shouting, the Ottoman sultans who had exercised power for seven centuries were relegated to history.

Within the week, Colonel Refet had taken over in Constantinople, leaving the Sultan powerless in Yilditz but determined to remain there, until rumours reached him that he might be put on trial. By now the old Sultan trusted no one except the conductor of his palace orchestra who happened to be the father of one of his five wives. In the greatest secrecy the conductor went to see Harington, the British Commander-in-Chief, who was making preparations to pull out British troops. He was shivering with fright when Harington saw him in his cold, bare, cream-painted office; his verbal message was that the Sultan wanted British protection. Harington, not wanting to be accused of 'abducting' the Sultan, demanded a letter, and when the Sultan had written this he laid his plan.

Shortly before dawn two days later an ambulance arrived at a back door of the Sultan's palace. The Sultan, his small son, and one eunuch shuffled through drizzling rain with a few bags, as an English medical orderly let down the steps at the back of the ambulance. The Sultan was carrying an umbrella which jammed in the ambulance door. Peevishly he refused to close the umbrella because of the rain. Finally a British officer held it over his head and handed it to him when he was inside the vehicle. At the quay a pinnace waited to take the Sultan to the battleship *Malaya* where the Admiral received him with proper ceremony, until the Sultan suddenly screamed with rage at the eunuch. One suitcase was missing. In his high, piping voice the eunuch protested that it was not his fault. Eventually the bag was found in the pinnace, and hugging it close to his chest like a child the Sultan took it to his cabin. The contents were safe – luckily, for the bag contained the Imperial coffee-cups, each one of solid gold.

An hour later, on the morning of 17 November 1922, the last of the Ottoman sultans sailed away, to live in the obscurity of a villa at San Remo. His cousin Abdul Mejid, a son of Abdul Aziz, became Caliph of All the Faithful.

The Sultan had made one last request to Harington; he would be grateful if, at an opportune moment, the general would kindly arrange for his five wives to follow him into exile. (He appears to have forgotten the gardener's daughter.) Harington was able to oblige him, and a eunuch shortly arrived in Constantinople to chaperon them on their journey to Italy. There was no need for secrecy – indeed, their departure was public – but it did result in a quaint cable reaching the British Embassy in Constantinople. It had been despatched by an American impresario, and it read, 'Hippodrome New York could use wives of ex-Sultan. Kindly put me in touch with party who could procure them.'

*

Power was now within Mustafa Kemal's grasp, but despite the ambition which never ceased to motivate him another emotion was gnawing him. He was tired of Fikriye, not only because he had become fascinated by Latife, but because he had been told that she was seriously ill with consumption. So, when he ordered Fikriye to enter a sanatorium in Munich for treatment, it was not only because she was ill, but also because he had become tired of her. He had no patience with illness, either in himself or in others. In the past she had distracted him, but the time had come to end the affair.

Yet, almost as soon as he had packed her off, Mustafa Kemal realized that his bed at Chankaya needed warming. From time to time he imported the ladies of the town (and the occasional young boy) but according to Colonel Arif, still his crony after dark, these evenings often ended in violent scenes in which Mustafa Kemal threw everyone out, cursing and screaming at them in drunken rages.

It seems certain that he was haunted by two things: the memory of Fikriye, probably the only woman with whom he had ever been deeply in love, and the memory of another woman, who had refused him. Only this can explain what happened next.

Without warning he ordered his driver to prepare his car for a long journey. Within an hour he was driving through the night at top speed half-way across Turkey to Smyrna. From the town he raced up the Bornova hills, the road lined with gardens, until he reached Latife's house. He knocked. There was no reply, for she was in an upstairs room. He pushed open the door, ran up the stairs, uttered no word of greeting, but spoke as though ending a sentence he had started during the fire of Smyrna. As the astonished Latife told her friends later, he merely said brusquely, 'It is agreed. We will marry now – at once. No delay, no ceremony. No invitations.'

It was too late that night so he left the villa, returning impatiently soon after dawn. Then, 'He hurried her out into the road, caught hold of the first bearded priest on his way to his mosque, and ordered him to marry them, there, at once, in the street, without delay.'

For their honeymoon the couple toured the war-torn countryside ravaged by the retreating Greeks, talking to peasants, civil leaders, troops, spending the nights wherever there happened to be a convenient inn or tent. Mustafa Kemal told no one he was married. Not until Latife rode beside him 'like an adjutant' at a formal review of the Army did his officers realize she was his wife.

Fikriye heard of the wedding by chance. In Munich, though desperately ill, she had been fêted almost as royalty by the Turkish community, who knew all about her relationship with Mustafa Kemal. Indeed, she boasted that as soon as she had recovered they were to be married. When a 'friend' told her of the marriage, 'She went quiet and lax, her body fell back against the pillows like a rag doll and her large eyes darkened with shock.'

What the friend did not tell her was that the first thing Latife did when she reached Mustafa Kemal's home outside Angora was to throw out Fikriye's carpets, tear down her curtains, and remodel her garden.

*

One of the curious anomalies of Mustafa Kemal's career is that, like Hitler later, he was lauded by the masses yet disliked by many thinkers who did not trust his judgement. It is probably true to say that Mustafa Kemal, like others of genius before him, suffered from time to time from *folie de grandeur*. He found it impossible to imagine that any other man in Turkey could play his self-appointed role. And once this had become an integral part of his basic thinking, of his creed, he became convinced that any means justified any end.

He was horrified when people compared him with Mussolini, his contemporary. 'Is it not amazing that I should be placed beside that mountain of complacency,' he said. 'That hyena in jackboots, who could destroy the Abyssinian savage without a moment's regret. I have fought for my people, but, my God, I have fought most of all for *our* innocent savages.'

Mustafa Kemal did differ in one fundamental respect from Mussolini (and later Hitler). Time and time again he reiterated that Turkey had no 'territorial ambitions'. But he meant it – and proved it. Once the Turco-Greek war was ended he made peace with the Greeks, however brutal his methods, which involved wholesale exchanges of population. He renounced all pan-Turkish, pan-Ottoman and pan-Islamic ideologies. All he demanded was for Turkey to take her place in the comity of nations.

To this end he had long been convinced that Turkey must become a republic. For weeks he promoted this philosophy among his closest supporters – many of them now intellectuals, a different breed from the early members of the Nationalist Party in their rough sheepskin coats.

Mustafa Kemal slowly wore the opposition down, stressing always that Turkey must be 'modern'. (When an old priest asked him what the word 'modern' meant, Mustafa Kemal replied simply, 'Old man, it means being a human being.') He sounded out world opinion by airing his views in an interview with a Vienna newspaper, arguing that Turkey was already a republic in all but name. He cited the United States as the greatest example of a democratic republic where every man had the same opportunities in life, where every man was 'a human being'.

Like any astute politician he first outlined the new provisions to his party members, who turned out in full force expecting a marathon speech. In fact Mustafa Kemal spoke only briefly, not because he was tongue-tied but because he had been fitted that morning with a new set of false teeth which were too loose. But he did have one ally who spoke for him – his Minister of Justice, who argued (with truth, but not the whole truth) that the new constitution 'involved no innovation, but sought only to clarify the existing law'.

He swung the party, and after that the acceptance of a republic by the Assembly was a foregone conclusion. Mustafa Kemal was unanimously elected President, though there were nearly a hundred abstentions. As a salute of 101 guns celebrated the birth of the Turkish Republic on 29 October 1923, Mustafa Kemal became the most powerful man in Turkey. He could appoint his own prime ministers and cabinets; he was commander-in-chief of the forces. He now had absolute control of his people, his army, his country.

*

One problem still nagged. His dream of a modern Turkey was still stifled by the religious fervour of the average Moslem, steeped in the tradition of centuries. Mustafa Kemal himself believed in no God, and, as he said to Colonel Arif when they were drinking together one night, 'Religion is like a heavy blanket that keeps the people of Turkey asleep, that stops them from waking up, from moving forward.' And on another occasion he said, 'The religionists are fond of declaring that the mills of God grind slow, but all I can say is that God has lived long enough to have heard of electric power.'

His dream was to outlaw religion, and he began with the new Caliph, Abdul Mejid, an agreeable man of fifty with no political pretensions yet conscious of the dignity of his position, even though he was not, of course, a sultan. Abdul Mejid delighted in pomp and ceremony for its own sake; he enjoyed the cheering crowds lining the streets of Constantinople each Friday when he drove in state to the Mosque, his retinue blazing with colour and pageantry, sadly missing from the austere post-war life of Turkey. One Friday he wore the old headgear of Sultan Mahomet, Conqueror of Constantinople. Another time he girded on the famous sword won by his ancestor, Selim III. Finally – and this was the last straw to Mustafa Kemal, sitting glowering in Angora – he crossed the

Bosporus in an ancient boat, rowed by fourteen oarsmen dressed in white breeches and black zouave jackets, with a helmsman in green and gold; the prow of the boat was decorated with a large silver phoenix, and at the stern fluttered the Caliph's personal standard.

This latest gesture coincided, unfortunately for the innocent Caliph, with a request for an increase in his stipend, which Mustafa Kemal refused tartly. 'I regard it as an impertinence that you should expect the Turkish people to support any further an anachronism,' he replied.

Those who were political opponents, opposed to the creation of the Republic, were delighted at the way in which Mustafa Kemal was being flouted. Even Mustafa Kemal might have hesitated to act had not an extraordinary chance presented itself, in the form of a letter from the Aga Khan, published in Constantinople newspapers, protesting at 'the indignities' against the Caliph. Mustafa Kemal seized on it. The Aga Khan, he said, might be an important Moslem, but he lived in England, wore English clothes, kept English racehorses, was friendly with English politicians. 'In fact,' said Mustafa Kemal, 'he is a special agent of the English.'

Foreigners in Turkey must have thought the Turkish people, even more so the Assembly, incredibly naive to believe such ridiculous nonsense, but in fact they certainly did. Exaggerating the facts, blending them skilfully with fiction, Mustafa Kemal warned the Assembly that this was a major attempt to destroy the Republic and restore the Sultan to power. 'Before very long,' wrote Irfan and Margarete Orga in *Ataturk*, 'they had begun to regard the Aga Khan as the sinister symbol of British policy intent in splitting Turkey in two. With Mustafa Kemal's warnings in their ears they saw the Nationalist cause lost and the people divided into two camps – those for the Caliph and those against.'

Mustafa Kemal immediately banned all Abdul Mejid's colourful processions. His stipend was cut by nearly fifty per cent. A new law provided the death penalty for sympathizers who hoped to see the Sultanate restored.

What followed was inevitable. On 3 March 1924 Mustafa Kemal presented a Bill to Parliament abolishing the office of Caliph – 'this tumour of the Middle Ages', as he called it. It was passed without debate, and Abdul Mejid was unceremoniously bundled off to Switzerland where he suffered one last indignity; he was held up for some time at the frontier because polygamists were not allowed in the country.

The following month the religious courts were abolished. Soon Turkish became the official language of the country, and Angora became the official capital. As Mustafa Kemal 'celebrated' the occasion in Chankaya, one of his oldest comrades in arms from the fighting days in Salonika, Tewfik Rustu, arrived unexpectedly. In an excess of fervent devotion, he compared the new dictator with the Holy Trinity.

'Father, Son and Holy Ghost?' said Mustafa Kemal who had a sense of humour. 'Yes, it's true – but don't tell anyone.'

*

There can be little doubt that Mustafa Kemal's incredible zeal was largely fostered by the utter misery of his private life. Despite his public success, he was now middle-aged, growing a paunch, and he was lonely.

Within a month of their marriage, Latife discovered he had been to a brothel. A woman of considerable intellect, with a background of European scholarship, it did not take her long to realize that Mustafa Kemal had married her for only one reason – because it was the only way he could bed her. Once he had achieved this, he lost interest. 'Latife was a politician, too, and she was too clever for him and used to put him in his place,' his bodyguard remembers.

Mustafa Kemal would not tolerate an aggressive woman, and Latife liked to play the role of a wife trying to control her erring husband, a woman who shared his closest confidences; she liked to give the impression that she also influenced his decisions. Mustafa Kemal was furious when she told Ward Price of the *Daily Mail* (in impeccable English), 'If I tell you anything, you may consider it just as authoritative as if my husband had told you.'

But perhaps most of all he hated the manner in which she tried to stop him drinking – something Fikriye had never done. And there was a curious reason for his anger. From boyhood he had suffered from chronic constipation and he believed alcohol relieved it.

When they fought, 'Both she and Mustafa Kemal were equally imperious and she was as caustic-tongued as he was.' Their quarrels increased until finally he decided they must part. He wrote out in his own hand and then signed a deed of divorce, and sent the briefest of announcements to the Assembly and the newspapers. Then he told her to leave.

Soon he was having several open affairs with the wives of prominent men, including the wife of a pasha who complained to Mustafa Kemal that people were beginning to talk, 'although I know the insinuations are only based on rumours'.

'I know you,' shouted Mustafa Kemal. 'You've been intriguing against me. Yes – I *have* had your wife. I took her to teach you a lesson.'

At this time Fikriye was still desperately ill with tuberculosis in the sanatorium, but as soon as she read of Mustafa Kemal's divorce she hurried back to Turkey. She told nobody, she left no message. Once in Angora, unknown, unheralded, she made straight for Chankaya.

When she arrived late at night she was on the verge of collapse. Mustafa Kemal was certainly inside, for his adjutant, Rusuhi, remembers the frantic banging on the door. He went to open it. 'She was distraught when I saw her,' he remembered later. 'She asked to see Mustafa Kemal but I refused to let her in. Her appearance alarmed me, and I thought she might attempt to do him an injury. I felt it was my duty to prevent her from going in.'

Whether or not Mustafa Kemal was told that Fikriye was at his front door we shall never know. Next morning the guards found her in an alley near the house with a bullet through her heart.

From this moment the personality of Mustafa Kemal slowly changed. Within months Ali Fethi, who had fought with him from his first successes, remembered, 'He was gaunt and angular. His eyes pierced through one, cold and penetrating but indifferent. It seemed as if he no longer cared about anything.' When finally Mustafa Kemal forced himself to meet his public again he was a different man. The old smile, the winning ways which had beguiled peasants while masking political acumen, had vanished. 'In its place grew a cold destructiveness. He appeared unsmiling, authoritative, heartless.'

Even his old friends deserted him – including the dashing Arif who had fought with him in Gallipoli, and then in Anatolia. And for Arif – for so many years his closest friend – there was to be a finale to life as dramatic as that of poor, ill-starred Fikriye.

*

Turkey – the modern, reformed Turkey – was going through a bad time.

It might be an independent republic, but it was also a hungry one, for food was scarce, credit was vanishing; the Greeks and Armenians, who had controlled many of the business firms in the country, had been killed or banished, and the Turks bungled even elementary economics. Taxes increased; crops rotted because the farmers had been called up for army service. A wave of discontent swept the war-tired country, yet Mustafa Kemal seemed not to notice.

Not until the primitive Kurds in the mountains near the Persian frontier rebelled – with banners crying, 'Down with the Infidel, long live the Sultan' – did Mustafa Kemal act. He murdered them, 'with the cruelty and the ferocity with which the Turks of the Sultan had massacred Greeks, Armenians and Bulgars'. Then he sent in special Tribunals of Independence under a deceptively gentle-looking judge called Bald Ali, a man who was to modern Turkey what Judge Jeffreys had been to Britain's Bloody Assizes. Thousands were tortured, jailed, executed, culminating in the public hanging of sixteen chiefs in the great square of Diarbekir.

Even his closest friends could not stomach these excesses, and Colonel Arif was among several politicians who resigned from Parliament to form the Progressive Republican Party in opposition. Mustafa Kemal waited, planning revenge on those who had deserted him, and the moment arrived in the spring of 1926 when a fanatic called Ziya Hursid boasted that he was planning to assassinate Mustafa Kemal. How far Arif was actually implicated it is difficult to say, but it does seem certain that at one stage Hursid visited his house.

On 14 June Hursid arrived in Smyrna two days before Mustafa Kemal was due to make a state visit. Hursid had money, friends – and a supply of bombs, which he put under the bed of his hotel room overlooking Mustafa Kemal's route. The night before the procession one of his accomplices informed the police. Hursid was woken out of a drunken sleep, the bombs were discovered, and he was arrested.

That in itself was bad enough, but it was followed by wholesale arrests of prominent politicians, who were rounded up and thrown into prison. Among them was Colonel Arif.

A farcical trial, reminiscent of the trial in which Midhat Pasha had been found guilty of a murder he never committed, was held in the Alhambra cinema. There was no proper procedure. No defence was allowed, as Bald

Ali, a man not unlike the popular conception of Mr Pickwick in appearance, invariably sentenced men to death with a smile that was almost beatific.

Arif was seated in the second row of prisoners, heavily manacled, but smiling with ice-cold cynicism and with 'the arrogant expression of a man against whom nothing could be proved'. He scarcely troubled to listen to the damning evidence, after which Bald Ali coughed to clear his throat and with a gentle smile sentenced Mustafa Kemal's best friend to death.

Mustafa Kemal himself signed the death warrants. When he came to the name of Arif, the only sign he gave (a momentary pang of conscience perhaps?) was to stub out the half-smoked cigarette with his thumb. Then he signed, and lit a new one.

Some of the alleged conspirators were hanged immediately; others died with a macabre touch, for on the night when the comrades who had helped him to build the new Turkey were executed in Angora, Mustafa Kemal held a splendid ball, to which the entire diplomatic colony was invited. He had had a dress suit sent out from the London tailors he had started to patronize, and seemed to be in the best of spirits. There was plenty of sweet champagne (dry vintages were not popular) and he forced everyone to dance the new-fangled foxtrot as the male guests and the band sweated in their unaccustomed tight collars in the heat of an August night. Mustafa Kemal never stopped 'tearing his partners round at a great pace, and giving them drinks between the dances'.

In the great square of Angora, four miles away, a dozen arc lamps shone down over the heads of the vast crowds, outlining eleven massive triangles of wood. In silence the condemned men, dressed in white smocks, hands tied behind their backs, the nooses already round their necks, lined up on the outside of the prison wall which formed one side of the square. As Mustafa Kemal's guests danced, each man was given the opportunity to say a few last words before the beaming Bald Ali. One prayed, one recited a poem. Only then could Bald Ali rush back to the ball and report to Mustafa Kemal that his enemies were dead.

When the last of the guests had departed, Mustafa Kemal played poker until dawn. Then he 'walked across and looked out of a window. His face was set and grey, the pale eyes expressionless; he showed no signs of fatigue; his evening clothes were as immaculate as ever.'

The last thing he did before going to bed as the hot dawn came up over the brown, burnt-up plains was to call his adjutant and bodyguard and issue an order, to be passed to all who would meet him, that Arif's name was never to be mentioned in his presence again.

*

With the last of his enemies gone, Mustafa Kemal, in a furious outburst of energy, decided literally to change the face of Turkey. Despite rioting all over the country, he insisted on banning the fez – an extraordinary move in a community so profoundly religious that a Moslem's headgear was as important to him as his daily ablutions. Unruffled, Mustafa Kemal toured the country in a straw panama hat, to the Moslems the age-old symbol of the Christian.

'Some of us,' he told a meeting at Kastamon, 'object to wearing a hat but we are stupid to do so. Why should a hat be so obnoxious to us, but a fez – a Greek symbol, a relic from Byzantium – be permissible? And the robes you wear and the baggy trousers, these are relics of Byzantium too, retained by the Ottoman princes who destroyed our young men on the battlefields of the world – do you know where they came from originally? From the Byzantine priests, the Greek priests and the Jewish rabbis! Long ago only the priest wore the turban to show he was a scholar, but after a time anyone and everyone wore it so that they could cheat the people. It is disgraceful for a civilized people to seek help from the dead.'

Old people tied handkerchiefs on their heads before putting hats on top, until the police tore the handkerchiefs off. Peasants in Anatolia who had never seen a hat wore ancient discarded bowlers or straw hats or cloth caps from Russia. In Smyrna a farmer found a deserted Greek shop filled with women's beribboned hats left behind during the panic of the exodus. He sold them in his village, but not to the women. All the male villagers wore ladies' summer hats on their way to market, even when working in the fields.

Mustafa Kemal would work himself into a fury every time he saw a man wearing a fez. When the Egyptian Ambassador arrived wearing one at a diplomatic reception in Angora, Mustafa Kemal strode up to him and shouted, 'Tell your King I don't like his uniform.'

Soon Mustafa Kemal abolished the veil. 'I have seen many of our sisters cover up their faces the moment a man approaches,' he told a meeting at Inebol. 'Surely this causes them acute discomfort in hot weather? Why are we men so selfish to let them do this? Let them show their faces to the world, let them have the chance to see the world for themselves. There is nothing to be afraid of. No nation can progress without its women. Do the wives and daughters of the civilized world behave like this? Of course they don't!' But this took longer, particularly in the country districts where a young girl who obeyed the law usually received a thrashing when she returned home. In the end Mustafa Kemal concentrated on the towns and left the villages to absorb change more slowly.

After abolishing the harem and polygamy he provided another startling innovation – co-educational classes in Constantinople, to study the nude in art.

He also imported Western classical music, and decided to compare the merits of Turkish and European music himself by ordering two orchestras to play in turn at the Park Hotel in Constantinople. The evening was not altogether successful, for Mustafa Kemal kept interrupting each orchestra, ordering the other to play a few bars until finally, aided by more than a few glasses of raki, he got up and shouted, 'I'm leaving – now you can both play together if you like.'

His other reforms were far-reaching. By adapting the Swiss civil code he introduced the westernized week with Sunday as the day of rest, irrespective of a man's religion; before, Friday had been the weekly holiday for Moslems, Saturdays for Jews, Sundays for Christians, making a convenient long weekend for many. Next the salaam was forbidden, and the handshake took its place.

He abolished the old calendar system in which a Moslem century consisted of only ninety-seven years. Until he introduced the Gregorian calendar, the hours had been counted from the hour of dawn, which varied, so that it was not uncommon for a man to ask, 'What time is midday today?' Now the day started at midnight. In his effort to bring Turkey into line with Europe, he standardized the time, and introduced metrication.

Perhaps his most remarkable innovation was to 'invent' a language, and then stump the country teaching it with chalk and a blackboard. His professors had produced a Latin phonetic alphabet in the astonishing time of six weeks, and Mustafa Kemal was the first man in Turkey to learn it. There were problems; all foreign words had been ruthlessly discarded and no one knew the new Turkish words that replaced them, let alone how to spell them in the new language.

Anxious to impress the *intelligentsia* of Istanbul, the one-time peasant boy took up residence in the palace of a sultan, the rococo Dolmabache. There he gave a reception with champagne, cigars and, on a dais, a blackboard. He wrote his own name in the new alphabet, then frowned at the unfamiliar word in disbelief. Schoolchildren stepped forward to show their prowess.

He seemed indefatigable. Soon all foreign schools had to employ a high percentage of Turkish teachers, however ill-informed they might be. No new ones could open. Religious leaders from foreign countries were commanded to appear in conventional clothes, instead of their ornate robes of office. Most professions were closed to foreigners. Beggars were outlawed, and it was made an offence to laugh at the insane. Names were changed week after week – Izmir for Smyrna, Ankara for Angora.

Even the name Constantinople was changed. The great city which the Greeks and Romans had called Byzantium, the Arabs 'The Threshold of Felicity', the Scandinavians 'The City of Girth' – the queen of cities, steeped in power, intrigue and colour – became Istanbul, a drab Turkish corruption of the words on the old Greek signposts, 'To the City'.

*

During all these years there were remarkable parallels between those two arch-enemies of the past, Turkey and Russia. The Russian revolution in 1905, the Young Turks in 1908, had both sprung from the same original passions – a deeply rooted desire for democratic government at a time when the equivalent of Britain's Industrial Revolution was changing the face of the two empires, each half-European, half-Asian. Each had reached a moment of destiny after losing a succession of wars. The parallels went further. Both separated Church from State. And while Constantinople became Istanbul, and a new capital was built out of a primitive village on the steppes, St Petersburg became Petrograd, then Leningrad, and the capital was moved to Moscow. In both cases the move was symbolic, the sign not only that each country wanted to blot out its tarnished history but wanted also to signalize to the world that it was making a fresh start.

There was, however, one vital difference between the two countries. A massive ideology underlay the tremendous events in Russia, often paralysing the Bolshevik attempts to introduce reforms, to get things done. By contrast Mustafa Kemal, as he Europeanized Turkey, unceremoniously nationalizing banks, introducing rural electrification, was never hampered by mystical theories which had to be earnestly debated. Since the basis of Mustafa Kemal's ideology was to produce a modern, westernized Turkey, he could bulldoze any measures, however startling, through Parliament simply because reform was the only creed he preached.

*

Among Mustafa Kemal's last reforms was to ban the titles that had been a part of Ottoman history for centuries – Pasha, Bey, Effendi, all coming from the Arabic language. And then he passed a law which made surnames obligatory – and they had to be Turkish. Until 1934 people had merely added their profession or their place of birth to their name, so that a gardener (Bostangi) called Ali who hailed from Angora would be called either Bostangi Ali or Ali of Angora.

Now all that changed overnight. Mustafa Kemal discarded both his names, which were of Arabic origin. Luckily he found a Turkish word meaning 'strong' that differed from Kemal by only one letter, so Kamal became his first name. For a surname the National Assembly and the Turkish nation bestowed on him the word he preferred above all others – Ataturk (Father Turk). From that moment he became Kamal Ataturk.

He was changing, of course. He was becoming pompous and inordinately vain. In 1921 he had proudly boasted that he owned nothing. 'Now he grew miserly and close-fisted.' The modest farm which had grown almost naturally in the fields around Chankaya had become a model farm boasting the finest breeding stock in the Middle East. He loved to play the role of gentleman farmer, but an autocratic one. When faced by a shortage of water he sent for an engineer and told him to construct a new reservoir; one of his friends suggested shaping it like Lake Geneva. To Ataturk the idea was good, but he made one change. He ordered it to be modelled to scale on the Sea of Marmora. (The Gulf of Izmit was left out to reduce the cost.)

He was drinking more than ever, gambling or womanizing; but, though his debauchery was coffee-table gossip throughout Turkey, it did not harm his reputation. Indeed, less fortunate men admired it, for to the

Turks, 'His chief vice was the national vice. Lechery had been the oldest boast of their ancestors.'

Inevitably, the old sickness which he caught in Sofia caught up with him. He had never troubled to cure it properly, a long process involving patience, before the days of penicillin injections. It had spread to his liver. To ease the pain he drank more than ever, despite his doctor's orders. He was lonely, and by 1938 it was obvious that even his constitution was not strong enough to withstand the grave illness that was gripping him. Behind his back his doctors sent for Dr Fissinger, a French specialist who immediately diagnosed cirrhosis of the liver and told Ataturk bluntly, 'You may be a great commander who has won great victories, but I am now your commander.' Even Ataturk was stunned into a sense of reality and gave up drinking, went on a diet, and agreed to spend three months in bed, getting up only for half an hour a day. He sent to England for a special *chaise longue* on which he could lie while reading or writing, but after a month he was surreptitiously getting up. After that, nothing could save him, not even the love and care of his ADC, Salih, who had been his friend since long before the campaign in Gallipoli, and who now never left his side.

It has been suggested by some Turkish historians that possibly Ataturk in his heart did not wish to be cured, preferring to make a grand exit while at the peak of his career, remembering the old Turkish proverb, 'When the roof of the house is completed the Angel of Death knocks at the door.' The Turkish Republic was now fifteen years old, and its founder, ironically, spent the last days of his life in a huge bed on the second floor of Dolmabache Palace, surrounded by French furniture, the last great rococo extravagance of the decadent sultans he hated.

He died at five minutes past nine on 10 November 1938, in a room overlooking the Bosporus. He was fifty-seven. Later in the morning, as the stunned people of Constantinople wept openly in the streets, Salih, his old friend and ADC, went quietly to a back room in the Dolmabache Palace and shot himself through the heart. He had no desire to live without his master.

All that day and throughout the night that followed, the silence of death smothered the city like a blanket. Black crape covered the city, draping the statues, the windows, the photographs of the man who looked down from every corner, every public room.

For three nights the body of Ataturk lay in state in Dolmabache, the ebony coffin covered with the flag of Turkey, the catafalque guarded by officers with drawn swords, as hundreds of thousands of Turks filed past. For most of them, mumbling 'Ata, Ata', it was probably the first time in their lives they had ever been in the close presence of the man they called Father. And, since in Constantinople one can never escape the history of a once-great empire, it was also the first time most had ventured into the past, to breathe the atmosphere of an empire's greatness as they filed through the gardens leading to the palace doors. How many, one wonders, realized that the flowers lining their path had been planted in 'the filled-up garden', reclaimed from the Bosporus nearly five hundred years previously by sixteen thousand Christian slaves. The paths led into the vast rococo throne-room of the Dolmabache where the corpse lay under the giant dome of the palace built by Sultan Abdul Mejid, the flamboyant spendthrift who demanded only one thing of his architect, that his palace must surpass any other in the world; where sherbet had once been served in golden goblets; and where later the wretched and terrified Abdul Hamid had lavishly wined and dined the German Emperor while he himself ate only a simple pilaff prepared in his private, poison-proof kitchen.

After three days of lying in state, Ataturk's body was taken from the home of the ruler he so despised. Every inch of ground on the route was covered; on every stout branch of every tree, on every dome, on every minaret men perched, anxious to catch a glimpse of the funeral procession, with the coffin borne on a gun carriage drawn by soldiers, one officer behind carrying only one medal on a velvet cushion – that of the War of Independence.

In sombre slow march, the procession moved past a squat granite-grey building with the sun filtering through stained-glass windows, in which lay the body of a man Ataturk might well have admired, Barbarossa, the red-bearded pirate who in the time of Suleiman the Magnificent had turned the Mediterranean into an Ottoman lake; savage, cruel, relentless no doubt, but, like Ataturk, a man of his time.

The long procession reached the bridge spanning the Golden Horn, the ferry boats clustering around, squeezing for space, each crammed with human beings, looking down from the upper decks on to the sparkling water, with its two bridges, one built by Mahmud, another reformer, son of Aimée Dubucq de Rivery who first brought European culture to the Ottoman Empire. At the end of the bridge the gun carriage wheeled left towards a pier and a waiting gunboat. The streets approaching the shimmering water had, of course, been cleared, but there was a momentary interruption in the slow procession, and for that brief moment the remains of Ataturk rested at the corner of Seraglio Point, at the apex of the triangle of land that formed the Grand Seraglio where so much history had been written: where Roxelana had persuaded Suleiman to make her his wife, and where she had plotted the death of his favourite son; where Mahomet III had his nineteen brothers strangled; where Murad IV in one year caused twenty-five thousand of his subjects to be executed, many by his own hand; and just behind the procession, if one looked carefully with a knowledge of the harem, were the windows of the infamous Cage, out of which Ibrahim peered for twenty-two years before becoming the most detestable of all the Ottoman Sultans.

Ataturk had expressed a wish to be buried in his beloved Ankara, so it had been decided to take the body first by sea to Izmit at the eastern tip of the Sea of Marmora. The Turkish vessel prepared to leave Seraglio Point, where ships of all nations lay at anchor, including the *Malaya* which had carried the last Ottoman sultan to an exile in Italy.

The coffin arrived at Izmit that evening and was transferred to Ataturk's presidential train, his private saloon the only carriage ablaze with light as the blackened train set off on the winding journey across the plains and mountains of Anatolia. This was the cradle of the Ottoman Empire, across which Murad marched for 110 days to Baghdad, there killing the bravest Persian in single combat before taking the city and massacring sixty thousand people; and it was here, where the darkened train now rumbled, that Ataturk himself had routed the Greeks in the great battle of Sakkaria, and had later led his soldiers back to Constantinople, passing under the shadow of Mount Olympus, with its inexhaustible supply of snow which for centuries had cooled the Sultans' sherbet. Here Ataturk had rested before setting off for the Dardanelles to challenge the British occupation forces in bloodless confrontation at Charnak.

Lord Kinross, his biographer, describes, in *Ataturk*, that last night how the 'peasants in their thousands crowded down to the track to await the train and see the last of their "father". They waved torches and poured their scant rations of petrol on the ground, setting light to it,' as the train puffed towards the township where Ataturk had loved the sad Fikriye and where she had met a violent death; where he had settled down as a married man with Latife, only to divorce her; where he had dined and danced through the night while eleven of his old friends were hanged publicly in the main square. But, above all, the train was carrying him to the village in the mountains of an empire which he had transformed into the capital of a country he had forged. He had taken a great empire, born out of courage, crumbling through debauchery, and in half a generation he had, in the words of Kinross, 'transported his country from the Middle Ages to the threshold of the modern era and beyond'.

Postscript

All is changed now. The bustling city of Istanbul, with its two bridges spanning the Golden Horn and its interminable traffic jams, is too busy searching for tomorrow to spare a thought for yesterday. History for the modern, westernized state of Turkey began with Ataturk, and the magnificent court of the sultans is now remote to the ordinary man in the street.

Through the courtyards of the Grand Seraglio, now one vast museum, schoolteachers on summer days shepherd long files of chattering children; the teachers watch anxiously to make sure that their charges follow the route, marked with neat cards, that all sightseers must follow. They look as harassed as their British counterparts in the Natural History Museum, and the children, one may be sure, regard this outing not so much as a practical history lesson as a day away from the hateful routine of the classroom.

To the average Turk old Constantinople is almost too familiar. As he screeches and brakes at the corner near St Sophia, or past the vast underground cistern, virtually unchanged, where the last of the Janissaries were drowned, he is too concerned with stray pedestrians to notice his surroundings. Perhaps the tourists, obediently following the multilingual guides through the dark passages and bright rooms of the harem, are able to absorb history more readily. Armed with guidebooks and cameras, they are making an expedition into a world of lost splendour, of an opulence that has all but vanished in our modern world.

On the edge of the Hippodrome, round which the Byzantines staged their horse races, and where the Sultan Murad shot an arrow from one end to the other, there are several stone benches, but they are rarely occupied, for the Hippodrome has run to seed since those days. At one end a group of urchins play football. An old, old woman sits on a nearby bench feeding pigeons, one hand clutching the black shawl which drapes her head, ready, one feels, to draw it instinctively across her face if any of the public photographers with their ancient cameras should approach too close. In the hot August sun, the occasional lizard darts out from the stones that have lain there since the days of Constantine. As still as death, its eye watches for an insect, it darts and is gone into the brown, crumbling walls of the city.

It is hard sometimes, sitting there in the shadow of the great and beautiful mosques, of the Seraglio itself, to realize that this was once the heart of a tyrannical empire so formidable that the Western world trembled at its might; despite the centuries of greatness, of conquest and oppression, of the intrigues of the 'favoured women' in the harem, of the miseries of its millions of subject peoples, it might all have been nothing more than a bad dream.

Notes on further reading

A bibliography, with its long string of titles in alphabetical order, can be a snare for the general reader concerned with enjoying a book rather than studying, for some of the most exciting titles can camouflage the dullest texts; so I am passing on to the general reader the titles of a few books which I found rewarding in research but also highly enjoyable.

The simplest guide to the political history of the Ottoman Empire is Eversley and Chirol's *The Turkish Empire*. It covers the years from 1288 to 1922, and every important date and event is recorded. It was my bible for two years. Von Hammer's definitive *History of the Ottoman Empire* is more detailed and authoritative, but though invaluable to the scholar is hard going.

The most fascinating aspect of my research lay in searching for details of everyday life in the changing Empire, and I found a wealth of material in dozens of old books. I can recommend the following: *Travels in Europe, Asia and Africa* in three volumes by that inquisitive busybody, Evliya Effendi; *Turkish Letters* by de Busbecq; *The Sultan and His Subjects* by Davey, and Sir Paul Rycaut's classic *History of the Turkes*. Many ladies did their best to penetrate the harem, and Lady Mary Wortley Montagu gives many fascinating descriptions in her *Complete Letters*. The best book on the harem is unquestionably N. M. Penzer's *The Harem*. It abounds in anecdotal material, is well illustrated, and though out of print now is still obtainable at many libraries. A recently published book, *The Palace of Topkapi* by Fanny Davis is concerned more with the Seraglio as it is today, but she skilfully interweaves stories of the past with the reconstruction problems of the present, and the book is beautifully illustrated.

Several books have been written about Suleiman and Roxelana, of which two, each called *Suleiman the Magnificent*, make fine reading. One is by Harold Lamb, the other by R. B. Merriman. For those interested in a detailed analysis of how Suleiman ran his government of slaves, there is the more serious *Government of the Ottoman Empire in the Time of Suleiman the Magnificent* by A. H. Lybyer, but it is rather specialized. Aimée, the French sultana, is vividly described in one chapter of Lesley Blanch's delightful *The Wilder Shores of Love*.

Several war correspondents involved in the battles for Plevna wrote their accounts, but I found them too discursive and one-sided. There is, however, one masterly book: Rupert Furneaux's *The Siege of Plevna*.

The two books on Abdul Hamid which I most enjoyed were Joan Haslip's *The Sultan: the Life of Abdul Hamid*, and Alma Wittlin's *Abdul Hamid, the Shadow of God*; while Sir Harry Luke, who could never write a dull book on Turkey, takes us through this period into that of the Young Turks in *The Old Turkey and the New* and *The Making of Modern Turkey*. *The Young Turks* by E. E. Ramsaur outlines their aspirations and failure, while Henry Morgenthau, American Ambassador to Constantinople when the First World War broke out, gives fascinating pen-portraits of Enver and Talaat and a detailed account of the Armenian massacres in *Secrets of the Bosporus*.

Ataturk was the subject of several biographies shortly after his death, but most were shockingly bad, possibly because they were deliberately written to shock. We had to wait until 1964 before the definitive story of his life and times appeared. It was *Ataturk, the Rebirth of a Nation* by Lord Kinross, and every page is compulsive and absorbing reading. One particular aspect of Ataturk's 'reign' is well written in *The Smyrna Affair* by Marjorie Housepian.

These are some of the books which I really enjoyed, and that, after all, is as good a reason as any for reading a book.

Books consulted

ABBOTT, G. F, *Turkey, Greece and the Great Powers* (London: Robert Scott, 1917)

AHMAD, FEROZ, *The Young Turks* (Oxford University Press, 1969)

ALDERSON, A. D, *The Structure of the Ottoman Dynasty* (Oxford University Press, 1956)

ANDERSON, M. S, *The Eastern Question 1774–1923* (London: Macmillan, 1966)

ARMSTRONG, HAROLD, *Turkey in Travail* (London: John Lane, 1925)

ARMSTRONG, H. C, *Grey Wolf (Mustapha Kemal)* (London: Arthur Barker, 1932)

BARKER, CAPT B. GRANVILLE, *The Passing of the Turkish Empire in Europe* (London: Seeley Service, 1913)

BARKER, THOMAS M, *Double Eagle and Crescent* (New York University, 1967)

BENJAMIN, S. G, *The Turk and the Greek* (New York, 1867)

BENSON, E. F, *Crescent and Iron Cross* (London, 1918)

BIERSTADT, E. H, *The Great Betrayal* (London: Hutchinson, 1924)

BLANCH, LESLEY, *The Wilder Shores of Love* (London: John Murray, 1954)

BRANDIER, M, *The History of the Imperial Estate of the Grand Seigneur* (London, 1635)

BUSBECQ, OGIER GHISELIN DE, *Turkish Letters* (Oxford University Press, 1927)

CASSELS, LAVENDER, *The Struggle for the Ottoman Empire* (London: John Murray, 1966)

CASTLE, WILFRID T. F, *Grand Turk* (London: Hutchinson, 1943)

CAVAVELAS, J, *The Siege of Vienna* (Cambridge University Press, 1925)

CHISHULL, REV EDMUND, *Travels in Turkey and Back to England* (London, 1747)

COECK, PETER, *The Turks in MDXXXIII*, ed. Sir William Maxwell (privately printed, 1874)

COLES, PAUL, *The Ottoman Impact on Europe* (London: Thames & Hudson, 1968)

'CONSUL'S DAUGHTER AND WIFE, A', *The People of Turkey*, 2 vols (London: John Murray, 1878)

COVEL, DR JOHN, *Early Voyages and Travels in the Levant* (Cambridge: Hakluyt Society, 1893)

COWLES, VIRGINIA, *The Russian Dagger* (London: Collins, 1969)

CREASY, SIR EDWARD, *History of the Ottoman Turks*, 2 vols (London, 1878)

CUDDON, J. A, *The Owl's Watchsong* (London: Barrie & Rockliffe, 1960)

DAVEY, R, *The Sultan and His Subjects* (London, 1897)

DAVIS, FANNY, *The Palace of Topkapi* (New York: Charles Scribner's Sons, 1970)

DAVIS, W. S, *A Short History of the Near East* (London: Macmillan, 1923)

DAVISON, RODERIC H., *Reform in the Ottoman Empire* (Princeton University Press, 1953)

DEVEREUX, ROBERT, *The First Ottoman Constitutional Period* (Baltimore: Johns Hopkins University Press, 1963)

DJEMAL PASHA, *Memories of a Turkish Statesman 1913–1919* (London: Hutchinson, 1922)

DONALDSON, H. E, *Ibrahim Pasha* (New York: privately printed for a Columbia University thesis, 1911)

EDMONDS, C. J, *Kurds, Turks and Arabs* (Oxford University Press, 1957)

EVLIYA EFFENDI, *Narrative of Travels in Europe, Asia and Africa in the Seventeenth Century*, 3 vols (London: Oriental Translation Fund, 1834, 1846, 1850)

ELLIOT, SIR CHARLES, *Turkey in Europe* (London: Edward Arnold, 1900)

ELLIOTT, FRANCES, *Diary of an Idle Woman in Constantinople* (London: John Murray, 1893)

ELLISON, GRACE, *Turkey Today* (London: Hutchinson, 1928)

EMIN, AHMED, *Turkey in the World War* (New Haven, Conn.: Yale University Press, 1958)

ETON, W., *A Survey of the Turkish Empire* (London, 1801)

EVERSLEY, LORD, AND CHIROL, *The Turkish Empire from 1288–1914–1922* (London: T. Fisher Unwin, 1922)

FARLEY, J. L, *Modern Turkey* (London, 1872)

FINLAY, GEORGE, *History of Greece* (Oxford University Press, 1877)

FLACHAT, *Observations sur le Commerce et sur les arts d'une Partie de l'Europe, de l'Asie, de l'Afrique et même des Indes Orientales* (Lyon, 1766)

FREEMAN, EDWARD A, *The Ottoman Power in Europe* (London, 1877)

FROEMBGEN, HANS, *Kemal Ataturk* (London: Jarrolds, 1937)

The Fugger News Letters, 2 vols (London: John Lane, 1924, 1926)

FURNEAUX, RUPERT, *The Siege of Plevna* (London: Anthony Blond, 1958)

GARNETT, LUCY M, *Turkey of the Ottomans* (London: Putnam, 1911)

GIBBONS, H. A, *The Foundation of the Ottoman Empire* (Oxford University Press, 1916)

GRAVES, PHILIP P, *Briton and Turk* (London: Hutchinson, 1941)

GROSVENOR, E. A, *Constantinople*, 2 vols (London, 1895)

HAMMER, JOSEPH VON, *History of the Ottoman Empire* (Paris, 1841)

HARINGTON, GEN SIR CHARLES, *Tim Harington Looks Back* (London: John Murray, 1940)

HARVEY, A. J, *Turkish Harems* (London, 1871)

HASLIP, JOAN, *The Sultan : the Life of Abdul Hamid* (London: Cassell, 1958)

HEMINGWAY, ERNEST, *The Fifth Column* (London: Jonathan Cape, 1939)

HEPWORTH, REV GEORGE, *Through Armenia on Horseback* (London, 1898)

HERBERT, W. V, *The Defence of Plevna* (London, 1895)

HOUSEPIAN, MARJORIE, *The Smyrna Affair* (New York: Harcourt Brace Jovanovich, 1966)

HUBBARD, G. E, *The Day of the Crescent* (Cambridge University Press, 1920)

HUTTON, W. H, *Constantinople* (London: Dent, 1900)

JARMAN, T. L, *Turkey* (Bristol: Arrowsmith, 1935)

JONES, D, *A Compleat History of the Turks*, 3 vols (London, 1701)

KEITOVOULOS, *The History of Mehmed the Conqueror* (Princeton University Press, 1954)

KEMAL, ISMAIL BEY, *Memoirs* (London: Constable, 1926)

KINROSS, LORD, *Ataturk, the Rebirth of a Nation* (London: Weidenfeld & Nicolson, 1964)

KNOLLES, RICHARD, *The History of the Turkish Empire 1679–99* (London, 1700)

LAMB, HAROLD, *The March of the Barbarians* (London: Robert Hale, 1941)
    Suleiman the Magnificent (London: Robert Hale, 1952)

LANE-POOLE, STANLEY, *Turkey* (London, 1888)

— *The Life of Lord Stratford de Redcliffe* (London, 1890)

LARPENT, SIR GEORGE, *Turkey, Its History and Progress from the Journals of Sir James Porter* (London, 1854)

LEWIS, BERNARD, *The Emergence of Modern Turkey* (Oxford University Press, 1961)

LEWIS, G. L, *Turkey* (London: Ernest Benn, 1955)

LEWIS, RAPHAELA, *Everyday Life in Ottoman Turkey* (London: Batsford, 1971)

LUKE, SIR HARRY, *The Making of Modern Turkey* (London: Macmillan, 1936)

— *The Old Turkey and the New* (London: Geoffrey Bles, 1953)

LUSIGNAN, PRINCESS ANNE DE, *The Twelve Years Reign of Abdul Hamid II* (London, 1889)

LYBYER, A. H, *Government of the Ottoman Empire in the Time of Suleiman the Magnificent* (Cambridge, Mass: Harvard University Press, 1913)

MCCOAN, J. CARLILE, *Our New Protectorate : Turkey in Asia*, 2 vols (London, 1879)

MACFARLANE, CHARLES, *Turkey and Its Destiny*, 2 vols (1850)

MANGO, ANDREW, *Turkey* (London: Thames & Hudson, 1968)

MAXWELL, SIR ROBERT, *Life and Letters of the 4th Earl of Clarendon* (London: Edward Arnold, 1913)

MAYES, STANLEY, *An Organ for the Sultan* (London: Putnam, 1956)

MELLING, A. I, *Voyage Pittoresque de Constantinople* (Paris, 1819)

MENZIES, SUTHERLAND, *Turkey Old and New*, 2 vols (London, 1880)

MERRIMAN, R. B, *Suleiman the Magnificent* (Cambridge, Mass: Harvard University Press, 1944)

MIKUSCH, D. VON, *Mustapha Kemal between Europe and Asia* (London: Heinemann, 1931)

MILLER, BARNETTE, *Beyond the Sublime Porte* (Newhaven, Conn: Yale University Press, 1931)

— *The Palace School of Muhammed the Conqueror* (Cambridge, Mass: Harvard University Press, 1941)

MILLER, WILLIAM, *The Ottoman Empire and Its Successors 1801–1927* (Cambridge University Press, 1927)

MONTAGU, LADY MARY WORTLEY, *Complete Letters* (Oxford University Press, 1965)

— *Letters during Travels* (London, 1789)

MOOREHEAD, A, *Gallipoli* (London: Hamish Hamilton, 1957)

MORGENTHAU, HENRY, *Secrets of the Bosporus* (London: Hutchinson, 1918)

MOURAD BEY, *Le Palais de Yilditz et le Sublime Porte* (Paris, 1897)

MULLER, HERBERT J, *The Loom of History* (London: Museum Press, 1959)

MUNDY, PETER, *The Travels of Peter Mundy in Europe and Asia 1608–1667* (Cambridge: Hakluyt Society, 1907)

NICOLSON, HAROLD, *Lord Carnock: a Study in the Old Diplomacy* (London: Constable, 1930)

OECONDMOS, DR LYSIMACHOS, *The Martyrdom of Smyrna and Eastern Christendom* (London: Allen & Unwin, 1922)

ORGA, IRFAN AND MARGARETE, *Ataturk* (London: Michael Joseph, 1962)

OSMAN BEY, *La Turquie sous Abdul Aziz* (Paris, 1868)

PALLIS, ALEXANDER, *In the Days of the Janissaries* (London: Hutchinson, 1951)

PARDOE, MISS, *The City of the Sultan*, 2 vols (London, 1837)

PEARS, SIR EDWIN, *Life of Abdul Hamid* (London: Constable, 1917)

PENZER, N. M, *The Harem* (London: Spring Books, 1966)

PORTER, SIR JAMES, *Turkey, Its History and Progress*, 2 vols (London, 1854)

POSTEL, GUILLAUME, *De la République Turke* (Poitiers, 1560)

RAMSAUR, E.E, *The Young Turks* (Princeton University Press, 1957)

RAMSAY, SIR WILLIAM, *Impressions of Turkey* (London, 1897)

— *The Revolution in Constantinople and Turkey* (London: Hodder & Stoughton, 1919)

RANKE, LEOPOLD, *The Ottoman and Spanish Empires in the Sixteenth and Seventeenth Centuries* (London, 1843)

REIS, SIDI ALI, *The Travels and Adventures of Admiral Reis* (London, 1899)

REMAK, JOACHIM, *Sarajevo* (London: Weidenfeld & Nicolson, 1959)

REMALEDDIN BEY, D. J, *Sultan Murad V* (London, 1895)

ROSENDALE, REV H. G, *Queen Elizabeth and the Levant Company* (Oxford University Press, 1904)

RYCAUT, SIR PAUL, *History of the Turkes to 1699* (London, 1700)

SANDERS, LIMAN VON, *Five Years in Turkey* (Annapolis: U.S. Naval Institute, 1928)

SHAH, IKBAL ALI, *Kemal – Maker of Modern Turkey* (London: Herbert Joseph, 1934)

SHERLEY, SIR THOMAS, *Discours of the Turkes* (London: Royal Historical Society, 1936)

SMITH, ALBERT, *A Month in Constantinople* (London: David Bogue, 1851)

STOYE, JOHN, *The Siege of Vienna* (London: Collins, 1954)

SYKES, SIR MARK, *The Caliphs' Last Heritage* (London: Macmillan, 1915)

THORNTON, THOMAS, *The Present State of Turkey*, 2 vols (London, 1809)

TOTT, BARON DE, *Mémoires* (London, 1786)

TRUMPENER, ULRICH, *Germany and the Ottoman Empire* (Princeton University Press, 1968)

TUGAY, E. F, *Three Centuries* (Oxford University Press, 1967)

UPHAM, EDWARD, *History of the Ottoman Empire till 1828*, 2 vols (Edinburgh, 1829)

WALDER, DAVID, *The Chanak Affair* (London: Hutchinson, 1969)

WEBER, FRANK G, *Eagles on the Crescent* (Ithaca, N.Y.: Cornell University Press, 1970)

WHITE, COL CHARLES, *Three Years in Constantinople*, 3 vols (London, 1845)

WITHERS, ROBERT, *Edited Version of Grand Seigneur's Seraglio* (London, 1650)

WITTEK, PAUL, *The Rise of the Ottoman Empire* (London: Royal Asiatic Society, 1938)

WITTLIN, ALMA, *Abdul Hamid, Shadow of God* (London: John Lane, 1940)

WORTHAM, H. E, *Mustafa Kemal* (London: Holme Press, 1930)

YOUNG, GEORGE, *Constantinople* (London: Methuen, 1926)

Documents

BON, OTTAVIANO, *A Description of the Grand Seigneur's Seraglio* (Venice: Library of St Mark, 1625)

BRASSEY, THOMAS, MP, *The Eastern Question* (London, 1877)

BROWN, JOSEPH, QC, *The Idolatry, Superstition and Corruption of the Christians of Turkey* (London, 1877)

CHISHULL, REV EDMUND, *Antiquitates Adriaticae* (London, 1728)

Constantinople reports 1730; Constantinople reports 1736 (Public Record Office 97/26 and 97/28)

COOPER, JOSEPH, *Turkey and Egypt (Consular Reports on the Slave Trade)* (London, 1876)

Dispatches from Envoys in Constantinople, Vienna, St Petersburg and Paris (Public Record Office 97/25–31; 80/54–8; 78/207–21)

'The Armenian Question', speech, 1898

The Bulgarian Horrors (London, 1876)

GLADSTONE, W. E, MP 'The Eastern Question', speech, 1877

Lessons in Massacre, Conduct of Turkish Government in Bulgaria (London, 1877)

Greek Atrocities in Turkey (Constantinople: Ministry of Interior, 1921)

HIEROSOLIMITANO, DOMENIC, 'Relations della gran citta di Constantinopii' (MSS Room, British Museum)

LARA, CHRYSSAPHIDES AND RENE, 'The Last Sultan of Turkey', *Nineteenth Century and After*, June 1909

Parliamentary Papers in the Eastern Question (London: HMSO, 1854)

Reports received from HM Ambassador and Consuls relating to the Christians in Turkey. Presented to House of Commons, 1867 (Public Record Office)

RICHARD, HENRY, MP, *Evidences of Turkish Misrule* (London: Eastern Question Association, 1877)

TAYLOR, SEDLEY, *The Conduct of HM Ministers on the Eastern Question* (London: Liberal Central Association, 1877)

VAMBERY, ARMENIUS, 'The Future of Constitutional Turkey', *Nineteenth Century and After*, March 1909

    'Personal Recollections of Abdul Hamid and His Court', *Nineteenth Century and After*, June 1909

'Vindex Veritatis', *That Unconscionable Turk* (London, 1877)

Index

Nicholas and Alexandra £1·25
Robert K. Massie

'Robert Massie makes the whole world-shaking drama all too humanly understandable – the long wait for an heir to the throne; the discovery of his haemophilia, the dreadful suffering the parents had to watch in their child; the ensuing royal dependence on the miracle-working, sex-ridden Rasputin . . .' HARPER'S

'Contains every imaginable ingredient for a runaway literary success . . . grandeur and misery; romantic love; a glittering court; absolute power over one hundred and thirty million people; Byzantine intrigues; mysterious illnesses and evil influences; an intimate view of great power politics; war and revolution; the violent and horrible death of almost everyone concerned' SPECTATOR

A History of the English People 52½p
R. J. Mitchell and M. D. R. Leys

'This is social history at its best, a superb compiling of information about the details of daily living which political, economic and military historians must ignore. It is the fruit of profound scholarship, but it does not smell of the academic lamp' NEW YORK TIMES

'The authors have dug deep and most profitably . . . The illustrations are a thing of beauty, stretching from illuminated medieval manuscripts down to George Stubbs and John Leech, while the indexes, by subject and place-name, are enough to show that there is something here for nearly every human interest' TIMES LITERARY SUPPLEMENT

'This is a volume of real enchantment that you will want to own, to refer to and to reread, particularly in your favourite passages, for years to come' SPHERE

Charles Edward Stuart 95p
David Daiches

'Excellent . . . a deftly drawn historical background, and against it a nicely painted portrait of a boy who grew up with one single stubborn purpose in his mind . . . That his adventure brought misery and disaster to the Highlands cannot be denied, but it gave them a story of infinite gallantry, of invincible loyalty, and to reread the story starts yet again sheer astonishment that the Prince could do so much' ERIC LINKLATER, GUARDIAN

'Brilliant . . . makes it possible to understand both the strengths and weaknesses of Bonnie Prince Charlie's expedition . . .' ANTONIA FRASER, SUNDAY TIMES

'Splendidly told . . . The author brings to bear on the Prince and on the events a historical imagination which is infused with a deep affection for the nation of Scotland' SCOTSMAN

The Steel Bonnets 95p
George MacDonald Fraser

Were your ancestors among the great raiding families from the six counties on either side of the Border Marches? George MacDonald Fraser, creator of the *Flashman* sagas, has produced an immensely entertaining and informative portrait of the guerrillas in steel bonnets.

'A remarkably successful book on a fascinating subject, well organized and well written' TIMES LITERARY SUPPLEMENT

The Young Elizabeth 40p
Alison Plowden

A vivid account of the first twenty-five years of the life of
Elizabeth I – years frequently shadowed by danger and the fear
of death . . .

'The intrigue, violence and flaming horror of what life was like
for a Tudor Princess is more than adequately conveyed . . .
Elizabeth would, I am sure, have blessed Miss Plowden . . . A
beautiful book' BOOKS AND BOOKMEN

'Vastly interesting . . . wholly informative and very entertaining'
THE TIMES

'Well researched, detailed, most readable' EVENING STANDARD

You can buy these and other Pan books from booksellers and
newsagents; or direct from the following address:
Pan Books, Cavaye Place, London SW10 9PG
Send purchase price plus 15p for the first book and 5p for
each additional book, to allow for postage and packing

While every effort is made to keep prices low, it is sometimes
necessary to increase prices at short notice. Pan Books reserve the
right to show on covers new retail prices which may differ
from those advertised in the text or elsewhere